DATE DUE

PRINTED IN U.S.A.

Survivors of Slavery

MODERN-DAY SLAVE NARRATIVES

Laura T. Murphy

 COLUMBIA UNIVERSITY PRESS   NEW YORK

COLUMBIA UNIVERSITY PRESS
Publishers Since 1893
New York   Chichester, West Sussex

cup.columbia.edu

Library of Congress Cataloging-in-Publication Data

Murphy, Laura T.
    Survivors of slavery : modern-day slave narratives / Laura T. Murphy.
        pages cm
    Includes bibliographical references and index.
    ISBN 978-0-231-16422-1 (cloth : alk. paper) — ISBN 978-0-231-16423-8 (pbk .: alk. paper) —
    ISBN 978-0-231-53575-5 (ebook)
 1. Slavery—History—21st century. 2. Slavery—Case studies. I. Title.

HT867.M67 2014
306.3'620905—dc23

                                                                            2013038839

Columbia University Press books are printed on permanent and durable acid-free paper.
This book is printed on paper with recycled content.
Printed in the United States of America

c 10 9 8 7 6 5 4 3 2 1
p 10 9 8 7 6 5 4 3 2 1

COVER DESIGN: Bryce Schimanski
COVER IMAGE: Ingram Publishing/SuperStock

References to websites (URLs) were accurate at the time of writing.
Neither the author nor Columbia University Press is responsible for URLs
that may have expired or changed since the manuscript was prepared.

CONTENTS

THE LISTENING ABOLITIONIST

EARLY ABOLITIONISTS UNDERSTOOD THAT THEY were working toward a revolution. When the first antislavery movement began in 1787, slavery was perfectly legal and had been a stable and pervasive part of most societies for thousands of years. It was supported by religion and was a key part of national economies. Leaders assured populations of its legitimacy and importance. The argument was made again and again that slavery, like the turning of the seasons or the growing of crops, was simply part of the natural order of things. It is hard for us, people of the twenty-first century, to grasp this fundamental acceptance—the popular understanding that, like death and taxes, slavery was a permanent part of the human condition.

In trying to convey and justify the revolution of abolition, writers in the nineteenth century would sometimes point to a Bible verse that illustrated a world turned upside down. It spoke of the last days when things were to be made right and illustrated that transformation by stating, "In those days I will even pour out my spirit on my slaves, men and women, and they will prophesy" (Acts 2:18 and Joel 2:29). The idea that slaves could have voices and use those voices in powerful ways was—and is often today—revolutionary. In the past, it was an idea so radical that it required the authority of a religious text in its support. Today, people still find it hard to hear the true and powerful voices of slaves. That is why Laura Murphy's careful attention to their words and stories is critically important.

The current antislavery movement, the movement that we hope will be the last such movement in human history through its eradication of slavery, has emerged at a time that is confused and troubled. Humanity, largely through its own activities, has created a profound crisis shaking the global economy and society and spinning off conflicts in the way a great thunderstorm seeds tornados. But the first abolitionist movements were also born in a time of great upheavals, national revolutions, devastating and long-lasting wars, violent colonial expansion, and the enormous and genocidal crime of the transatlantic slave trade. Yet in that time of militarism and inhuman commerce, the new movements, in opposition to the moral economy in which they evolved, valued the voices of the powerless and honored those who had suffered.

But as antislavery movements grew, their revolutionary fervor could fade. Gradualism could challenge immediatism, and earnest concern and discussion could replace liberation as the primary activity of abolition. For some parts of the contemporary antislavery movement, there is a similar threat of incipient stultification. While liberators and survivors risk their lives to help others to freedom, some "antislavery" groups and international organizations spend their time focused on the circular activities of awareness raising and fund-raising, harvesting through sensational pleading the means to continue their plea. It is in this context of a maturing movement that the guidance and voices of those who have been enslaved are most needed. As the power of the antislavery movement grows, there is a need that truth will speak to and guide that power.[1]

In this book, Laura Murphy provides the channel by which the voices and the lived experiences of slaves and former slaves might reach us clearly[2] and convey their truth and guidance. This is important because slaves are silenced in slavery, often brutally and finally. In freedom, two other forces work to mute slaves. The first is a social context that resists the challenge of freedom. Around the world, the majority of slaves live where enslavement receives at least partial support from local elites. Systems of oppression and discrimination, gender suppression, ethnic violence, religious prejudice, and bias according to caste, class, or race are the weft into which the warp of slavery is woven. To end slavery it is necessary to change the systems that allow slavery to exist. Freed slaves understand the calculus of oppression perfectly and will condemn its constituents. But these systems of hierarchy and oppression serve the powerful well, and speaking against them carries a risk. In the countries where slavery is most prevalent, local elites and government officials often prefer that freed slaves simply move away, but if they must stay, then they should be grateful, obsequious, and silent. Yet, remarkably, this social pressure and suppression are less effective than the second force at work that mutes former slaves: the sense of shame and dislocation that wells up from within the slave's own being.

Those who have been enslaved share many of the psychological sequelae of those subjected to sexual violence. Like a victim of rape, the former slave often feels shame. In both cases, the shame is irrational; neither victim has done anything wrong—indeed, both have been very seriously wronged. But the stigma of enslavement, the products of long-term denigration and abuse by slaveholders, press upon the mind and emotions of freed slaves and stifle their voices. The voices in this book have risen above that shame or, just as likely, have spoken even as it has tormented them. Is it any wonder that there might be clumsiness of expression or disjointed phrases when we know a former slave is speaking in spite of his or her pain? The hurt that sometimes bursts through survivors' words simply reflects the ache they still feel. Overcoming this shame can be a long process, but the very act of speaking and writing can be restorative. As Toni Morrison put it, "Freeing yourself was one thing; claiming ownership of that freed self was another."[3] That fact adds a special dimension to this book. These voices, these narratives, are both the truth of slavery and a way to resolve and vanquish the pain of slavery for freed slaves.

Vanquishing the pain of enslavement is an act that is sometimes sabotaged by the modern antislavery movement—an important theme that Murphy addresses in her discussion of the narratives and that Minh Dang makes clear in "Letter to the Antitrafficking Movement" in this foreword. If those who benefit from the systems that support slavery want their freed slaves absent or silent, modern "antislavery" groups that feed on publicity and sensation want their slavery victims to be attractive, pathetic, and grateful.

When survivors are manipulated and groomed for public presentation, the result is that our ears are stopped and muffled by our preconceptions. In our imagination, we "know" what slavery is like, we feel we understand the lives of slaves, and we apply our certain but deeply imperfect knowledge to all slaves. When we do so, we make a serious error. Slavery is a multilayered relationship. To become enslaved usually involves *social* relationships determined by power differences that make a person vulnerable to slavery. Once someone is enslaved, slavery is also fundamentally an *economic* relationship; a slaveholder's primary aim is to profit from his or her control over the slave. And between the slave and the slaveholder, taking a form marked by dependency and manipulation, slavery often becomes an *emotional* relationship. Each case of slavery is a unique expression of these layered relationships that is then further shaped by the culture, time, and place where it is found. The result is that no two cases of slavery are the same, and the range of variation in slavery is as wide as it is in other human relationships.

When we typecast freed slaves as pathetic victims, however well meaning that action might be, we deny the unique truth of each lived experience of slavery. We once again steal the individuality of the person who has been enslaved. If we do so to make slavery meet our own emotional, social, and economic needs, then we are not serving freedom—only ourselves. The antidote to this hubris is to be guided by those who know slavery best and appreciate freedom most: the survivors of slavery.

The guidance given us by freed slaves is not always comfortable. We want our slaveholders to be beings of pure evil, but freed slaves will tell us that slaveholders are people, too. We want our former slaves to be wise and patient, even though they are confused by freedom, angry at injustice, and dismissive of our slow and inadequate response to slavery. Our current antislavery movement still waits for its Frederick Douglass or Harriet Tubman, for a survivor with a true voice of great power. But it is important for us to remember that however we may honor Douglass and Tubman today, the previous antislavery movement often found these figures difficult and controversial. The voices in this book will push us to go faster than we are going, to give more than we are giving, and to be as radical and forceful in achieving freedom as slavery is powerful in its brutal practices.

If we listen, we'll be better abolitionists.

Kevin Bales
St. Saviours, Isle of Guernsey

JULY 2012

AN OPEN LETTER TO THE ANTITRAFFICKING MOVEMENT

MARCH 2013

Dear respected members of the anti-human-trafficking movement,

As a U.S. citizen and survivor of child abuse, incest, and domestic sex trafficking in the United States, I write to you to communicate my deepest wishes for how we approach our antitrafficking work. Over the past three years, I have publicly shared my story of slavery and freedom in venues large and small across the United States. I have met college students, teenagers, mothers, fathers, clergy, professors, service providers, and many others working to fight modern-day slavery. Through my presentations and conversations, I have developed a working set of **guiding principles for the antitrafficking movement.** I urge all of us to take heed of these principles because our adherence to or refutation of them will deeply affect the work that we do and the impact we have.

Principle Number 1: Rehumanize Survivors. I have often described my experience of trafficking as being like that of a caged animal at a zoo—an exotic creature that people could see from afar but could not touch. People who paid my owner were given special privileges to use my body for their entertainment. My movements were restricted and monitored, and my environment was not native to me. I was isolated from others in my own species. Although this simile fits, I have come to find that I also often felt like an alien. I always knew that I resembled human beings because of my two eyes, two arms, two legs, and same general body shape; however, it appeared as if I were not thinking or living like other human beings I witnessed.

The majority of my healing work thus far has focused on reconnecting with my humanity and the humanity of others. I have had to learn (or relearn) that I am human, that I was always human, and that the people out there—you as well as those who hurt me—are also human. My basic relationship to who I am, what I can expect of others, and what is possible in the world was damaged. As we incorporate survivors into the antitrafficking movement and encourage them to be at its forefront, we need to recognize their humanity. In a recent training, one of the participants asked me, "How do we as allies in this movement love survivors the way they need to be loved?" I responded, "How do you love yourself? I do not need you to love me any differently than you love yourself, and if you do not love yourself, then you cannot love me."

When people hear the stories of survivors, they oftentimes separate themselves from the survivor. Thoughts pass through their head such as, "Wow, I could never have gone through that. That person is so amazing. My life is nothing compared to that. My trauma was not *that* bad." It is these thoughts that often lead to actions that further isolate and alienate survivors from common humanity.

Survivors are *no different* than you are. You are no different than I am. Just because I have stood on the street corner soliciting sex does not mean that I cannot understand you and you cannot understand me. If you were born to my parents and put in the exact same situation, you would be writing this letter right now. Find a way to relate with survivors. You do not need to have gone through what they went through to imagine what they might experience. Also, share your own story—your own story of learning to love and trust, to cope with shame, to experience joy, and to discover your life's purpose.

One last thought on this point: when asking survivors to share their story publicly, pay attention to how this process may contribute to their continued dehumanization. What are your plans for the story? Are you merely curious and want to hear their story for personal consumption? Why must you see a survivor to believe the issue exists? Other than his or her story of slavery, what other knowledge and expertise might you ask the survivor to share? Are you compensating the survivor for his or her time and incidentals, just as you might a conference keynote speaker? What would you need or want for yourself if you were sharing your own story?

Principle Number 2: Get Out of the Box. As I was growing up, my prized possessions fit into about four shoeboxes. These shoeboxes contained report cards, notes from friends and teachers, pictures, choir concert programs, and magazine clippings. These items were pieces of my identity that were not celebrated by my parents while they were busy abusing me. I had to hide essential parts of my identity. What did not fit in a shoebox or could not be represented by an object, I buried deep inside my soul, hoping to reveal it someday in my unknown future. My parents and perpetrators forced me into the boxes of bad daughter, prostitute, whore, hurtful child, and on and on. In order to fit those boxes, I was made to contort myself into unfamiliar forms and to put on a mask as disguise. In my healing process, I have come to adorn new masks and to hide in new boxes, primarily those of victim and survivor. Today, about seven years after my escape from slavery, I am learning that I need to let others know about the hidden parts of myself and the parts of me that do not fall under the label *survivor*. I am a lover, an artist, a social scientist, a friend; I love poetry and peer-reviewed articles; I enjoy being physically active and going to street fairs. Through sharing all parts of my story and who I am, I can free myself from a life confined to recycled shoeboxes.

I invite our movement to join me in breaking down the boxes that we live in. I invite us to challenge the restrictions we put on our ways of being and thinking. Let's think outside the box about how we do our work. What is *not* being said? Whose story is *not* being told? Right now, awareness of domestic-minor sex trafficking, also known as commercial sexual exploitation of children, is growing in the United States. We need to remember the lesbian, gay, bisexual, and transgender youth and the boys who are also subjected to sex trafficking. We need to remember that women as well as men are buying and selling children. Many people associate trafficking with people in Southeast Asia or abroad working in brothels or being sold into factories, but we need to remember the international citizens who are sold into slavery in the United States—those who were promised a legitimate job as a nanny or a restaurant or farm or garment worker and instead were tricked into debt bondage. Unable to speak English and not knowing anyone or anything about their new environment, survivors of debt bondage don't talk to people about what has happened to them because of immigration concerns. Once these individuals are able to escape, they may be permanently dislocated from their home country and families. We need to remember that U.S. citizens are perpetrators of slavery, just as foreigners are.

What is human trafficking about when we look beyond sensationalized stories? How is *human trafficking* less fit a term for what is truly slavery? How is "modern-day slavery" different from historical slavery? Or is it different at all?

Principle Number 3: Sing a New Song. Many of us know what it's like to have a song stuck in our head. For survivors, the song is often one of humiliation, shame, and degradation: "You slut! Who do you think you are? You're good for nothing, only to be used. You think anyone will believe you? You asked for it. You liked it. Why didn't you just leave? Shut up! I don't want to hear you. You mean nothing. No one will love you. You should be grateful." And on and on.

It is time for us to sing a new song—to raise our voices in unison and drown out the old verses. Let's sing songs like the following: "You were born an innocent child. It wasn't your fault. I am so sorry. You were mistreated. You are strong and resilient. How are you feeling? It's okay to feel angry. It's okay to cry. You deserved better. I love you."

However, as we all know, songs are not easy to uproot from our memories. They are deeply engrained as neuropathways in our brains, and though it is possible, it takes many new experiences to rewire our brain. After nearly twenty-one years of slavery, I have lived only 25 percent of my life in freedom. That means that 75 percent of my life was spent hearing lies and insults. On April 16, 2026, the balance of my days on this earth will finally reach 50 percent in slavery and 50 percent in freedom. As I write this letter, that is more than thirteen years from now.

For every interaction that communicated to me that I was worth nothing, I need to practice and surround myself with experiences that breed self-worth. I cannot take self-worth for granted. I must work for it. I am learning that self-love in adulthood does not come from the outside. As a child, I needed my parents to love me so that I could feel loveable. Today, I find that love from the outside goes only so far. Although it is helpful to experience the love of others, no matter how many times I am told that I am beautiful, intelligent, loveable, and wonderful, self-love does not just seep through my skin via osmosis. I must work for it. I must see these qualities and own them for myself.

Until the balance of my days tips toward freedom, the words and songs of others bring comfort and shed doubt on my false beliefs about who I am. They help me see myself when my vision is clouded by the images laid out by my perpetrators. They are whispers in my ear as I develop my own voice. I am as worthy as any other being on the planet just because I am. I am a human being, not a human doing.

In the "doings" of our movement, we now have our own recycled song— that of the three P's: *prevention*, *protection*, and *prosecution*. Although I do not minimize the importance of these three P's, I suggest that we transition to embracing three additional P's: *preparation*, *partnership*, and *promise*.

Preparation. People from all walks of life are entering the antitrafficking movement. Prevention efforts include training of law enforcement and service providers, but I also argue that preparation goes beyond learning statistics and warning signs. Preparation must include a self-reflective and emotional component. How prepared are people to hold the horrors of human trafficking? How prepared are people to hold the horrors while celebrating the joys? How informed are people of their motivations? Are we here to "save" participants because we think they have sinned? Or do we see our own futures as intertwined with the futures of survivors of human trafficking? What stereotypes do we bring to this work? What stereotypes are we reinforcing? As a former service-learning professional, I am adamant about training and supporting those who serve in communities and those who work for social justice. How will we sustain this movement for the long term? How will we ensure that those who do this work do not succumb to their despair but find ways to embrace it, share it, and move on?

Partnership. I already witness service providers coming together to share best practices. I see law enforcement working with service providers to ensure survivor safety. I see survivors coming together to provide support to one another and to assert their voices in our movement. I urge all of you to continue to partner with survivors—to ask survivors not just about their stories, but also about their policy recommendations, their ideas for improved intervention, as well as their hopes and concerns for the movement. I also ask that members of our movement do not seek to divide and separate survivors by focusing only on sex trafficking or on labor trafficking or to overemphasize international survivors or domestic survivors; rather, I ask that you face the complexities of this issue, refrain from reducing diverse experiences into a neat package, and portray both the similarities and differences in survivor experience. Partnership is defined as having joint interest—I ask that you build relationships with survivors and find joint interests with them.

Survivors are critical to the movement because every successful social movement is guided by those directly affected by the injustice. I urge the movement to invest in the training and leadership of survivors of human trafficking. Survivors have much to contribute, and we must support their healing and autonomy as they take center stage in antislavery efforts.

Finally, as we lift up survivors, I ask that we work to avoid entrenching a divide between survivors and nonsurvivors. Just as I am weary of a movement led only by service providers, I am weary of a movement led only by survivors. I know so little about freedom that my experiences are limited. How can I expect to know the *true* boundaries of what is possible? Nonsurvivors similarly have a limit to what they can know about the experience of slavery. By working in partnership, however, we can utilize our individual strengths and account for the gaps in our partners.

Promise. I speak not of a contract or agreement that one makes with another, but rather of *potential*. Prevention, prosecution, and protection do not address much about the future for survivors of human trafficking. If survivors successfully put their perpetrators in jail and then sufficiently feel safe in their homes and communities, what comes next? What about the rest of their lives? What about their hopes and dreams and their potential to live life beyond their years of slavery? After more than thirty years of imprisonment, the character Brooks in the movie *The Shawshank Redemption* (1994) committed suicide shortly following his release from prison. He did not know how to live in freedom. He had adapted to a restricted form of living. How does this apply to survivors of slavery? They must consider long-term support and services to ensure (re)acclimation to freedom. We must consider the potential for thriving, not just surviving.

Principle Number 4: Address Emotional Poverty and Profits. By now, we all have heard that human trafficking is a multi-billion-dollar industry. It thrives because it is a business—because traffickers can make monetary profits by selling human beings again and again. Although laudable efforts have been made to interrupt the financial gains from human trafficking, it appears that money can't be the only problem. If it were really an issue of money, just as if world hunger and poverty were merely an issue of money, we would throw our money at the issue and end human suffering.

Why does human trafficking persist? I argue that we are at a time of extreme *emotional poverty* and that traffickers receive *emotional profits* from their deeds. It is *gratifying* for traffickers to feel a sense of domination. I understand that for most of us this idea is hard to grasp. Why would a human being enjoy dominating and inflicting pain on another person? It is because by inflicting pain and dominating others, traffickers can deflect their own pain, pass on their own history of trauma, and avoid their own emotional suffering.

This happens every day among "regular" people. It is rooted in our society and our biology that we seek to harm those who have harmed or wish to harm us. We carry an eye-for-an eye mentality. When we've had an emotionally rough day at work, we come home and argue with our families. We yell at the dog, we rage while driving, we hate people of a particular faith or race or sexual orientation, and so on. We displace our own pain, and so do traffickers. So let's not put traffickers into some subhuman/nonhuman category of people. We all are seeking some emotional release. We feel emotionally empty, and so we use others to fill us up. We use drugs, sex, food, TV, and, yes, the enslavement of others to fill an emotional need that we don't think can be gratified otherwise. Emotional poverty does not just happen—it is developed over many years. How have we deprived our children and ourselves of love, connection, empathy, and freedom? How does this deprivation sustain itself through our family dynamics, schools, communities, businesses, and institutions? If we do not fill our emptiness through harmful ways, what do we do with it?

I have had to learn to sit with it. To grieve that the emptiness I carry is from the past and cannot be filled. Now I must create fullness in my present and my future. I am very troubled by the fact that my parents made hundreds of thousands of dollars from exploiting my body. However, more than troubled, I am plagued by the fact that they completely disregarded my humanity. It was the fact that another human being, let alone my parents, refused to have a relationship with me—with my humanity—that caused my psychological, emotional, and existential wounds. My humanity was sacrificed for other people's emotional gratification. Financial gratification is only temporary. Money doesn't buy happiness, so a trafficker may seek to earn more and more money, hoping that it will fill that emotional hole. It won't. And while they are on an impossible quest to extinguish their feelings of emptiness by using other people as objects of gratification, many people's basic human rights are robbed, spit on, and disrespected.

Principle Number 5: Peace Is in the Pain. In my weekly therapy sessions, I am reminded of my need to grieve for the losses of my childhood. Like my perpetrators, I will seek to regain my irretrievable losses if I do not grieve for them. Grief acknowledges that there *is* emptiness—that there is loss. I recently heard the term *disenfranchised grief,* and it resonated with me. Though I know nothing of its origins and definitions, I have used this term to name the unacknowledged and unwitnessed sorrow that I experienced as a child. Enfranchisement is the empowerment of a vote. Disenfranchisement is a silencing. Disenfranchised grief is a silenced pain that I walk around with. I try to hide it, I face it in small and large doses, and time and time again I am surprised at the depth and the quantity of grief that I experience.

How *do* I grieve for my losses? I have lost *so* much. I lost parents. I never truly had parents. I had slave masters. I lost an entire childhood and all of the appropriate developmental stages, countless hours of playing and relaxing, years of sleep, an experience of the basic goodness of human beings, and an experience of my own basic goodness. The loss brought about by the trauma I endured cannot be regained. Because I missed so much in my childhood, I am often living from a place of scarcity—scrambling to "get" as much out of life as I can. When I'm trying to "get," however, I'm not really being in my life or enjoying it much. Days come and go, and I don't feel fulfilled. So no matter how much I do now and how full I fill my days, more does not make up for the less, the lack, the loss.

Grieving for my losses will help me pursue goals that are possible rather than goals that are *im*possible (like making up lost time). Grieving frees me of the pain and burden I've carried alone for so many years and opens up space for new adventures and joys. Grieving brings me true peace with what I have suffered and where I am now. In our movement, how do we sit with the grief of survivors? Or do we even sit at all? Are we too eager to "take action" that we forget that sitting and listening are actions? Are we too afraid to feel the depth of our own pain and thus try to avoid the depth of another's sorrow? So often when I share the pain of my experience, people remind me of how great my life is now. They tell me great things about myself. Some unique few cry with me. They cry for themselves *next* to me. They do not cry *for* me, but *with me*.

Grieving is not just for survivors. Grieving is for all of us. We all live in a world where violence pervades our everyday ways of relating with each other. We have experienced violence, and we have enacted violence—whether big or small. What losses does the antitrafficking movement need to recognize? What sorrows are we avoiding?

Principle Number 6: Survivor Stories Are Not Enough to Sustain This Movement. The first time I shared my story publicly was in April 2006 at a poetry reading in Berkeley. I was taking "Poetry for the People," a course designed and taught by the late June Jordan, a scholar, activist, and writer. It was my last semester of my undergraduate degree, and I was in the midst of emancipating myself from my slave masters. When I finally broke free, I felt liberated, and poem after poem about my years of enslavement began to flow out of me. The poem that I read nearly seven years ago seems an appropriate ending for this letter and my final guiding principle. In that poem entitled "My Name Is Revolution," I end with this:

> this poem is about revolution
> because even when I write these words
> I am not supposed to be alive

I am not supposed to be free
I am not supposed to be anything
but my parents' slave

this poem is about revolution
this poem
these words
my stories
must continue
or
I will not exist
I write
so
I exist
I write
so
I claim a life that was stolen from me
my name is Minh Dang
every time I speak
I speak a history
of incest
I speak a history
of slavery
I speak a history
that generation after generation after generation
continues to overlook
chooses to ignore as something rare
child abuse is not rare
slavery is not rare
I will not be silent
I will not
be silent
I
will
not
be
silent

I write so that I exist. I write for myself, and I speak for myself. I have learned that in sharing my own journey, I empower others to do the same. From my own experience of doing social justice work, I have come to believe that fighting for others is *not* enough. I am adamant that any pursuit of social justice must coincide with our own pursuit of personal justice. Individual healing and community healing *must* go hand in hand. As Dr. Martin Luther King Jr. said, "Injustice anywhere is a threat to justice everywhere." If we tolerate a lack of self-love in our own lives, how can we truly promote self-love in the lives of others? If we enact micro- or macroaggressions on the people nearest to us, how do we also enact these aggressions in the world at large?

My story is not enough to sustain this movement. It is surely not enough to sustain you. I hope that each of you finds a way in which you have been dehumanized. Then you can begin to empathize with the survivors of human trafficking. I hope that each of you also takes the courageous step of looking at how you have dehumanized others, whether in big or small ways. Then you can begin to empathize with perpetrators of human trafficking. Empathy and understanding is *the* difference between surviving and thriving. Empathy counteracts the severe alienation that a human being feels when he or she is treated as an object. Empathy counteracts an "us" versus "them" mentality.

In the words of aboriginal activist Lilla Watson, "If you have come here to help me, you are wasting your time, but if you have come here because your liberation is bound up with mine, then let us work together."

With deep gratitude and a fire in my belly,
Minh Dang
Berkeley, California

ACKNOWLEDGMENTS

THERE ARE NOT SUFFICIENT WORDS to express the enormity of my gratitude to the courageous people who choose to tell their stories of enslavement. This book is a testimony in nearly forty voices to the horrors of
slavery, to the audacity of survival, and to the enormous responsibility of
freedom. The people who have written or told their stories for this collection have my humblest admiration and thanks for their willingness to share
their stories despite the immeasurable pain it takes to narrate slavery. Their
narratives of freedom are an inspiration and an encouragement to me to
continue to work toward the abolition of modern slavery.

I must also thank the organizations and activists who have contributed their time and their work to this collection as well as to the modern abolitionist cause. Thanks to Free the Slaves—especially Kevin Bales,
Peggy Callahan, Ginny Baumann, Judy Hyde, Jody Sarich, and Terry
Fitzpatrick—and to the Coalition to Abolish Slavery and Trafficking
(CAST)—the Survivor Advisory Caucus, Vanessa Lanza, and Kay Buck.
These two organizations provided contacts and interviews for substantial
parts of the book. Polaris Project, Protection Project, the Albanian Association of Girls and Woman, and World Vision International provided access
to narratives as well. Thanks to Laura Lederer for her help in contextualizing some of the narratives and for decades of service to this cause. My
gratitude also goes to Christopher Shay and Inge Bell for being willing to
share their work for this project as well as to Rod Soodalter, Bridgette Carr,
and Sandy Shepherd for their help in understanding the issue and for putting me in contact with people who were crucial to the completion of this

THIS BOOK IS A COLLECTION OF modern-day slave narratives. It marks the reemergence of a narrative genre that many of us thought had died with the last of the survivors of legal slavery in the Americas. Slavery unfortunately did not end with its abolition in any country in the world. Instead, it went underground. It often operates under different and more obscure names, such as *conscription, trafficking, peonage*. But the basic elements of slavery—the forced labor, the lack of pay, the inability to escape—remain the same. And the drive to tell the story of slavery remains as strong among survivors today as it did during the antebellum period.

Since the turn of the twenty-first century, increasing attention has been paid to these situations of forced labor, and we are calling it by its rightful name: *slavery*. As concerned global citizens slowly come to realize that slavery still exists and always has existed in our midst, survivors of slavery are increasingly coming forward to report and reflect on their lived experiences of enslavement. Thus, in the past decade or so, the slave narrative has been reborn.

This book is an open condemnation of the global crime that is modern slavery. It has two explicit goals. The first is to find an audience for the courageous survivors who have chosen to testify to their experiences of enslavement and provide an impetus for activists, scholars, students, and citizens to work to eradicate these contemporary forms of bondage. The second, complimentary goal is to engage the narratives from a scholarly perspective that understands these testimonies of modern slavery as the primary documents of the emerging field of modern slavery studies and the now radically

Each story documents an individual's unique experience of enslavement in his or her own words. These narratives provide us the opportunity to learn of slavery and its effects directly from those who have experienced and escaped or still live its horrors. As many of the narrators insist, the first-hand accounts of survivors of slavery are crucial for any informed discussion of the issue and to the formation of policies and practices that respond to it. Too often we rely on abstract statistics to guide our understanding of political issues such as this one, but the voices of survivors contextualize those statistics in real, lived experience.

The goal of this collection is to present as faithfully as possible the unembellished reflections of people who have experienced slavery firsthand. For that reason, no professional creative writers have been employed in this project as amanuenses (or ghost writers) for the survivors, and no contributors were prompted to write any particular narratives for this volume. As a result, some translations sound choppy, or the narrators do not utilize what we might want to call "proper English." The stories sometimes leave out the very details we were expecting to hear. In order to get as close to the narrators' voices as possible, they remain unaltered except for some changes in punctuation when necessary for understanding, particularly in the case of orally delivered narratives, and some changes in the presentation of numbers, capitalization, and compound terms. The occasional inserted word or phrase is marked in square brackets when orally transcribed narratives are less clear in the transcription than they are on video. Perpetrators' names have been omitted to avoid legal repercussions.

Some slave narratives available to readers in other volumes have been written or embellished by professional writers in the expectation that amplified drama renders the experience of slavery more realistic or more compelling. Other collections have abbreviated or condensed the narratives or removed the interview apparatus to focus more clearly on particular aspects of the narrator's story. Some collections have been commissioned by particular organizations, churches, or political groups. By contrast, a wide assortment of narratives from a variety of different sources have been collected here and kept in their original form in pursuit of the goal of representing the breadth of experiences of enslavement in the world today. When narratives have been abbreviated for the sake of space, the omissions have been indicated clearly. (All ellipses in the text indicate a pause in the speech of the narrator, not a deletion.) The focus on variety and fidelity to the original story is meant to create a more multifaceted and accurate composite image of slavery today, while recognizing that each narrative individually has its own limitations, impulses, and politics associated with it. The expectation is that this method will provide more useful materials for scholars, activists, and others who read these narratives now and in the future.

The primary limitations on creating this collection have been lack of access to survivors and sensitivity to their privacy. In collecting these narratives, I had access only to those people who have already publicly discussed their experiences through the media or through nonprofit organizations. Out of sensitivity to the fact that many people are hesitant (to say the least) about sharing their stories (whether that be out of fear for their safety or because they simply want to put the experience of slavery behind them), I did not contact survivors who had not publicly testified about their experience, and I asked organizations to recommend only those survivors who had expressed interest in having their stories widely shared. Although the slave narrative has a long history of effectively mobilizing abolitionist movements, sensitivity to survivors of slavery was the first priority in creating this collection in order to avoid exploiting people who were not ready or interested in sharing their stories.

Unfortunately, this editorial choice means that there are many people whose voices could not be included here, even many who might have been interested in sharing their experiences. People who have no access to nongovernmental aid organizations, those who have never had access to a legal system that would record their stories, those who do not have access to the Internet or have never had the ability to share their stories with others cannot be included here. Thus, this book represents the voices of a particular group of slavery survivors—those who have managed to make their voices heard—but it should also be a reminder of all of those who have not had that privilege.

Although the narratives have been altered only very slightly in the editorial process, this does not mean that they come to us unmediated. They were originally written or told in a wide variety of circumstances and thus reveal different investments in the telling and recording of the stories. As Sidonie Smith and Kay Schaffer remind us, the activists and scholars who use first-person narratives as a means of informing the public of human rights violations choose and "package" very particular stories that they think will speak to or appeal to their target audiences.[11] Congressional leaders and lawyers are similarly selective in the cases they bring before hearings and the court. Smith and Schaffer appropriately urge us to question what power relations were involved in the production of the narratives, what political or cultural circumstances might have been involved, what audiences were intended to hear the stories, and what expectations the narrators had for the stories they tell.[12] In order to give the reader a better sense of the varied rhetorical situations that encourage the production of these narratives, a wide variety of testimonies have been included here, and contextual information is supplied in introductory remarks and tables preceding the narratives. Readers are encouraged to ponder these issues as they read and analyze the narratives.

Some of the survivors first submitted their testimonies to judicial or legislative bodies. In these narratives, survivors often employ the language of the courts in order to have their claims heard and adjudicated fairly. In other cases, survivors recounted their stories for nonprofit organizations that support their activist work or that have helped to liberate people in their region. These narrators often make a plea for further support from the organization and its donors or shape their narratives in a way that encourages increased commitment to abolition, much like nineteenth-century slave narrators did. Still others wrote or told their stories as a means of healing their own pain, and these stories often show the markers of a greater internal deliberation or contemplation of the experience of slavery. All of these stories are shaped by the desires and interests of the narrators' and collectors' intended audiences. Some of the stories were written by survivor activists who heard about the publication of this volume and wanted to participate, but even in those cases the stories are shaped by the narrators' notions of what this book would be and what constitutes a compelling and convincing story of slavery and survival. The interests and pressures expressed in all of these responses to varied narrative contexts are themselves important parts of the experience of enslavement and liberation.

The contexts in which the stories are told are also crucial for understanding the narratives themselves. Each situation of production generates a different language, a different tone, and a different mode of narration. Many of the narratives submitted by nonprofits have been through the mediation of translation, which means that we have access only to the rendering of the narrator's voice that an interpreter makes available. Some nuances and details can be lost in this process. The very questions that the interviewers ask shape the stories that people tell and how they tell them. The people who were present during an interview may have influenced what a narrator chose to tell of his or her story as well. Even the choice and arrangement of the narratives into chapters for this project reveals something about how the editorial process informs our understanding of the narratives and slavery in general. In these many ways, the creation of the archive of slavery is itself shaping the production of the narratives, and this aspect of the production cannot be mistaken or forgotten.

When scholars began to look to nineteenth-century slave narratives to better comprehend antebellum slavery, they had to commit themselves to rhetorical and contextual detective work, a literary archaeology of slavery, in order to understand the intent, meaning, and politics that informed those stories. The table that precedes each narrative in this collection is meant to provide the context that will aid readers in making sense of the investments and conditions that may have influenced the narrator's story or the version of it that is available to us. Without these contexts, we risk seeing the slave narrative as a genre that stands outside of space and time. A primary aim of this book is to give readers an apparatus that will help them situate the modern slave narrative in the precise political, historical, and cultural spaces from which it was born as a way of encouraging more sensitive, culturally specific, politically informed engagement with this complex genre and the overall issue it represents.

Regardless of the motivations the narrators may have had in telling their stories, the narratives collected here represent the testimonies of people who have been enslaved in the past twenty years. They are the voices of slavery and freedom today. This book is an archive of a global crime we thought was long ago eradicated. It is proof to us now and to future readers that slavery still exists and that there are survivors who are speaking out in order to abolish it once again.

SLAVE NARRATIVES: PAST AND PRESENT

Social movements that aim to eradicate injustice are deeply indebted to the stories that survivors tell of their personal experiences. No social movement can make a case for itself without the testimony of the people who have survived injustice and lived to tell it. In the nineteenth century, slave narratives were an important and powerful component of the antislavery movement in both Great Britain and the United States. As William L. Andrews writes, "Nineteenth-century abolitionists sponsored the publication of the narratives of escaped slaves out of a conviction that first-person accounts of those victimized by and yet triumphant over slavery would mobilize white readers more profoundly than any other kind of antislavery discourse."[13] More than simply a tool of white abolitionists, however, the slave narrative became a way for former slaves to prove both their literacy and their desire to emancipate themselves and others. Autobiography provided the slave narrator a venue through which to "*write* himself into the human community through the action of first-person narration," as Charles Davis and Henry Louis Gates Jr. put it.[14] The slave narrators' words insisted upon their individuality, their humanity, their citizenship, and their agency in a world that attempted to deny them those basic rights. Their narratives engaged and mobilized politicians and activists to support their movement for freedom for all people. These early narratives have more recently become an important source for scholars' understanding of slavery and abolition in the nineteenth century.

Despite the differences in the forms slavery takes today, the stories in this collection bear a striking resemblance to the narratives told by nineteenth-century African American survivors of the antebellum plantation system. Indeed, the way people narrate their experiences of slavery has changed less than one would suspect, given the fact that few if any of these narrators had ever heard of Frederick Douglass before they wrote or told their life stories. Like their predecessors, the authors who tell their stories of twenty-first-century enslavement, either here or in other works (see "Suggestions for Further Reading and Viewing" in appendix C), often begin with a story of their origins, of their existence *before* they knew slavery, thus insisting on their humanity, on their right not to be enslaved. Although nineteenth-century narrators repeatedly remarked that they were "*born* a slave" rather than free, their focus on birth and parentage was part of a claim to a humanity that preceded and exceeded their experience of slavery, according to James Olney and Francis Smith Foster.[15] The twentieth- and twenty-first-century narrators likewise typically remind their audiences that they were born free and insist on the same thing—that they have a right to their freedom despite whatever experiences they may have had between being born a human purportedly endowed with liberty and their current status as a freed citizen.

Modern-day slave narrators, like nineteenth-century narrators, also describe in unsurprising detail the cruel people who played integral roles in the perpetuation of their enslavement, the threats against their friends and family, and the widespread corruption that allowed slaveholders to constantly tighten their grip on the enslaved. They tell the tales of the slaveholders' refusal to provide for their needs, the denial of their religious and educational rights, and the extraordinary abuses they witnessed being enacted upon other enslaved people around them.

Perhaps more interesting, however, is the fact that whether their testimonies include the experiences of people who were enslaved along with them or of the people they have helped as activists since becoming free, narrators often relieve themselves of the pain of reliving their own experience by telling the stories of other victims they have known. Former slaves often avoid expressing too explicitly their own suffering by describing how brutally other people were treated (as is evident, for example, in James Kofi Annan's depiction of young boys in the fishing industry in chapter 7), and they often describe others' heroic (but often failed) efforts to escape (such as the tragic failed escape depicted in Sina Vann's narrative in chapter 8). The stories depicting others' suffering is often code for the narrators' own suffering and can tell us much about what the narrators refuse to describe about themselves. Cambodian Somaly Mam, for instance, is explicit about her discomfort in talking about her time as a sex slave. Instead, she often speaks about the victims she is aiding as an activist or the headway she has made in legislation against trafficking. Through this circumventive form of narration as well as through their activism itself, the narrators gain some control over slavery.

Though it may seem counterintuitive, the exploration of the actual *work* performed as a slave is often kept short, perhaps because of the difficulty narrators have in expressing and reliving the pain of that time in their lives. Instead, as in many nineteenth-century narratives, much time is spent describing plots to escape, failed escape attempts (as discussed in chapter 4), and then the final successful attempt that gained the narrator his or her freedom (which is shown throughout the book, but most clearly in chapter 5). Paul Lovejoy has noted this focus on freedom in the nineteenth-century narrative as well and has argued that perhaps we should dispense with the "slave narrative" moniker for many narratives and begin to call these texts "freedom narratives."[16] Indeed, modern slave narrators speak of their escapes in extensive detail, while often leaving the experience of the actual work of slavery in the shadows, revealing the way the genre is shaped as much by silences as by what is made explicit on the page. This is the case for forced sex workers in particular, who almost never describe an encounter with a client in any detail but instead dwell for the majority of their narratives on the physical and psychological abuse by their pimps and their plots to escape. By analyzing both the narrators' words as well as the events and emotions that remain marginalized in the narratives, we can begin to sketch the contours of a genre that can encompass both the historical narratives and the contemporary ones.

Throughout this collection, chapter introductions discuss the narrative and genre conventions that emerge from these new slave narratives, interweaving information and statistics about modern slavery useful for contextualizing the experiences described by the survivors. Each chapter pursues a particular theme or trend in slave narratives that tells us something about the binding characteristics of this varied phenomenon called "modern-day slavery" and instructs us on how to fight it. The chapters also reveal something about the experience of creating an image of oneself after slavery and finding the means to tell that story. The fact that the slave narratives of the nineteenth, twentieth, and twenty-first centuries share so much is critical to our understanding of slavery itself as well as to our understanding of the narrative strategies people employ to describe slavery. This collection of first-person narratives of slavery provides us with a unique opportunity for understanding the ways survivors engage the experience of enslavement and trauma through writing and storytelling.

It also provides us an opportunity to effect change ourselves. The primary goal of the slave narrative of the nineteenth century was to encourage antislavery activism and to educate disbelieving Northerners about the true perils of the slave system in the South. These first-person narratives of torture and abuse moved audiences around the world to legally abolish slavery slowly but surely over the course of the nineteenth century. The new narratives given here and elsewhere perform the same activist ambitions, urging readers to take action to ensure that the laws that now make slavery illegal all over the world are enforced and that people who are exploited are protected. The narratives collected here are a call to action.

DEFINING SLAVERY TODAY

Part of the difficulty in eradicating slavery and, indeed, in narrating it is that most people in the world do not understand what it means to be enslaved today, and they are hesitant to believe that slavery still exists. Many people wonder whether what we are seeing (or even what they are personally experiencing) today is actually slavery. It is important that we are clear about this. The people who are enslaved today, the people who have chosen to tell their stories here, would easily be recognized as slaves even if we were using the definition of slavery that is familiar to us from nineteenth-century plantation slavery in the Americas. What the people who are considered enslaved today have in common with antebellum American slaves is that they are forced to work against their will, often well beyond their capacity to work. Their labor, the fruits or products of their labor, and the profit from their labor are not their own, though others typically profit enormously from that labor. Though they may want to quit their "jobs" and move on to better situations, they are not allowed to, and they are almost always threatened with violence or other abuse if they attempt to walk away. When they do try to leave, the word they must use to describe this effort is *escape*. Though they all may not have self-evident "owners," they are forced to work without pay and under threat of violence, which renders them enslaved.

The existence of slavery today may be hard to detect because slaves are no longer bought and sold in open markets (or even in secret ones), for the most part. Not all slaveholders legally "own" their slaves. In fact, it is even more lucrative for slaveholders *not* to own people.[17] Slave traders and traffickers often falsely offer to provide an education to the children of impoverished families but instead put the young children to work in the fishing industry or industrial farm until they are no longer able to perform the work or until they die. No money need be exchanged when the promise of an education is proffered. In this way, the slaveholder has made absolutely no investment in the labor the child has provided. To purchase a person outright would cost a trafficker more and would be more difficult or dangerous. Because enslaving a person and utilizing his or her entire capacity for work costs little or nothing and can often be easily negotiated, especially in the most impoverished regions of the world, Kevin Bales has dubbed modern-day slaves "disposable people."[18] When slaveholders spend so little on labor, they begin to imagine the worker as disposable, expend-able, fully exploitable. Ownership and purchase are thus not the funda-mental characteristics of enslavement; rather, it is the forced extraction of labor for another person's profit that is essential in defining slavery.

It might also appear that some people we are calling slaves had the oppor-tunity to "choose" their occupation or position and therefore seem to have "chosen" the conditions in which they labor. Women around the world often find themselves in dire economic straights that force them to regard their bodies as their only capital. On the vast spectrum of what constitutes choice, they indeed choose to become sex workers. Some commercial sex workers argue that they do not feel exploited by their work. Others do feel exploited by sex work—much more than most other people feel exploited in their jobs—but they willingly tolerate it because they are able to make a living by doing it. These people are not enslaved. The men and women whom we are characterizing as enslaved here may have at one time decided that sex work was acceptable employment for them. However, what marks them as enslaved is that when they do find work in the sex industry, they are held to that work by force, and when they decide to quit, they find that they are not free to leave—that quitting their jobs means *having to escape*, and a failed escape can mean punishment, violence, even death.

The same is often true of other workers—agricultural workers in the United States, for instance. Though many laborers willingly immigrate to the United States (legally and illegally) in search of opportunities for employment, some employers take advantage of their relative vulnerability as immigrants and force them to work without pay. In agricultural areas, some farms are quietly operated using forced immigrant work pools. When these workers realize that their situation is exploitative, that their bosses are not paying them, that they are being housed twenty to an apartment, that they have been duped, they also realize that if they attempt to quit their job, they will be beaten or even killed. Though many of the people who are enslaved today did seek out work, they realized too late that they had not found legitimate employment but instead were not paid and were prohib-ited from quitting—in other words, enslaved.

POWER AND THE WORD SLAVERY

Though it is clear, then, that slavery does still exist even into the twenty-first century, it is appropriate that most of us are hesitant to use the word *slavery* loosely. Much of our anxiety over the issue is related to our reverence for the African American victims and survivors of the transatlantic slave trade. It is crucial that we pay respect to the pain and suffering that enslaved people endured throughout history and that their descendants have endured as we witness the legacy of injustice worldwide that is the result of past slaveries.

Yet this is also precisely why using the word *slavery* in the modern context is so important.[19] What we are doing is establishing that the violation of a human's right to self-determination and to his or her own labor is a consistent characteristic of slavery, whether we are talking about the antebellum American context or a vast spectrum of other slaveries around the world throughout history or the varied contemporary manifestations of slavery today.

We must call this contemporary violation against humans "slavery" because that is precisely what it is. By using the word *slavery*, we honor the struggles of those who had to live through slavery in the past by saying that we have not forgotten those struggles and will not stop before *all* slavery has been eradicated in the world. To call this particular form of injustice by its rightful name, *slavery*, is to recognize the power of language to indicate the gravity of the problem today. When people say that the victims of slavery today live in "slavelike" conditions, they underestimate the extraordinary experience of those who are forced to work without the means to escape, and at the same time they exonerate those who are willing perpetrators of the modern slave trade. We cannot hesitate to call slavery by its real name when we see it; doing so reminds us that the work of abolition is still incomplete.

Using the word *slavery* compels us to articulate the common denominators that characterize it over time and space, as has been done here. Evoking this term requires our precision and responsibility. As Joel Quirk has argued, however, the work of abolition is a long-fought, multinational, and multifaceted series of battles that have precedents in many contexts—with both positive and negative consequences—that we must take into account as we struggle to address it today.[20] A nuanced portrait of slavery today, situated in the context of these historical global slaveries, must be informed by the unique and varied experiences of survivors from around the world who nonetheless prove that using the word *slavery* is just as important now as it was in the world-changing global abolitionist movements of the nineteenth century.

Because of the power of the word *slavery*, it is important to distinguish it from other forms of exploitative labor. In fact, millions of people working around the world today are forced to tolerate excruciatingly exploitative working conditions in order to survive the hardships of poverty. Many people work multiple jobs for less than a living wage and cannot feed their families. Many people do not have reasonable alternatives to the physically abusive working conditions they endure in their current employment. As global citizens dedicated to the eradication of suffering and inequality in our world, we need to address these dire circumstances. However, when we talk about slavery, it is important to recognize that we genuinely do mean people who are trapped in inescapable forced labor, being paid nothing or only enough to keep them alive to work another day.

When people use the word *slavery* to mean something that is painful but not forced or inescapable, they diminish the power of the word. Using the word as a metaphor to represent the worst possible things imaginable also undermines its political power. Some American political organizations and legislators, for instance, have tried to define all sex work as slavery in an effort to mobilize the word's political power. They believe that if they mark all sex work as slavery, then people will understand how horrific the conditions of the sex industry can be. They are not always describing inescapable forced labor, however. What those movements seek to do is to encourage people to act by *comparing* the problem they are addressing—for instance, the sale of sex, alcohol abuse, violent marriages—to slavery in a way that is suggestive of the horrors associated with the issue, but not indicative of actual slavery. In this way, the word *slavery* has been so overused in our culture that it has lost much of its power of meaning and has thus become a word that encourages us to doubt its validity when we hear it. These metaphorical uses diminish the word's capacity to have a political impact. Like the casual use of the word *rape* to mean anything that seems abusive, cruel, or over the top, the word *slavery* will lose its impact if we keep using it as a flimsy weapon against our workaholic colleagues or our political foes. Utilizing it to represent forced labor, however, is a powerful statement against extraordinary oppression.

Recent media coverage of prostitution has had a similar watering-down effect. MSNBC's series of sensationalist reports with titles such as *Sex Slaves in America*, *Sex Slaves in the Suburbs*, and *Sex Slaves: The Teen Trade* use flashy images, superficial dramatizations, and ominous music to scare the populace into protecting their innocent daughters from harm.[21] Though it is true that commercial sexual exploitation is a very real threat around the world, these programs sensationalize sex slavery, creating an almost tantalizing image of the women and their experiences. The programs appear to use slavery primarily as a way to create shocking and melodramatic programming for weekend viewing. This naive and dangerous approach to the problem promotes a generalized view of all sex workers as victims and diminishes the political power of the appropriate use of the word *slavery*. By exaggerating and melodramatizing, such programs misinform the public and encourage activism that can do more harm than good. Film portrayals of modern slavery are similar. Recent Hollywood films and television programs that have portrayed modern-day slavery make it seem as if all enslaved people are innocent girls tricked into the sex industry, though a lucky few can be saved by a brawny and caring action hero—always a man and often a father. They simplify the nature of modern slavery and propose naive and sexist solutions to a complicated global phenomenon. In this way, the word *slavery* is again being used in a metaphorical way—it is not being used to provoke thought about actual forced labor, but simply to highlight the latest titillating scandal that media outlets can sell to audiences voracious for shocking programming.

All of this tells us that we must commit serious energy to radically shifting public understanding of slavery in the modern context and begin to use this word that has such a great impact with the full force that it can muster.

OVERVIEW

The chapters in this book could have been organized in many different ways—by forms of enslavement, by gender, by geography, and so on. However, the themes ultimately chosen were generated through careful attention to the stories themselves. The chapters represent themes that arise again and again in slave narratives regardless of the varying conditions, locations, or experiences of enslavement. Each chapter presents a single theme that draws the stories together, though each individual narrative certainly tells a unique tale. And the chapters are organized in such a way that we can come to a better understanding of the trajectory by which people are enslaved against their wills, the way they struggle to understand their enslavement, the suffering they experience as a result of their captivity, their intrepid desire to challenge their captors and to fight for freedom, and the barriers they encounter and successes they enjoy once they have liberated themselves.

Every third chapter presents a case study that integrates the themes of the previous two chapters by means of a collection of several interrelated narratives that have emerged from a particular site of enslavement or freedom. This case study allows the reader to see one instance of slavery elaborated in detail from several different perspectives (in one instance, even from the perspective of the traffickers themselves). Each narrative is a star that, when seen as part of a constellation connected to and shaped by all of the other stories, provides us with an image of what slavery looks like today and how it is told.

However, the portrait being drawn here is not an uncomplicated or uncontested one. Even the character of freedom is complicated by these narratives as we begin to understand the way slavery haunts many survivors for much of their lives. Despite the persistent afterlife of slavery, this book's trajectory is a positive one. The chapters move from captivity into freedom and on to activism in a course that tracks the determination of the survivors who tell their stories here. This narrative arc is deliberate. The liberation of enslaved people around the world *is* possible, and the people who tell their stories in this book make clear some of what we need to know to abolish slavery. The "freedom narratives" that we encounter here represent a collective call to action that does not deny the very real and very tragic circumstances that the majority of enslaved people still endure. However, these narrators' freedom and activism force us to insist on every human being's right to liberty and to the fruits of his or her own labor.

The first chapter, "The Allure of Work," explores the ways people are made vulnerable to the slave trade by their desire for work. As Bales reminds us, people are all too often lured into enslavement by the simple question "Do you need a job?" The stories of Rambho Kumar, a child from India who worked at a carpet factory, and Quang Thi Vo, a woman from Vietnam enslaved in a factory in American Samoa, reveal how family illnesses, debt, and poverty can lead people to accept even the most suspicious of work contracts. Chapter 1 illustrates the fact that slavery is not something that simply happens to the poorest of people in non-Western countries, nor does it happen only to those who are naive. In fact, it appears that just about anyone who is looking for reliable, paying work can be targeted by people who offer false opportunities. In a world in which legitimate work is becoming increasingly scarce, these stories remind us of the vulnerability of all the world's citizens to criminals who offer employment as a lure.

"Slaves in the Family," chapter 2, illustrates the way in which the rhetoric of family is problematically mobilized to justify complete power over other humans. In each of the stories presented here, traffickers use terms of familial bonds, such as *mama* and *sister*, to enforce the relationships between slaves and their traffickers in ways that imply a natural bond between them. In the case of Helia Lajeunesse, the system of *restavecs* (forced child laborers) in Haiti is based in a familial system by definition, wherein wealthier citizens adopt impoverished children as their own. Helia's story calls into question the limits of such family bonds when she and the neighbors realize she is not, in fact, treated like the other children in the family. In Sopheap's case, an "aunty" forces her to beg on the streets of Cambodia but demands that Sopheap hand over all of the donations. Even Sopheap's own family won't let her return from her life of enslavement because they are so convinced of the aunty's good will. Shamere McKenzie's story tells the familiar tale of a pimp who used love and well-being as a lure and then manipulated the rhetoric of family and the notion of home to entrap his victims. All of these stories point to the pernicious relationships that are fostered in the system of modern-day slavery, providing insight into the means by which slave "masters" maintain their captives' subordination.

In chapter 3, the first of our three case studies, we meet three real people who have intimately experienced the slave trade together: a forced sex worker, the man who trafficked her, and the house "mother" in the brothel in which she was enslaved. In these stunning interviews by Inge Bell, a German investigative journalist and author, we go inside the world of sex trafficking to better understand the means by which so many women are held as forced sex workers in eastern Europe. The young women describe the circumstances in their lives that made them vulnerable to sex slavery. The trafficker knows precisely how to convince women to do his bidding, and the brothel "mother" attempts to assuage the pain of enslavement by doting on her "children." Through these narratives, we see how the forces of work and family described in the previous chapters intersect to make people vulnerable to enslavement.

In chapter 4, "Painful Defiance and Contested Freedom," we learn how difficult it can be simply to walk away from slavery. Many may wonder why enslaved people do not escape the first chance they get. These stories of attempted resistance and escape show that the physical and psychological abuse in slavery can prevent people from being able to find a way out of bondage. For Marsha, persistent resistance on her part resulted in her earning less money for her trafficker, so he increased his abuse to keep her docile and profitable. As a result of the decline in revenue, he drugged her and resold her to an even more brutal pimp, who refused her food if she refused to work. Inez's story shows that even after an escape, slavery still follows a survivor into freedom. In her testimony before the U.S. Congress, she admitted, "No woman or child would want to be a sex slave and endure the evil that I have gone through. I am in fear of my life more than ever. I helped to put these evil men in jail. Please help me." These stories indicate the ways freedom can be challenged and challenging even after a person has escaped enslavement. Even when survivors are physically free of captivity, many still do not experience complete psychological or emotional liberation from their captors.

In the two longer narratives that constitute chapter 5, "Community Response and Resistance," we meet two men who, together with their fellow laborers, refused to be held in bondage. Through community deliberation, they manage to strike back against their enslavers. For Given Kachepa and his friends, members of a Zambian boys choir who were forced to work for a religious ministry in the United States, it was only through a group strike that they were able to stand up to their bosses' abuses and threats. Miguel's narrative explores one of the first legal cases to utilize human-trafficking law in the United States. In a revealing collective voice, Miguel depicts a group of disparate agricultural workers who came together to fight for their rights. Though many people manage to escape their enslavement on their own, this chapter is indicative of the way collective action (and even collective psychological support and thought) can affect the structures of power that maintain slavery.

The second case study, chapter 6, is entitled "Mining Unity." Here we read the testimonies of several mine workers who toiled in a rock quarry for generations without any pay beyond subsistence. It took community organizing to help each individual imagine the possibility of freedom for him- or herself. After revolting against the quarry owners, the workers managed to attain a property lease through legal channels, and they now own a quarry and its profits for themselves. Their stories are followed by interviews with the local community organizers who helped the miners to free themselves and take back the means of production. In the last unfortunate testimony in the case study, however, a woman who remains enslaved in a nearby rock quarry laments her fate and the continued difficulty of resistance for most bonded laborers in India.

In chapter 7, "The Voice and Silence of Slavery," we take a careful look at the language with which former slaves manage to articulate their pain after the right to express their thoughts and experiences has been stolen from them in slavery. For several of the contributors, including P, it is much too difficult to describe the events that happened to them as a result of trafficking, and they often explicitly point to this unspeakability. For James Kofi Annan, a former child slave who now protects children from the life of slavery that he led and rehabilitates those who have experienced that life, it is primarily through telling the story of the children he has saved that he manages to express his own traumatic experience. Silence has long haunted the memory of slavery, and these narratives explore the limits and possibilities of those silences as the contributors use that silence to speak to the utter horror of an enslaved life.

For the writers and activists included in chapter 8, "Becoming an Activist," all of the struggles and pains described in the previous chapters are familiar. Anywar Ricky Richard, Somaly Mam, and Sina Vann are survivors of human trafficking who have turned their suffering into their life work— they have dedicated their lives to using their stories to help others avoid or escape from slavery. All of the contributors in this chapter have taken a public stand, endangering themselves and their families, to speak out against the governments, criminal syndicates, and property owners who make slavery possible in the twenty-first century. The varied approaches outlined by these survivors provide evidence of the importance of locally generated methodologies in fighting human trafficking. They are also a testament to the way survivors are genuinely at the center of effective anti-slavery activism today, just as they were in the nineteenth century. These stories are an inspiration to all people interested in abolishing slavery, for they prove that even a person who has been denied power can stand up and make a difference.

The final case study brings this collection to a conclusion that weaves all of the previous threads together. The stories collected in this chapter are interviews by and about members of the Survivor Advisory Caucus of the Coalition Against Slavery and Trafficking (CAST). All twelve caucus members are survivors of modern slavery, and they work together on a committee that develops strategies and programming for one of the most successful antislavery organizations in the United States. This collection of interviews, in which survivors ask questions of other survivors, shares many of the early chapters' themes and concerns. However, these stories are different because they were developed in a therapeutic storytelling workshop that the survivors organized themselves. Together, these women developed the courage to tell and record their stories. They wanted their narratives to be published so that their life stories could be transformed into activism. This storytelling workshop is a replicable model for other organizations that are supporting survivors of trafficking.

In the epilogue, "Twenty-First Century Abolitionists—What You Can Do to End Slavery," readers will find an extensive and detailed list of actions they can take to help combat slavery. It is easy for us to imagine that had we been alive in the eighteenth or nineteenth centuries in any one of the many places in the world that legally permitted the ownership of one human by another, we would have been abolitionists. In this chapter, readers are provided the opportunity to respond to this centuries-old blight on our human landscape. As Sunit Singh, a nongovernmental organization consultant whose interview is included in chapter 6, suggests, "Research and action must go side by side. I mean, in that sense I am equally involved in this project because I feel that it is not a question of simply freeing the laborers. It's the question of liberating ourselves also, the research community, the academic community. We must also understand what the reality is and how to participate in the process of transformation, which is part of our society, part of our economy in which we are living. If we are committed to build a free society, if we are committed to make our democracy strong, we must participate in such transformation processes sincerely and honestly." The goal of the epilogue (and of the whole book, for that matter) is to convince readers to find their own role in these "transformative processes" that are currently working to eradicate this global injustice. Contact information for organizations that are already doing this work are listed in appendix A, and signs of enslavement to look for are described in appendix B.

1

The Allure of Work

IN OCTOBER 2009, AMERICANS LAMENTED the steep rise in the unemployment rate following the mortgage crisis and the subsequent economic recession. The unemployment rate that month hit a peak at 10.2 percent, the highest it had been since 1982.[1] In 1933, as a result of the Great Depression almost one in four Americans was out of work,[2] but that staggering statistic did nothing to ease the pain of those twenty-first-century Americans who were without work. Just as it did nothing for the additional 4 million Americans who were not being counted in the unemployment statistics because they had been unemployed for so long that they no longer received unemployment benefits.

In response to this nearly unavoidable unemployment—and it no doubt was unavoidable, for if we consider that at least one in six Americans was unemployed or underemployed, then even the wealthiest American must have known someone who was affected by the recession—Americans were forced to find work or sustenance by any means necessary. Some of those who had the means moved to areas with higher employment potential, and many immigrants returned to their countries of origin, where they thought perhaps there might be more work. Some people started new business ventures or went back to school in hopes that a fresh start would dramatically change their lives. Some relied on the five years of social services benefits that our government provides to those citizens who are struggling to make ends meet. Some of them surely turned to selling their bodies because it was the only thing they undoubtedly owned. Some may have opted for and remained in jobs that were exploitative or abusive. Others may very well have resorted to criminal activities in their desperation to feed themselves and their families.

These were the difficulties that citizens of the United States faced in the recession. Imagine if you lived in Togo, however, where the average per capita income is less than a dollar a day, and very few young men have a job or hope of getting one. On workdays, crowds of adult men gather informally in the streets and markets, listless and unsure of what to do next. In nearby Liberia, 85 percent of working-age adults are unemployed. In Asia, Nepalis face 46 percent unemployment, and Turkmen 60 percent.[3]

What do able-bodied, hard-working people do when there simply aren't enough jobs to go around? As with Americans facing the economic downturn, a number of options might help a person avoid the bind of unemployment. Most people would admit that they would do anything to pay for their children's education, to maintain their family's health, to put food on the table. But what happens when there just isn't enough work for everyone to be able to afford to do those basic tasks?

In so many of the cases of modern-day slavery that we encounter, the only lure a trafficker needs to convince someone to walk into enslavement is the simple offer of a job. In the narratives collected in this chapter, the writers found themselves unemployed or needing medical care or wanting to help a family member or simply hoping that they could provide a better life for themselves or their families. When introduced to the possibility of a job that could genuinely change their lives or be the key to their survival, these narrators were willing (as many people would be in their situations) to take a risk, sign an unusual contract, believe a smooth-talker, take burdensome loans, or entrust their children to distant family members.

Quang Thi Vo left her native Vietnam for a factory job in the United States, where she hoped she would be able to work to support her child and extended family back home. Instead, she was taken to American Samoa by a fraudulent employment agency, and when she got there, she was abused mentally, physically, and sexually. She was held captive by the company and was unpaid for her work. Her story reveals how a desire for better opportunities in other countries can lead working adults to accept even the most suspicious of work contracts, and the debts they accrue trying to get there can keep them bound to their traffickers long after they manage to emancipate themselves.

It is easy for most young people to imagine that they could never be caught in the trap of slavery, but the stories collected in this chapter might convince them otherwise. Katya was a college student in Ukraine when a legitimate summer job in the United States lured her away from her family and into a life of slavery. Katya had learned about trafficking and had been vigilant to ensure her own safety. She'd done her homework and had found a safe opportunity to study English and wait tables. Nonetheless, people she knew from her hometown convinced her that the program was moved to Detroit, where they forced her to work in a dance club and give them all of her pay. She knew how to protect herself from the fraudulent work agencies that are all too common in eastern Europe, but she hadn't been prepared to protect herself against familiar faces from back home. For O, an abusive father made any job outside her home seem positive until she found that the abuse continued there as well. Like so many other people in her situation, she sought a job that would help her leave behind the painful existence of her youth. These decisions to seek a better life unfortunately made Katya and O easy prey for men who pretended to be their saviors.

Rambho Kumar, a child from India who worked at a carpet factory, shows us how even children are vulnerable to the temptation of a job if that job will mean that they can help their family out of poverty and illness. Kumar's family thought that he would be educated during the day and work in the evenings when he moved to the city. Like many impoverished families all around the world, Kumar's parents were willing to allow him to leave home on the guarantee that he would be educated and learn a trade, but Kumar was never allowed to go to school. Instead, he spent every waking hour working on a dangerous loom to produce carpets. Even when he was injured, he was forced to continue working. The allure of a job and a future career was enough to convince his family that he should take a chance. For Kumar, that gamble led to slavery.

When we remind ourselves that the most essential aspect of slavery is the work, then we begin to understand better how it is that people can be tempted by an offer that eventually leads them into bondage. Work is the candy that traffickers use to tempt adults and children into captivity. Of course, no one suspects that they won't be paid or that they won't be allowed to leave their place of employment. The allure of work alone is often enough to entice a person in need to let his or her guard down and take a chance.

One complicated aspect of forced labor is that it can go unnoticed. It is often difficult to tell the difference between forced labor and a regular job. Katya worked in a strip club, where some relatively nice guys visited without realizing they were watching slaves dance until the girls told them so. Quang Thi Vo and Rambho worked in factories, which produce the clothes we wear and the rugs we walk on, but consumers rarely ever inquire about the working conditions of the people who make the goods they buy. O was just one among so many young girls who have turned to selling sex—no one ever looked carefully enough to see that she was being forced to work on the street. Our naive ignorance of the fact of forced labor often makes enslavement difficult to detect.

In the late nineteenth century, when the slave trade was abolished on the west coast of Africa, people distinguished between legitimate and illegitimate trades—between, say, the trade in palm oil or cocoa and the trade in people. Still today, selling a person is clearly seen as illegitimate, but how can we detect the difference between legitimate free labor and illegitimate slave labor? How can a person spot a slave when a slave often looks simply like a person who is working? There are too many stories collected here—and far too many that couldn't be collected here—for us to allow the work of slaves to remain in the shadows.

Work is a central component of human life, something we all rely on to support ourselves in so many ways. Even those of us who are lucky enough to love our jobs tend to go to work primarily because we want to be able to provide certain things for ourselves and our families—shelter, food, and clothes are immediate necessities, but we also work to gain money for our hobbies, to be able to travel to visit family, and no doubt for luxury goods. Nevertheless, choosing our work is a form of human agency that some of us often take for granted. Work is not only essential to us financially; in most cultures, it is considered crucial to our well-being, to our sense of ourselves, and to our participation in our communities.

Slavery is *forced* labor. When a person is forced to work against his or her will and without pay—as all slaves are—traffickers and slave owners excise agency and desire from work. Slavery is a perversion of work. It converts something constructive of identity, social value, and community participation into something that is destructive of those very same processes. It takes a simple human desire to be employed and makes people vulnerable to other people's predatory and self-serving desires.

In her testimony before the U.S. House of Representatives International Relations Committee (during which she used the pseudonym "Vi"), Quang Thi Vo describes the advantage of being able to choose her own employer after her escape. She writes, "Here I am free to choose where to work. If dissatisfied with one workplace, I can always go to another one." The notion that one has the capacity to choose one's own job is essential to most notions of freedom. Even in the most exploitative of situations, most people are free to walk away from their jobs if they feel abused or are unpaid. The people in this book were unable to walk away from their work when they realized it was not what they had chosen. Their employers robbed them of this simple freedom.

Illustrating how important work is to people's sense of self, many of the contributors to this book chose work as a way of taking control of their lives after slavery despite all of the pain associated with labor. The choice to work defines their notion of freedom. Katya currently works full-time and wants to go back to school. We will later meet Given Kachepa, who is thrilled to have a legal work permit in the United States after a fraudulent minister forced him to work here as a choir boy. He is now pursuing a degree in dentistry. All of the contributors to chapter 8 have turned their work into a way of preventing slavery. Work—legitimate work, paid work, chosen work—is a dream for so many people regardless of their particular circumstances. The desire for a life defined by good work, not defined by the perversion of it, fuels these narratives and the lives of people who were made to suffer as a result of forced labor.

QUANG THI VO

Origin: Vietnam   *Trafficked in/to*: American Samoa

Form of enslavement: Forced factory labor   *Current status*: Free

Source: "Vi," testimony at the *Implementation of the Trafficking Victims Protection Act Hearing Before the Committee on International Relations*, U.S. House of Representatives, November 29, 2001, 107th Cong., 1st sess., 1 Cong. Rec., Serial No. 107-63, 156–60 [2001].

Context: Quang Thi Vo worked for the Daewoosa company, which was using American Samoa as a site for the production of clothing to be sold to major American retailers. The owner of the factory was sentenced to forty years in prison on charges of involuntary servitude, money laundering, and extortion for holding more than two hundred people captive. Vo, using the pseudonym "Vi," provided testimony before the U.S. House of Representatives International Relations Committee on the Implementation of the Trafficking Victims Protection Act on November 29, 2001. She was assisted in preparing and presenting her testimony by the organization Boat People SOS (see appendix A). The names of Vo's traffickers have been changed for legal reasons.

I arrived in American Samoa on July 22, 1999. Two other groups of Vietnamese workers had been brought to this island before us. When I signed the contract, Tour Company 12 (TC12) told me that I would go to the U.S., and its deputy director promised that I would be paid $408 a month. I had to borrow $4,000 to pay TC12 and another $2,000 to pay the company official in charge of recruitment. We were taken to American Samoa, not the U.S. As soon as we landed, our passports were confiscated.

At Daewoosa, I had to work from 7:00 A.M. often to 2:00 A.M. and sometimes to 7 A.M. the following day and also on Saturdays and Sundays, without pay. We had no money to buy soap, amenities, or food. We had to pay about $200 per month for meals, which Daewoosa should have provided according to the contract. Meals at Daewoosa consisted of a few cabbage leaves and potatoes cooked with a lot of water. Those who were at the head of the line could get some cabbage and potato; latecomers got only water. Hungry, we planted some vegetables to supplement our meager diet, but Mr. Kung, president of Daewoosa, destroyed our garden. Undernourished, I lost thirty-five pounds and weighed only seventy-eight pounds.

Working and living conditions at Daewoosa were very suffocating. There was no ventilation. Workers sat next to each other. It was very hot. We were not allowed to step out for fresh air. The supervisor even kept count of how many times we went to the toilet.

We lived thirty-six people per room. Another worker and I shared one tiny bed. We could only sleep on our side. If we lay on our back, we would pile up on each other.

Most of us were women. At night Mr. Kung often came to our room and lay next to whomever he liked. Once he forced me to give him a massage right in our bedroom. He called pretty ones into his office and forced them to have sex with him. Three women have publicly denounced him for that. Once, several of his customers arrived in American Samoa; Mr. Kung pressed several female workers to sleep with them. They resisted. At the workplace, he regularly groped and kissed female workers in front of everyone.

There were three pregnant women among us. Mr. Kung demanded that they undergo abortion. He fired them when they refused. Evicted from Daewoosa, they had to seek refuge at a local church.

Movement at Daewoosa was very restricted. Everyone leaving the compound was searched by American Samoan guards. Female workers were groped all over their body. Those who protested were strip-searched.

Those coming back to the compound after 9:00 P.M. were beaten up. Once I was slapped.

Mr. Kung used big American Samoan guards to terrorize us. Once several workers staged a strike because they were not paid. He threatened that he would send these guards to short-circuit the electric cables and cause a fire to kill all of us. Everyone was fearful because two female workers, Hanh and An, involved in a lawsuit against Mr. Kung had just disappeared.

On November 28 of last year, there was a dispute between the supervisor and a female worker. Mr. Kung ordered the supervisor: "If you beat her to death, I will take the blame." The supervisor dragged the female worker out. Other workers came to her rescue. The American Samoan guards, already holding sticks and scissors, jumped in and beat us. Everyone was so frightened. We ran for our life. The guards paid special attention to the five or six workers known to have supported the lawsuit against Mr. Kung. They beat them the hardest. Ms. Hien, the key witness in this lawsuit, was held by her arms on two sides by two guards; a third guard thrusted a pointed stick into her eye. She has now lost that eye. A guard beat a male worker with a stick, breaking his front teeth and bleeding his mouth. Another male worker was pinned to the floor and repeatedly beaten at the temple, his blood spilling all over the floor. The next day, FBI agents took picture of the bloodstains. During the assault, Daewoosa's lawyer and the police were there but did nothing. Only when the lawyer representing the workers showed up did the guards stop the beating.

From 1999 to the above incident, TC12 and International Manpower Supply—another Vietnamese company hiring workers for Daewoosa—forced us to continue working without pay and threatened to send us back to Vietnam if we disobeyed. Everyone was deeply in debt; if sent back to Vietnam, how could we pay our debt? Since my arrival to the U.S., I have sent every dollar earned back to Vietnam to pay my debt. However, this has barely made a dent because the interest rate is so high—50 percent per year.

My parents in Vietnam are very worried; their hair has turned all grey. They told me that it is fortunate that I have come to the U.S.; otherwise we would be in a hopeless situation. If [I were] sent back, it would be hard for me to find employment. My previous workplace will not take me back. Because of my involvement in the prosecution of Mr. Kung, I am afraid of running into trouble with the government if repatriated to Vietnam.

I am getting used to life in the U.S. Here I am free to choose where to work. If dissatisfied with one workplace, I can always go to another one. I have been thoroughly helped in my first steps towards a normal life. I find everyone to be kind. I now live with a Vietnamese family without having to pay rent. That family offers me employment. They take care of my food, transportation, and other things. They also give me a phone card to call my family in Vietnam once a week.

I have received the certification letter from the Department of Health and Human Services for public benefits. I have a temporary visa, which will expire on October 30, 2002, and a work permit. I work at a nail salon in D.C. to pay my debt. If allowed to remain in the U.S., I would like to go back to school because in Vietnam I had to stop schooling at seventh grade. I also wish to be reunited with my child left behind in Vietnam.

I am thankful to everyone who has helped get me out of American Samoa and everyone who has assisted me in my new life in the U.S.

KATYA

Origin: Ukraine   *Trafficked in/to*: Detroit,

Form of enslavement: Forced sex work   *Current status*: Free

Source: Katya's T-visa nonimmigrant-status application narrative, submitted to U.S. Citizenship and Immigration Services, 2005; reproduced with permission.

Context: The person known as "Katya" here submitted this narrative as part of her application for a T-visa, a type of visa the U.S. government has created specifically to aid victims of trafficking. Her attorney redacted parts of the narrative to avoid providing specific personal information that would identify either Katya (including her real name) or her acquaintances in this story. The traffickers' names have been changed for legal purposes.

My name is Katya. I was born on [redacted]. I am currently twenty years old and was born in Ukraine.

In the summer of 2003, I lived with both my mother and grandmother. My grandmother was old, and she became paralyzed, stopped eating, and was unable to use the bathroom on her own. In a short time, she became senile. She needed daily care. My mother worked as an accountant and was making around $130–150 per month, which absolutely was not enough for three people.

I was studying as a freshman at the Ukraine State University, majoring in physical education and sports. Every day after my classes, I had trained in athletics and pole vaulting. My mother started having problems with her heart, blood pressure, and had chronic bronchitis, which made it difficult for her to work. After I finished my first year at the university, I decided that I need to look for a job, as we had nothing to eat, we did not have money, we were in need.

Together with my best friend, Galina, we looked through the newspaper for jobs. We went to apply to be waitresses to a bar that was just opened in Kiev called "Paradise." When I arrived at Paradise, I met Vladimir, the owner. He told me that I couldn't be a waitress because I was too short, but that I could be a dancer instead. At that moment, I could not imagine myself as an exotic dancer. Nevertheless, Vladimir convinced me by promising me good money, $50–100 a day, which was very good in the Ukraine, and also to work on the days that I wanted. Instead of Paradise, Vladimir sent me to work at another one of his clubs, "Vegas." I guess he owns a lot of clubs.

I worked at Vegas three days a week. My mother did not even suspect that I danced. I did not want her to know about that. I told her that I worked as a waitress with Galina.

In one sad day, on November 18, 2003, my grandmother died, a person whom I loved very much. There were just two of us left, my mom and I. On the same day, I had a conversation with Vladimir, he told me that I have a chance in my life to help my mother, to earn money and see the United States. He said that it would be like summer break for me, for only three to five months. He told me that I would work in the U.S. as a waitress and that he would provide a place to live. He promised me good money, which I really needed at that time for me and my mother.

In December 2003, Vladimir introduced me to Dmitri and Sasha to talk more about going to work in the United States. I knew that Sasha was Vladimir's son. I did not know anything about Dmitri. I had seen them before at Vegas. Dmitri told me that I should find an English-language tutor to learn English. He paid for my English lessons, which lasted until April 2004.

In April 2004, Vladimir gave me the address of a company called "Kolizey." That company helped students to go abroad for summer break: to rest, to earn some money, and to see the country. When I met with Kolizey representatives, they gave me an option to choose the place of work. They also told me it would cost around $1,300, which included Kolizey services and tickets to the destination country. Vladimir gave me money for this program and told me it would not be a problem and that I did not have to pay him back. Vladimir told me to pick "Beauty Search Incorporated" to work for in the U.S. at my next Kolizey appointment, and Kolizey agreed. I was told I had to go through the American embassy first.

Before going to the embassy, Dmitri called me at home to prepare me for my embassy interview. He gave me questions and answers that could have been asked at the embassy in English.

I continued to work at Vegas during this process, and Vladimir, Dmitri, and Sasha kept talking to me about America and its future promise and the money I would earn. Only now I understand what good psychologists they were and how they were pressuring me.

Shortly before my scheduled departure to the U.S., I received a call from Kolizey, and they told me that "Beauty Search Incorporated," to which I initially applied, was not valid and that they would not let me go. Natasha, another girl who worked for Vladimir and was also traveling to the U.S., and I both went to Kolizey to try to find a different company to work for. Kolizey offered to fly us to Virginia Beach to work as waitresses. We had an interview and the next day, at 2:00 P.M., purchased the plane tickets. The flight would be out of Kiev–London–Washington. They said there would be a bus waiting for us at the airport to take us to Virginia Beach, where we would work. I called Dmitri and told him that I could not go to Detroit. He sounded upset at first but then told me not to worry and go to Virginia Beach anyway.

In May 2004, Natasha and I flew to the U.S. When we got to the airport in Washington, to my surprise I saw Dmitri at the airport. He told us that we were going with him, that everything worked out, that we did not need to worry, and that he would "take care of everything."

Dmitri bought us bus tickets to Detroit. Natasha and I rode the bus for a long time; it was very scary, not knowing English language, and the area frightened us. When we arrived in Detroit, Vladimir, Dmitri, and Sasha met us. They kept talking about how lucky we were and how they were going to take care of everything.

They brought us to a hotel, and in one moment *everything* changed. Once in the hotel, they told us that for bringing us to the U.S., we owed them money. Specifically, Vladimir told us that we had to give them back $12,000 each within two months. Natasha and I were in shock from learning what we got into, but that was not everything; the next thing they told us that the following week we have to go to work, and there everything would be explained to us. They bought a phone card for us and told us to call our parents. However, during our conversations with our parents, then and later, Sasha or Dmitri were always present, listening to what we said.

Within a week, Sash and Dmitri bought strip clothes and shoes for us. They found an apartment for Natasha and me, but also had their own keys to it. They told us that we were to work in a bar called "Cheetahs" from 2:00 P.M. to 2:00 A.M., two shifts from Monday to Saturday. They warned us not to tell anyone anything about ourselves, not to tell where we were from and where we lived, and which stores we went to. They said that if they were to find out we talked to anyone, we would have problems with our health and well-being.

It was hard work. We worked at Cheetah's Monday through Saturday, twelve hours a day. After the work, we had to give all of our money to Michael and Alex. I was very tired and never wanted to do anything. I became depressed very soon.

Monday through Saturday, I would wake up at 12:00 P.M., make breakfast, wash, put makeup on, fixed my hair, and at 1:00 P.M. a car would be waiting for us at the door. Sasha or Dmitri always took us to work and brought us back home. We worked till two o'clock at night; at 2:30 A.M. a car [picked us up] at the club, [and] we gave all the money and went home. Often after coming home, Sasha or Dmitri would force us to have sex with them. Dmitri would have sex with me, and Sasha would have sex with Natasha. We argued with them about this, but it was useless. We also fought about the money. Sasha and Dmitri kept telling us that they wanted each of us to make $1,000 a day, and if we didn't, they would yell and scream at us. And then around 4:00–5:00 A.M. we would go to bed with a hope for a better tomorrow. Every day I earned between $400 to $1,000, but I did not feel I made money since I never saw it.

On Sundays, Sasha and Dmitri told us it was our "day off." We were still not rid of them on Sundays. At 1:00 or 2:00 P.M., Sasha and Dmitri, sometimes both, would drive to our apartment and take us out for our manicures and pedicures. Then, they would take us to the mall; they would give us some cash for clothes, perfume, and makeup. We would have to give any money back we did not spend. We were not allowed to talk to anyone else or tell them about ourselves. Then Sasha and Dmitri would take us to a restaurant with them, where they would make fun of us. For example, they would tell me I wasn't holding the utensils right or make fun of something I said and just laugh at me.

In September, Svetlana, another girl from Ukraine, arrived in Detroit to work for Sasha and Dmitri and to be a dancer with us. Natasha and I told her about what happened to us. I think she was shocked. Later, sometime in November, another girl, Mari, arrived from the Ukraine to work for Sasha and Dmitri. We told her everything as well. Svetlana and Mari lived together in an apartment in another building in a similar "arrangement" to my situation with Natasha.

Some time after Mari arrived, all four of us became very ill. I think we all had bronchitis. I had a high fever, coughing, headache, body aches, and I lost my voice and could not speak. But Sasha and Dmitri had no feelings and made us work anyway. They would scream and yell at us until we gave in, always. I remember once, I bought an outfit at the club for $40 with money I earned that same night and told Dmitri that a customer bought it for me. After work, Dmitri took Natasha and I to the house that he and Sasha lived in and locked us in the basement. They set us down on the couch, yelled at us, threatened us, and raised their arms as if they were going to hit us. They yelled about money we owed them and said that if we did not make enough money for them, they would sell us to a prostitution house and get their money. They kept questioning me about the outfit I bought, and when I finally said I bought it, Dmitri hit me hard across my face with his hand. I had stars in my eyes, then it was dark, and only then I realized that he hit me. I could not feel my face. Natasha and I cried, asked to let us go home, yelled that we were tired. However, for them, we were not people, only dollar signs.

Dmitri and Sasha arranged for Natasha and I to live in an apartment with a TV, buy us nice clothes from the mall, and get our nails done. But we did not have a right to choose where we lived, right of freedom, freedom of speech, freedom of actions. Sasha and Dmitri had keys to our apartments. They controlled all of our movement and travel. They watched us and listened when we called our parents. They didn't let us make friends or tell anyone anything about ourselves. We couldn't keep any of the money we earned. We couldn't ask anyone for help.

After six months of slavery, Natasha and I thought we could go home. We estimated we had earned enough to pay Sasha and Dmitri back for what we "owed" them. We asked Sasha and Dmitri if we could go back to the Ukraine. Their response was that we "would break their business down" and that they would not allow that.

Once I asked Dmitri to take me to the airport to go home. He didn't really reply—he said something about it not being his business. But the next day when they came to pick us up to take us to work, Dmitri told me to stay home and wait for him. Later, he let himself into our apartment with his key, and he made me sit down in the living room. He asked me why I was not happy. I told him I wanted to go home, and I want the money I earned. Dmitri told me I owed him a lot of money and that I did not [have] any money and that there was no way back home. I started to cry and argued with him about this. He became enraged and ran towards me, raised his foot at me, but kicked the boom box next to me instead and broke it. I understood I could not solve the problem this way and never raised this issue with him again.

I had a young client at the club who came to see me once a week. I used his phone to call Ukraine; I told my mom what was going on. My mom told me to take my things and run.

The entire time I was working for Sasha and Dmitri, I never got enough sleep. Natasha and I worked on our escape plan for a long time. She said she would talk to one of her clients, Bobby, to help us. On February 12, 2005, after the night shift, at six o'clock in the morning, Bobby's car was standing outside our apartment. He took us to the Immigration Service, and that's how we got rid of Sasha and Dmitri. I told Immigration my story. I was still scared, however, since Sasha and Dmitri have a lot of connections in the Ukraine.

Since leaving the situation with Sasha and Dmitri, I have been telling my story to Lou de Baca of the U.S. Department of Justice and Kelli Hodges of the FBI during interviews. It has sometimes been difficult, but I know it is important.

I feel like going back to the Ukraine would be like going back to my own grave. Vladimir is still there with all of his clubs and associates. I am scared he would hurt me if I returned. The police there would never protect us, as they are corrupt. Vladimir got away with so much there.

Since running away from Sasha and Dmitri, I have fallen in love with this country. The laws work here, police are good, and there are people here who will help people like me. The government attorneys and FBI agents I work with really care about me and my case. I am trusting people for the first time. I feel safe and protected.

At the present time, I study English at Truman College in Chicago. I plan to take computer classes soon.

my country and live with her. I returned from Italy and am trying to start a new life here.

RAMBHO KUMAR

Origin: India   *Trafficked in/to*: India

Form of enslavement: Forced factory labor/ child labor   *Current status*: Free

Source: Interview conducted in August 2005 for the Free the Slaves' documentary *Freedom and Beyond: Bal Vikas Ashram*, directed by Peggy Callahan (2005); transcript reproduced with permission.

Context: This is a transcript of an interview conducted by Free the Slaves, a nonprofit abolitionist organization headquartered in Washington, D.C. Peggy Callahan, cofounder of Free the Slaves, interviewed eleven-year-old Rambho Kumar with the aid of a simultaneous interpreter (this translation is looser than in most Free the Slaves interviews) at Bal Vikas Ashram in Uttar Pradesh, India, where children who have been rescued from forced labor are provided with shelter, food, education, and health care until they are able to return to their families. Callahan reports that Kumar has now returned home to his family, but his life circumstances remain difficult.

CALLAHAN: Can you tell us how you came here?

KUMAR: I was working in the carpet industry, and then Mr. Rajnath and Supriya came with two policemen, and they got me from there.

CALLAHAN: Can you tell me what growing up in your village was like?

KUMAR: I used to work at home, and I also used to play. I used to go to the fields to work at times.

CALLAHAN: Did you have fun at home? What was your recreation like?

KUMAR: I used to play and roam around with the kids living nearby.

CALLAHAN: Did you have any brothers and sisters, and how many brothers and sisters did you have?

KUMAR: I have six brothers, including me.

CALLAHAN: How did you go to the looms?

KUMAR: A man named Shankar and the owner of the loom came and gave 700 rupees [about U.S.$13] to my house and got me to the loom.

CALLAHAN: Did you want to go to the looms?

KUMAR: I didn't want to go to the looms. I wanted to stay at home.

CALLAHAN: If you didn't want to go, how come you were made to go? Did your parents want you to go?

KUMAR: There was no money at home for us to eat and to have food, so my mother told me to go.

CALLAHAN: Were you very sad when you had to leave?

KUMAR: I was crying and saying that I don't want to go there.

CALLAHAN: What was your day like when you went to the loom?

KUMAR: For two days when I reached [there], they made me sit, and then they told me to learn how to use the machine and the loom. After that, they took me to use the loom, but my hand got cut. And when my hand got cut, the owner and his brother shut my eyes, and they put my finger in boiling oil and said that "now it's all right, now you get back to work."

CALLAHAN: Which finger?

KUMAR: This is the finger that got cut. [Holds out finger.]

CALLAHAN: What did the loom owner tell your parents? What did the loom owner promise to your parents? Where was he? What was he going to do to you?

KUMAR: He told my parents that he's going to take me, and he's going to educate me and make me do some work.

CALLAHAN: Did the loom owner tell your parents that you're going to be able to make some money and send it home?

KUMAR: He said that he's going to give me money, and he's going to make me work. He'll send money home. And then after some time after working, I can go back home. But after a very long time, he told me that I'm not going to be able to go back home ever.

CALLAHAN: How did you learn how to weave a rug?

KUMAR: The loom owner taught me how to make it.

CALLAHAN: What happened if you made a mistake while weaving the rug?

KUMAR: If any mistake was to be made by me, the loom owner used to take a stick and beat me up with that.

CALLAHAN: How was the school and the sending the money home that the loom owner had promised you?

KUMAR: I used to keep asking the loom owner, "When will I go to school?" and the owner kept telling me, "Now there is no school for you. Now you will spend the rest of the time weaving carpets."

CALLAHAN: How many hours in a day did you work, and what were your working conditions like?

KUMAR: I used to work from four in the morning till about eleven in the night.

[Translator asks several extra questions to clarify.]

KUMAR: There used to be about fifty people working, and it was a fairly clean place.

CALLAHAN: Did you get to have good food there? Did you get to go outside and play? What were your conditions there? What was your life like?

KUMAR: Over there I wasn't allowed to play or roam around or anything. I used to wake up in the morning at around four o'clock and go to work. At about ten o'clock, we used to get our first meal, which was not good. I didn't like the food over there. And then I would go back to weaving the carpets till about nine in the night—at nine in the night we would get our second meal. And that was all we did in the day: weaving the carpets, eating food, and going to sleep.

CALLAHAN: How long were you working there in the looms?

KUMAR: I worked there for one year.

CALLAHAN: What did you think about while you were working there?

KUMAR: I wanted to go back home. I thought I'll go back home and study over there.

CALLAHAN: Did you study in the village before going to the loom?

KUMAR: No, before going, I didn't study in the village.

CALLAHAN: When the raid happened in the loom, what were you thinking? What was happening around you? What did you feel about what was happening around you?

KUMAR: The owner used to tell us that if the police ever come, run away before they can catch you, so I knew that when the police come, I'll be taken away from there. And when I saw them coming, I was very happy. As soon as they came, the owner and his father and his brother and all the other people ran away. About ten of us were surrounded by the police. Six of them got away, but four of us were brought to the ashram. I was very happy when the police came because I knew that would be the end of my working in the loom.

CALLAHAN: Were you scared at all when the police came?

KUMAR: I wasn't scared at all because I knew they wouldn't do anything to us.

CALLAHAN: What is it like here at the ashram? Can you tell us the difference between here in the ashram and the loom where you worked?

KUMAR: I never used to like it there. We didn't have time for anything. I always used to want to get away. When I came here, I liked it because over here you get time to eat, you get time to play, to study. You have a time for everything over here. I really like it over here.

CALLAHAN: What is your favorite time over here? What do you like most about being here?

KUMAR: I like studying the most.

CALLAHAN: Are you eager to go home?

TRANSLATOR: He doesn't want to go back home.

CALLAHAN: Do you feel like going home?

KUMAR: I feel like going home, but I'm not going to go home right now. I am going to go home after six months.

CALLAHAN: How long has it been since you've seen your mother? And are you missing your family a lot?

KUMAR: I haven't seen my mother for the past thirteen months, and I miss my family a lot.

CALLAHAN: If you could tell people in the world about what happens to children in the looms, what would you tell them?

KUMAR: I won't let anybody go there even by mistake. I'll tell them that they hit you and they beat you, and I would not let them go there ever.

[Camera operator asks for another take because of a camera problem.]

CALLAHAN: If you could tell people in the world about children and their life in the looms, what would you like to tell them?

KUMAR: They hit the children over there, and if there's any mistake the children make, they beat them up. I won't let them go there.

CALLAHAN: We might go to your village and show this to your mother and your brothers and your family. Is there any message that you would like to give for any of them?

KUMAR: I just want to say that my days here are good, and there's no problem with anything. I'm liking it over here.

CALLAHAN: What would you like to do after you leave here? How do you think your life will be in the future? How it will be different after you leave here?

KUMAR: I want to go in my village and be a guard over there. And I think that if I get out of here, then I'll be able to study, and I'll be able to earn money.

CALLAHAN: Is there anything else you'd like to say?

KUMAR: I want to say that my father has passed away, and I have six brothers and my mother now living in the village.

CALLAHAN: Is it hard for your family in the village without your father?

KUMAR: It's difficult for food and water in the village. When my father died, we put 6,000 rupees [about U.S.$110] into expenses for his treatment, but still he passed away. Now we don't even have a place to stay over there in the village.

CALLAHAN: Do you want to help your mother in the future and find her a place to stay?

KUMAR: I want to help my mother find a house.

2

Slaves in the Family

IN THE NINETEENTH CENTURY, apologists for American slavery would resort to romanticizing life on their plantations, referring to the people who
lived there as their "family, black and white."[1] This self-deluding rhetoric
allowed slaveholders to justify their relationship of nearly complete power
over the people they held in bondage. As historian of slavery Ira Berlin describes, in the early nineteenth century when rising dissatisfaction with the
institution of slavery forced slave owners to rethink and justify their relationship to their supposed property, newspaper articles provided advice to
plantation owners on "how to best manage their slaves, with the language
of family serving as the medium through which slavery could be defended
before the world and justified to themselves."[2] This notion of the slave as
family compelled the slaveholders to supply some semblance of shelter and
safety for these members of the family, but it also provided them the opportunity and imperative to discipline their supposed "children." Slave men and
women were understood to be in a state of perpetual childhood and thus in
a relationship of need to the master-father of the family. This paternalistic
rhetoric, though not necessarily adopted by all slaveholders, allowed those
who did employ it to maintain what they considered unquestionable control over their slaves by insisting that the paternal authority bestowed upon
them was precisely what the slaves needed—the protective and disciplining
embrace of a father. It was in this way that the rhetoric of the family became
the explicit tool of the slaveholding class to maintain bondage.

The mythology of family still appears to pervade the discourse sur-
rounding slavery in many contemporary situations. By using the language

of family, the twenty-first-century slaveholder produces the illusion that he or she offers safety and protection, which ironically allows him or her the room to do nothing of the sort. As in the case of antebellum paternalism, the use of familial language expresses the type of bonds the master hopes to relay to the enslaved. However, unlike in the antebellum period, the modern trafficker's use of familial designations seems to exist entirely for the purpose of maintaining power over the enslaved. The use of familial designations such as *daddy*, *sister*, and *aunty* does not so much provide a justification for the use of slaves in the trafficker's hearts and minds but tightens the psychological chains around the person he or she has enslaved. In the narratives collected in this chapter, there seems to be no indication that the slaveholder believed the rhetoric he or she was producing. None of the traffickers described here seems to have been concerned about the politics of his or her work, any responsibility to the people he or she was holding captive, or the spiritual cost of enslaving others, as antebellum slaveholders sometimes were. The use of the rhetoric of the family reinforces the traffickers' will and power over the people being enslaved and allows them to be concerned about what is most important to them—making money and obtaining free labor.

For instance, many pimps require that the women they force to work for them use the word *daddy* to refer to them. If a pimp has control over several women, they must call each other "wife-in-law" and are supposed to treat one another like family, including by teaching each other the ropes of "the game," as Shamere McKenzie's story reveals. The rhetorical power of this language even convinced McKenzie to call her pimp's house her "home" even later while she was staying with her own uncle. By insisting on a false familial structure, a pimp can elicit the bonds that so many young people seek. McKenzie's pimp, like so many others, exploited both her need for paid work and her human desire for love and affection, turning the familial relationship into one of labor and bondage. Young women often feel as if they are betraying their own families, then, when they decide they want to leave "the life." Even long after many former sex slaves have escaped their enslaving pimps, they often continue to call their former pimps "daddy" and have a difficult time separating their enslavement from notions of family responsibility, commitment, and love. McKenzie's own escape was extraordinarily difficult and dangerous in part because of this familial mythology, and the repercussions—both psychological and mental—continue to haunt her even as she embarks on a career as an antitrafficking activist.

The slaveholder's use of "family" takes many forms. For Sopheap, who was enslaved as a beggar in Cambodia, the rhetoric of family was employed to maintain order among the children who were gathered to beg. Sopheap explains, "Because they couldn't control too many kids, there were lots of 'families.' In mine, they were different ages, some older and some my age." Sopheap was often put in charge of babysitting the other children, and when they misbehaved, she was blamed and tortured. Perhaps ironically, the notion of family insisted upon by the slaveholders' disciplinary structure did little to convince the child beggars of their responsibility to one another. The children often disregarded Sopheap's instructions, unapologetically allowing her to be beaten. The familial structure was merely a mirage—each child protected only himself or herself.

The former slave known as "F" here had a completely different experience of the rhetoric of family. A young man whose proposal of marriage she had refused kidnapped her one day as she was walking down the street. As in far too many of the narratives of eastern European forced sex work, the man attempted to use the institution of marriage and the role he hoped to assume as her husband as a means by which to legitimize his right to sell her body on the streets. When his misguided attempt to sway her through her interest in marriage did not succeed, he kidnapped her and threatened her biological family. In her narrative, she reveals, "One time when I could hardly withstand the torture, they threatened to kill my family and to kidnap my little sisters, who were only children at that time, so I accepted the work." Only through the manipulation of her concepts of family were her traffickers able to compel her to work in the sex industry.

In order to produce the illusion of the familial relationship in bondage, slaveholders often find ways to divorce their victims from the victims' own biological family. In so many of the stories collected in this book, slave traffickers prey on people who have lost their family through some tragedy, people who have broken away from their families out of rebellion, or people who have abusive familial situations.

When a familial break is not already evident, traffickers often induce the separation—through kidnapping, smuggling, and transport, but also through killing, torturing, raping, or trafficking the victim's family members.

Kavita's traffickers tortured her ten-year-old sister and forced Kavita to watch. She recounts the effects of this torture on her:

> When we came to the house we were in in Allahabad, they made every single effort to break the bond with me and my sister. I was tied and thrown into a room like a piece of furniture. I had clear instructions not to talk to my sister or to speak with her, to have no contact with her, almost like I didn't exist. I was nothing. Worthless, useless.
>
> In front of me, my sister was beaten up, tortured, made to work every day. I couldn't console her. It was crazy. This was my sister, somebody I would share every single moment of my life with. There was no bond.

Through the torture of her sister, the traffickers refused Kavita the only familial bond she had left in the world and left her feeling defenseless to their manipulations.

Some systems of slavery depend entirely on the perversion of familial bonds. Haiti's *restavec* system, for instance, provides a very interesting and particular case of slavery based in a familial structure. The French word *restavec* means "to stay with" in English. Through this informal and unregulated institution, poverty-stricken rural families place their young children in the homes of families with greater resources in the hopes that these families will provide the food and basic life necessities their children are unlikely to receive if they remain at home. Children are sometimes sent to "stay with" their relatives who live in more urban areas so that they can go to school. Other children are simply sent to live with wealthier neighbors or families who may even be strangers to the child and to the family in need. In most of these cases, the children are expected to work in the home of the family that is supporting them, and in many cases this expectation leads to abusive situations. *Restavec* children are typically not treated the same as other children in the family, despite the fact that they are often expected to call the parents "Mother" and "Father" or "Aunty" and "Uncle." They are not fed adequately, they are not allowed to attend school, they are not provided adequate clothing, and they are forced to work without pay from early in the morning until the very late hours of the night.

Helia Lajeunesse tells the story of her life as a *restavec* in this chapter, and she recounts that her life was a constant struggle to survive the torture of the woman she was left with when her mother and grandmother died. She was forced to do all of the cleaning in the house, but she was denied an education despite the fact that the other children were allowed to attend. The mistress's children were allowed to beat Helia and abuse her emotionally. The woman who was supposed to care for her thought of her as an animal and said so to her face. It was only through the intervention of the mistress's neighbors, who threatened to burn down the mistress's house, that Helia learned that a real *restavec* situation was supposed to genuinely mimic family relationships. Her neighbor condemned the mistress because, as she put it, "she should take care of her like she's any other child because maybe tomorrow when she could do something for you, she will say thank you."

The entire *restavec* system relies on the deceptive rhetoric of family in that it maintains its viability though the intimation that children are being cared for by people who would treat them as family. In this way, parents in impoverished rural areas can feel relieved in the expectation that their children will be cared for, but the flip side unfortunately is that rich people who take in these children can extract free labor at no personal or economic cost. The rhetoric of family allows this exploitation to continue and to remain concealed from those who innocently and hopefully send their children into fosterage. Helia presents an especially instructive case in terms of how culturally convincing this rhetoric can be. Despite her admittedly painful experience as a *restavec*, she later sent her young daughter to live as a *restavec* in the hopes that she might have the benefit of a wealthier family's resources and familial attentions. The rhetoric of family is, no doubt, a powerful and convincing tool.

Despite Helia's continued belief in the *restavec* system in general, she was always aware of the fact that she was in no way a part of her mistress's family. Indeed, in few cases of modern-day slavery is the rhetoric of family enough to fully convince an enslaved person that he or she has found a new familial bond, that he or she is being protected by the suspicious characters who have enslaved him or her. These narratives reveal that the very thing an enslaved person wants to be protected *against* is the person who is propagating this myth. The contradiction between the rhetoric of the family and the experience of enslavement is often all too evident. The survivors who tell their stories in this chapter never reconcile themselves entirely to the deception of familial bonds. It is clear from these stories that the violence that enslaved people endure throughout their time in bondage is constant and clear evidence of the lack of familial bonds and protections.

SHAMERE MCKENZIE

Origin: United States (native of Jamaica)   *Trafficked in/to*: United States

Form of enslavement: Forced sex work   *Current status*: Free

Source: Personal narrative written by Shamere McKenzie for this collection, (2012); reproduced with permission.

Context: Shamere McKenzie has recently emerged on the activist scene as a popular public speaker who travels the country talking to young women, college students, and faith communities about the dangers of sex trafficking in the United States. She testifies before legislative panels to assist in the creation of effective laws to prevent trafficking and punish traffickers, and she works for several nonprofit and governmental anti-trafficking organizations. McKenzie wrote this piece specifically for the collection, to which she was invited to contribute, but reflections of her experience as a public speaker are evident throughout. She works with Laura Murphy on the Survivors of Slavery project, a website that features survivor activists like herself (listed in appendix A).

I will never forget the day I met my trafficker. It was a cold but sunny afternoon in January 2005. As I crossed over Ninety-Sixth Street in Manhattan, New York, this car was approaching me. I stopped to look if it was my friend, who had a similar car, but this man came out of the car and introduced himself. Although he was not the typical guy I would talk to, he was extremely polite. That initial conversation made me completely forget how chubby he was. Nonetheless, we exchanged numbers. Within ten minutes, he was already calling my phone, but I was at work and had no time to speak.

Over the next several weeks, we had great conversations as we got to know each other (or should I say, as he got to know me). We had conversations about politics, single parents, the high number of men incarcerated, and how the government is building fewer schools and more jails. This was the kind of conversation I enjoyed. I became attracted to this man, as he had stimulated my mind. I easily looked past the fact that I was not physically attracted to him, especially when he told me he graduated from Morehouse College. He never told me his profession, as he said he wanted me to be with him for who he is, not what he does. In my mind, this was a well-educated, intelligent man, so he must have a great job. I began thinking that he must be used to females getting involved with him because of his profession and not for who he was as a person. Therefore, I never tried to find out what he really did for a living.

At this point in my life, I was working trying to save $3,000 I needed to go back to school at the end of January. When he learned about this, he immediately offered the money for me to go back to school. He said all I had to do was dance, and he would make sure I would go back to school. At that point, I was only making $10 per hour and really didn't see how I would make $3,000 in one month. Although I battled back and forth if I really wanted to dance, I agreed for him to help me. Many girls dance to pay for their college tuition, so this would not be a big problem. He told me to move to his basement apartment, as this would help me save, since I wouldn't be paying rent.

He bought me a dress and some dance shoes and then drove me to New Jersey to a strip club. At this club, the men were not allowed to touch the dancers, and within two hours I made $300. I was extremely excited because that meant I didn't have to dance for a long time before I got the $3,000.

That same night he took me to a house in Brooklyn, New York. The man at the door was very big and scary looking. He gave us each $20 to give the man at the door and told us to charge $10 for a wall dance and $20 for a lap dance. This was a three-story house, and men were on every floor. I quickly changed my clothes and began asking everyone if they wanted a dance. It wasn't very long before one guy asked me for oral sex. How rude and disrespectful, I thought, and I immediately got into a verbal altercation with this man.

My trafficker was watching the whole time and did nothing. Instead, he pulled me to the side and began yelling at me to go and do what that man had said. I then got into a verbal altercation with him. When I told him this wasn't something I wanted to do, he began choking me up in the corner, asking me if I think I would make it out of that house alive. He then told me, "It's $50 for oral sex and $100 for sex. Can be more but nothing less."

I quickly remember the big scary man at the door and went back over to the man. At this point, he didn't want to talk to me. I had just finished cussing him out. I explained to him that my life depended on him. He agreed to dance with me for five songs so I could get the $50.

That night when I got back to the house with my trafficker, I told him I wanted to leave because this was not something I wanted to do. The dancing I could do, but I could not have sex, let alone oral sex with men, which I thought was so disgusting. He told me I could not leave, but I began heading for the door. He doubled his fist and gave me the first blow to the face, and I swung right back. He began punching me in the face, kicking me with his

Timberland boots, and choking the life out of me, telling me if I leave he would kill me and my family. I woke up lying in urine on the kitchen floor. Never in my life had a man put his hands on me, and I started to cry. He immediately came into the kitchen and began to hug me and apologized. He said he didn't know what got into him, and he would never hit me again. He quickly reminded me he was just trying to help me get back to school. I believed him.

The very next day I saw him beating and kicking the life out of one of my "wife-in laws" (girls under the same pimp). I began to cry as I told another girl I wanted to help. "He can't beat her like that." She told me I would get in trouble if I did, but I didn't care. I thought that girl was going to die, and I wanted to help. I went into the living room and told him to stop; he is going to kill her. He immediately started pouncing on me and told me to stay out of pimp business. I went back to the other girl who had told me not to interfere. It was then she tried to tell me the rules of "the game."

"What had I gotten myself into? How am I going to get out without getting hurt? How am I going to get out without my family getting hurt?" These were all questions I asked myself. Things only got worse. One moment he tells me how much he loves me and the next he beats me to the point I feel like I'm going to die. Within a month I ran away.

I went to stay with my uncle. He [the trafficker] would chirp (walkie-talkie) the phone, threatening me. When I told him, "I'm going to the police," he told me he would let me talk to a girl who tried to call the police, but too bad, she can't speak right now. I immediately thought he killed her. I stayed at my uncle's house for two weeks, and he [the pimp] told me I better come back home before he start going after my family. I became fearful as I remembered the severe beatings he gave to me and other girls, and so I went back home.

While the other girls were at work, he told me I had to be punished because I was disobedient. As he raped me, I felt numb. As I lay lifeless, I wondered if things could get any worse. When he realized I was not responding to him, he began to sodomize me. The excruciating pain I felt was worse than a toothache. I begged him to stop, but he said I had to be punished. Blood began running down my legs, and I thought I was going to bleed to death. That did not stop him. He continued anyway, as I screamed and begged him to stop. When he was done, he laughed and said, "Bet you will never leave me again." I went in the shower and cried and cried until he came and told me to hurry. I had to get ready for work. "He must really be crazy," I thought. "How can I work after you just raped and sodomized me?" He didn't care. He still put me on the "track" (streets where the prostitutes work). That night I made no money. It was painful for me to walk and sit. When I got home, he beat me again for not making any money.

There were rules that I had to follow:

1. Don't look at or talk to another pimp.
2. Get in the street when a pimp is on the sidewalk.
3. Bring a girl home.
4. Tell no one that you have a pimp.

These were just some of the rules. Other rules were as simple as not talking back to him when he spoke. Of course, I couldn't keep up with that rule. I was always getting hit, as I had to have the last word. Another one was giving him all your money you made. If you got caught keeping as much as a dollar, you would get a beating. I remember on one occasion one girl had $5 crumpled in her purse, and when he searched us, he found it. He told her to strip naked, and he performed a cavity search. While [she was] naked, he took a belt and whipped her like a slave.

It was hard for me to bring a girl home. I didn't want anyone to experience the hell I went through. However, one day we were in the club, and there were no customers coming in. When he called to check in, he said to bring a girl home instead. We all started talking to this one girl, who agreed to come home with us. We left Connecticut early that day and drove her back home with us to New York. When she got to the house, she told him she was sixteen. He said she can't stay because he doesn't work with underage girls. The very next morning I drove her back to Connecticut.

By now you must be wondering how we got to Connecticut. Well, the money got slow in New Jersey, and we began working in New York. However, the police raided the strip club, and two of us got arrested. After that, he took us to Connecticut. This I hated the most. We had to be in Connecticut by 12:00 noon, leave at 2:00 A.M., and then work the track until 7:00 A.M. every day. While the other girls got to sleep to and from Connecticut, I was up driving. Many times I fell asleep behind the wheel to wake up right in time before hitting someone or something.

On one occasion, I told him I didn't want to drive anymore. He asked me to choose death or driving. At this point, death was the best option. I couldn't take the physical or psychological abuse anymore. The beatings were one thing, but being called a bitch every second and being told that you will never be anything but a prostitute was not something I could deal with anymore. So I told him to kill me. He placed the gun in my mouth and pulled the trigger. I thought I was dead until I started feeling the blows from the gun on my head. Why was I still alive? Why wasn't I dead?

The next stop was Dallas, Texas. We all got fake identification that we used in the airport. No one stopped us. We stayed in Texas for about two months. I ran away again in Texas but shortly returned home when he threatened to kill my family. The next stop was Miami, Florida. This was when my quota[3] got real high—$3,000. Working out of one of the biggest strip clubs in America, it was very easy to make this kind of money. By this time, I had been arrested four times for prostitution and was still looking for a way out.

While in Florida, he recruited one girl who was also Jamaican. She asked me to help her escape, and I quickly helped her, making her promise that if she should ever get caught, she would never tell him I helped her, or he would kill me. Of course, we went back and forth about me going with her, but I believed he would have killed my family. He didn't know where her family lived; he met her at a bar, so it was easy for her. While in Florida, I had met up with a bunch of Jamaicans from a big gang out of Jamaica. The leader normally came to the club, but he would never buy a dance or anything. One day when I ran away for the third time, I told him what was happening to me and asked him to help. He sent one of his guys to pick me up from the hotel I was staying, and the plan was to rob and kill my trafficker. As we were on the road going to the house where my trafficker was staying, I told the guy, "I can't go through with the plan." He put the gun to my head and told me not to waste his time. I begged him not to kill me, so he said I had to have sex with him and not tell the leader what happened. While having the gun to my head, he had sex with me, then dropped me back off at the hotel. My entire life flashed before me.

I came up with a brilliant idea—just stop making money, and he will get rid of you. Not so much of a wonderful idea. I went from bringing home $2,000 to $3,000 a night to bringing home $200. That was impossible in his eyes. He had been in the club and knew the clientele were millionaires. Nonetheless, he put me to work on South Beach. Instead of working, I met people and had fun until he caught me.

Another girl and I were at lunch with a guy when we saw him [the pimp], and we flew under the table. Unbeknownst to us, he had been watching us all day. He called us to the car and began beating on the other girl since she was in the front seat. After he dropped her off at another club to work, he asked me what I wanted to do. I told him I wanted to leave, and he said, "Cool. I will give you $5,000, and you can leave."

When we got to the house, he went upstairs, and I remained downstairs. I ran out the back door as I heard the click of the gun. While [I was] running in the gated community that we lived in, a man was in his garage playing with his daughter and asked why I was running. I told him that I was running from my exboyfriend, who was trying to kill me. He put me in a hotel, fed me, and let me call my mother.

I returned to New York but stayed with my best friend for fear that he would come after me. I had gotten an attorney to take care of my prostitution charges, got a job, and was in the process of going back to school when the FBI came to my house and arrested me. Immediately, I started to cooperate.

I spent three weeks in prison and was sent to a program for victims of sex trafficking. At this program, I received services to include counseling, housing, and other basic needs. Then I was offered a plea to the Mann Act— knowingly and willingly transporting minors across state lines for illegal purposes. MINORS!!! Yes, one of the girls was twelve years old, and because I drove, I had to take responsibility for my actions. I didn't willingly drive; neither did I know she was twelve years old.

I felt so stupid. How could I not know she was twelve? I did her makeup. Even if I knew, what could I have done? I took the plea and felt my life was over. Here I was being charged for something I was forced to do. My sentence was five years' probation and two hundred hours of community service. In addition, I had to register as a sex offender. I thought my life was over, and there was no reason to live. I dropped out of school and was about to attempt suicide when my best friend talked me out of it.

God had bigger plans for my life. I met Kevin Bales, who assisted me in starting a career in public speaking. Kevin not only showed me how to start but gave me the tools I needed to move forward. He still plays a key role in my life to this day. He introduced me to Jody Sarich and Laura Murphy, two phenomenal ladies who play a key role in my life today. They both have supported me every step of the way, ensuring that I am not only helping others but I am helping myself.

I had the opportunity to work for Tina Frundt at Courtney's House, where I am now able to be a mentor to another survivor—a survivor who looks up to me for strength when she is weak and knows that I am always here for her. However, I always remind her of her own strength and intelligence. She brings joy to my life and reminds me each day why I had to continue this fight.

Currently, I am the Protected Innocence Initiative policy assistant at Shared Hope International. Shared Hope's name speaks for itself. Before working for Shared Hope, I still had a bit of emptiness inside. However, the staff at Shared Hope each started making a deposit to fill that void. They didn't treat me any different from any other staff member because I am a survivor. Many people show sympathy to survivors and that makes me feel weird sometimes. The staff at Shared Hope treated me equal and transformed me into being more than a survivor. They empowered me while teaching me the diplomatic approach to being a part of the anti-trafficking movement. In addition, they encourage me to pursue my hopes and dreams.

It took me five years to start speaking about my experience. As I travel throughout the country and speak to various people on this issue, I now realize that I went through the trauma not for myself, but for someone else. I have had several wonderful opportunities because of being enslaved, some of which are mind blowing. It is still a struggle, but God has given me the strength to fight this battle, and as I continue to put my faith in him, I know he will never disappoint me. I just keep Jeremiah 29:11 on my heart each day: "For I know the plans I have for you, says the Lord, plans to prosper you and not to harm you, plans to give you hope and a future."

I believe I am the voice for those still enslaved, the voice for those who perished while enslaved, and the voice for those who are free but have not the courage to speak up. We all have a story. What are you doing about yours? I am determined to use my story to make a difference in the life of someone else, leaving a legacy in this world.

SOPHEAP

Origin: Cambodia   *Trafficked in/to*: Vietnam

Form of enslavement: Forced begging   *Current status*: Free

Source: Narrative collected and translated by World Vision International, 2003; reproduced with permission.

Context: World Vision International collected this narrative from Sopheap (a pseudonym) as a way of keeping a record of the children it was aiding in Cambodia. Sopheap was among thirty children chosen to participate in the Mekong Youth Forum on Human Trafficking held in Bangkok in 2010.

Until I was six, I lived under the care of my aunty and uncle. During the day, they all would go out to work, and then when they came back at night, they would always fight because they were tired from working. My aunty was very hard of hearing, and she had a terrible temper. If she could not understand what somebody said, she would just go straight away and beat them. This happened to me—sometimes my aunt and uncle would beat me very severely. My cousins also didn't like me, even though I liked them.

When I was three or four years old, my aunty sent me to Vietnam to be a beggar. I went with a lady who my aunty knew, but I had never met her before. She took me on a motorbike and then a boat. There were other people going to Vietnam with us, and they all were keeping an eye on me. When we got to the river, we caught a boat. I knew I was going to beg for money for my aunty. I would go begging for one month at a time, and then I would be allowed to go home again for a few days before my aunty would rent me out to another woman again. She forced me to go and beat me if I refused. I did this three times before I ran away.

When I was begging, some people would give me money, but some would look at me angrily or yell at me. My minders told me to say "thank you" and "food, food." We would sleep outside. The minders would feed us and let us sleep only if we made 30,000 dong [about U.S.$1.70]. If we didn't, then they wouldn't let us sleep or eat. This happened a lot. Usually they made me beg at night, and during the day I had to watch the others while they begged to make sure no one ran away. I was responsible for them. If someone disappeared, then I would get beaten. Sometimes one of the other children would be mischievous and hide. The first time this happened, the minders forgave me, but the next time we couldn't find a child, they beat me badly.

There were many other kids on the street, but only fifteen with me, all Khmer. Because they couldn't control too many kids, there were lots of "families." In mine, they [the kids] were different ages, some older and some my age. They would say I was weak and that they didn't need to listen to me, and it didn't matter if I was tortured. Once the other children were playing even though the woman minder had said we weren't allowed to play, and I was watching them, but I fell asleep. Then the woman came back and saw us, so she took me to a secret place and beat me very seriously. And the husband minder came back and beat all the other children, too. If I earned enough money, I could sleep and eat, but they warned us not to try and keep any of it—they would find it and beat us. I would start work begging in the afternoon and into the night. If I got the money quickly, I could get some sleep, but I would still have to get up at 4:00 a.m. to beg again—even if I had made my target.

It was very scary working at night. I was afraid of being arrested or sold again and of having my organs stolen, especially when I had to work late into the night because I didn't have enough money. I never got any money, but I knew my aunty got money from this woman every month. Once when she took me home, I saw her give my aunty 100,000 dong [about U.S.$5.71]. I told my aunty that they beat me and starved me, but she didn't care. When I told my uncle, he said I should keep quiet, or he would beat me. One day I chanced to meet a Cambodian mother who had come to Vietnam with her own child to beg. She felt sorry for me and advised me to start saving money to catch a boat back to Cambodia with her.

So I worked extra hours, not sleeping and going out alone until I had 50,000 dong [about U.S.$2.85]. I went with the lady, and it cost me 45,000 dong to come back home. When I got back to my village, there was no one at my house. A neighbor saw me and said, "You mustn't stay here, they will just keep making you beg, and it is not good. Run to the commune chief's house; he can help." So I took her advice and went to the commune chief and told him I didn't want to beg any more or live with my aunty, but wanted to go live in a shelter. The commune chief helped me.

When my aunty found out, she scolded me. She had not told anybody how she treated me. She asked me to come home, but I refused, and finally she agreed to that. Even though she did this to me, nothing has happened to my aunty or my uncle. I want to say to the government, "Please help destitute people before their poverty forces them to leave home to beg or to commit crimes. Please help them from falling into these traps, even if it's just by giving them advice."

F

Origin: Albania   *Trafficked in/to*: Italy

Form of enslavement: Forced sex work   *Current status*: Free

Source: Narrative collected and translated by the Association of Albanian Girls and Women, 2005; reproduced with permission.

Context: All of the personal and place-names in this narrative have been redacted or changed to help maintain the contributor's anonymity. For more context for the association's narratives, see O's narrative in chapter 1.

My name is F, and I am twenty years old. I was born in L——, a northern city of Albania. I have three sisters and two brothers as well as my father and my mother. We have always been living under a patriarchal mentality where the man of the family has the right to judge and decide for everything and everybody. We had good living conditions, though, so I managed to finish high school with an average of marks 8.7. My desire was to proceed to the university, and I was interested in pursuing law. During the summer after I finished high school, I started to work in a fast-food restaurant in order to help my family, as we moved from L—— to the capital city for a better life. In the meantime, I met a boy I used to like a lot, but my father did not allow me to see him, so I respected his wishes, and I broke with the guy.

After one month or so, a neighbor next to my house told my father that a cousin of hers was interested in marrying me. She told my parents he was rich and had serious intentions toward me. I could not stand this woman; indeed, she seemed to me a very cheating person. So I told my father I was not going to say yes to her and her cousin. I had other plans for my life than getting married. We quarreled for some days; then it seemed everything was settled down.

One day as I was coming back home as usual, a car stopped at my feet, and two men kidnapped me by force. They used violence; it was late afternoon, and with my bad luck nobody was walking by. They kept my eyes closed, and I found myself in the city of D——, near the seaside. We stayed there for one week. When I opened my eyes, I could easily tell who the persons were. One of them was the guy that was supposed to marry me. I could not believe my eyes at first, and then I understood their real intentions.

In the meantime, in D—— they abused me physically, sexually, and psychologically as well. Then we moved to the city of Vlora. Once there, we stayed one night only, and we left for Italy by speedboat. As soon as we arrived there, we met some other girls that were there for the same reasons.

We all had to work as prostitutes in the streets. For sure, I refused to work, but you would never believe what kind of people they are and what methods they use to keep you feeling as a prisoner, as a victim. One time when I could hardly withstand the torture, they threatened to kill my family and to kidnap my little sisters, who were only children at that time, so I accepted the work.

They took all the money I used to earn. I used to work every night in the streets and used to earn enough money for them, or this is what I believed. But they were never satisfied, and no deal was ever possible to make with them. So I started looking for ways to escape by myself. Once I tried to get hidden in the house of a priest, as he offered to help me. There were some other girls there as well. He called the police in order to help us. We stayed at the police station one night, and they deported us to Albania. But very soon the pimp found out where I was, and for a second time we went illegally to Italy in the city of M——, where I worked for about nine months.

During this time, I met with a guy who used to be my regular client. He used to behave well to me; he respected me and showed compassion for my story and experience. So by passing the time we became good friends, and then we fell in love with each other. He proposed that I leave with him, and I reflected quite well and escaped with him. I did not denounce anybody because I was still very afraid and unsafe. I lived with him for one year and a half. I met his parents and his sister. We did not tell them anything about my story. I was afraid they would prejudge me even though it was never my fault. I tried to contact my family in order to say to them I was living a normal life, but only my mother and one of my sisters were willing to talk to me. I had not spoken to my father and brothers for two years.

We decided with V (the guy I met) about the possibility of getting married one day, sooner or later, but I was still an illegal immigrant, without regular papers. So I decided to come back to my country. I went to the police and told them about my situation. They deported me to Albania. I went to live with the nuns for some time and then in a safe place in Albania. There they helped me to contact my family, to set up the relationships with them. This was a hard process at the beginning, but after time things settled down. Now, after some months, I get along well with them, although it's still not so easy. In the meantime, I contacted V to tell him I was fine. He promised to come and marry me here in my country in order to have the possibility of preparing the documents to go back with him to Italy. Now I am trying to start a new life with him as well as with my family.

KAVITA

Origin: India   *Trafficked in/to*: India

Form of enslavement: Forced sex work   *Current status*: Free

Source: Interview conducted for a Free the Slaves' video, 2004; transcript reproduced with permission.

Context: Peggy Callahan of Free the Slaves collected this interview (with the help of an interpreter) during the group's visit to its partner organization Sankalp in India. The work it does is featured in chapter 3. While working on their video *The Silent Revolution: Sankalp and the Quarry Slaves* (dir. Peggy Callahan, 2008), the Free the Slaves crew also visited a women's shelter in Allahabad, where they met Kavita and discussed her experience as a forced child sex worker. In this interview, Callahan occasionally directs her question to the translator, so she addresses the question in the third person.

KAVITA: When I ran away from my house, I had no idea about anything—where I would land, what I would do. I was just so scared that the fact I was actually taking a risk didn't enter my brain for a long time. It was only when I was waiting at the station that fear crept into my heart. I kept thinking, "Where will I go from here? What will I do?"

I didn't know anything. It was the first time I left the city of Ajmer. In fact, even when I came to the shelter, I was very scared. I refused to speak for the first two days. I just cried and cried. But now I'm happy—very, very happy. Happy at the life I'm leading over here and happy each time I think where I could have landed, landed in a place where my sister is right now.

Even though I am happy in the life and the activities that I do here, each time I think about my sister and what she has to go through in her daily life, I am just so hurt, so resentful and so angry. I am happy for my luck and my fortune, that I am where I am, but still angry at what she is suffering from.

CALLAHAN: Does she know where her sister is? Is her sister here in town?

KAVITA: When I ran away from that place, it was the very first time I had come to Allahabad, so I was not familiar with the names of the places or where her house is. I have descriptions; I have pictorial references; I know it was a village setup. The house where she was working was a big house. There was a shop close by, and that's about all I remember. I remember what it looked like, but not the exact location of it or the name of the place.

CALLAHAN: If she could tell people in the United States who don't understand that girls are trafficked and terrible things happen to them, what would she say to people to make them understand how horrible it is?

KAVITA: What I would like to say to the world is when it comes to children, they're small, they're innocent, they're vulnerable. They just like playing, laughing, having fun, and very often they are unable to comprehend the repercussions of what the elders are doing to them. When somebody told me they would take me to a better life, I trusted them, I believed them, and I went with them.

For example, my sister—the two of us we were living in a village. We were happy. Agreed, we were poor, and our parents had to struggle to give us a daily existence. But at least there was a bonding. There was love; there was affection. We were happy in what we were living in every day.

When we came to the house we were in in Allahabad, they made every single effort to break the bond with me and my sister. I was tied and thrown into a room like a piece of furniture. I had clear instructions not to talk to my sister or to speak with her, to have no contact with her, almost like I didn't exist. I was nothing. Worthless, useless.

In front of me, my sister was beaten up, tortured, made to work every day. I couldn't console her. It was crazy. This was my sister, somebody I would share every single moment of my life with. There was no bond.

People who do such things must understand that we are children.

And even though it's not acceptable, when they do such things to elders— that's somebody who's mature and can deal with this. We are so innocent, so vulnerable. Their impact on our soul is so deep. They must understand that. They must not do this to anyone, anywhere.

CALLAHAN: What was the very worst thing that happened? It sounds all so horrible. What was the worst thing?

KAVITA: The worst thing that probably happened to me was the death of my parents and the fact that after that I was separated from my sister.

Think about it. I am sitting in a corner, tied, a witness to the beating of my younger sister. Being elder, I'm unable to protect her. I can only hear her cries of pain. I can't talk to her; I can't console her. Nothing.

Each time I think about that, I just stagnate. My thoughts become still. I can't think beyond the fact that there's a possibility I can probably never meet her again. The pain is so deep. I'm at a loss . . . pretty much at a loss for words.

CALLAHAN: I'm so sorry. I'm going to change the subject. Can she tell us what they've taught her here? I believe they've taught her some really important things here.

KAVITA: What I've learned from this shelter is how to become a better human being. I've learned the values of empathy, the values of sympathy, the value of how to be sincere, to understand, and to comprehend what I am going through.

To deal with pain, not only mine, but of somebody else. How to respect somebody's emotions; how to know when to give them space. How to know to tell the person who's tormenting me, to explain to them what they're doing is wrong, always in a polite and yet effective manner. I've learned how to deal with myself and with others in responsibility.

CALLAHAN: What does she hope to do now when she grows up?

KAVITA: I want to grow up, and I want to study, and I want to study to become a nurse. I want to become a nurse so I can help other people and look after them in their hour of need.

CALLAHAN: One final question. She's fourteen now, how old was she when she left home?

KAVITA: I'm fourteen now, so when I left home, I was about twelve. But even though I was twelve, I was still very innocent. I hadn't seen life beyond my house, so I didn't know what to do next, where to go, how to deal with life. I was just a very protected twelve-year-old.

CALLAHAN: Anything else she'd like to say?

[Discussion off camera suggests that she might talk about how she was very distant and disturbed when she first came to the ashram. Callahan suggests that she can talk about that if she likes.]

KAVITA: Initially, when I entered the ashram, I would just weep inconsolably for days on end. Raddadi assisted me a lot at this point of time. She talked to me and would console me, tell me, "I know. I understand that you have a ten-year-old sister who has been left behind. I understand that your parents are dead. But you must also understand the fact that there's nothing you can do about this at this point of time. You're in a new place, a place that can teach you a lot. So maybe it's possible for you to try forgetting the past and move on."

Something somewhere down registered, and slowly and steadily I got out of the vacuum or the shell.

But even then I was just so emotional I would not want to study. I would see others around me opening their books, doing things, studying. But even though my mind was in it, my heart wasn't. So Raddadi encouraged me to just draw, something I will always do.

I've studied to class six. Therefore, initially I would help out the tiny ones. Any younger child I would see, [I would] help them out with the homework, with little lessons that I could do. And then there was a friend of mine, Sonia— I would steal her books and read from them.

So my interest developed. I began to read little by little, and now each time I see a book, I want to devour it. So now my interest in studies is definitely increased far more. It's a lot to do with Raddadi, with her encouragement, her wisdom, her knowledge, and the confidence that she gave me to start my life afresh.

HELIA LAJEUNESSE

Origin: Haiti	*Trafficked in/to*: Haiti
Form of enslavement: *Restavec* fosterage	*Current status*: Free

Source: Interview conducted in June 2007 for a Free the Slaves video; transcript reproduced with permission.

Context: This is the transcript of the responses to an interview done by Free the Slaves with Helia Lajeunesse, who is part of a women's group, Limyè Lavi, that works to end the institution of *restavec* in Haiti. Lajeunesse's own children were put into *restavec* fosterage when they were young, but with the help of Limyè Lavi, her children are now free as well. The transcription here is of the translator's words, so some of the difficulty with language is a result of that translation. Some information has been included in brackets when the translation of Lajeunesse's rendering of dialogue requires some clarification for understanding. The names in this transcript have been changed for legal purposes.

HELIA LAJEUNESSE: My name is Helia Lajeunesse. I was someone whose mother died when I was seven months old and left me as a tiny baby. My grandmother took me in because my father, when he impregnated my mother, he left. And my grandmother took care of me from that time until I was about five years old. Then my grandmother died. And then a neighbor took me in.

I was five years old when the neighbors took me in. But then I had to do all the work in their house. I had to go and get water even though I was so little I couldn't do anything really, but they decided that I should be the one to doing that work. I had to sweep the whole house, and I had to do all the dishes. They showed me how to cook food, but it was my own food that I cooked because when they made food for themselves, they didn't give me any of that. I was the one that went to bed the latest, and I was the one who got up first. As soon as it was four o'clock, I had to be on my feet to go and sweep the kitchen and to light the fire and wash all the dishes and put the water on for coffee.

When they would make their coffee, they said I couldn't do it because they said I wasn't clean enough to do it. And they would make coffee, but they wouldn't give me any—they would just drink it with their own children. Then they would tell me that I had to go behind the breadfruit tree to make my own food.

Sometimes the children of the house would hit me on my head even when I didn't do anything. And sometimes the children would set it up so that one would take the money of the other, and they would say that I was the one that took it.

All the children in this neighborhood were in school. There were four of them. But she [the mistress] said she wasn't going to put me in school because I was just an animal without any family. I stayed there because I didn't have anywhere else to go. I didn't know anybody in my mother's family till I was about eight or nine years old.

There is a marketplace that was very far away, so then I had to put a basket on my head and go very far and sell in that village so that I would bring back all the provisions for them. But the road for me to leave that marketplace to go back was very far. And after I had finished selling, they said I can only get ten cents out of the profit. But there was a type of bread that would sell four for fifteen cents, and they [the sellers at the market] would just give me three for ten cents. And then to eat just that so that I would to go all the way back home—it wasn't very close. And then she would have me do a lot of different errands, but the money she made off of the sales wasn't enough. She would say that I had eaten the profits instead of doing what she had asked me to do.

They would have horses that they had saddles for. She wouldn't saddle a horse for me. She said I had to carry it [everything] on my own head. There was water very far away, and I had to go down and get the water. It was very far down below a mountain. And I had to walk very far, very steep. And the clothes I had, if they got torn, she wouldn't buy anything new for me.

But I had other neighbors that looked, and they would say to the woman, "Regine, you should take care of her just like she was your own child." She would say, "Oh! I should take care of her like any of my other child of my own? No, she's just an animal without any family." But they say, "No, even though she's not your own child, you should take care of her like she's any other child because maybe tomorrow when she could do something for you, she will say thank you to you, too." But she'd say, "What's that going to be useful for me? What could she learn for herself that she could take care of herself?"

I just stayed there, and I was in a lot of misery. And I was just barefoot, too. And then when I was eleven years old—no, ten—there was a school that they closed in with some coconut leaves. The man who was making that school were close to the house. The children of this woman went to the good Catholic school. [The man would say,] "Regine, this child, we don't need any money for her to go to school because you say she's just an animal of the family. So all you have to do is buy a little milk. We'll help her as family." And so she said, "I should buy a notebook? What she's supposed to do with the notebook? When you have people like this that have no family, they're just like animals. We should just treat them like animals." The teacher would say, "That's not something that you should say because you have children." But she didn't agree.

And so one day she went away into the city, and her children were old enough they were going to be baptized. One day when she was going to be gone for three days, one day when I was washing the dishes in the kitchen, and the man called me, "Helia!" and [I] responded, "Yes, Mister." And he said, "When you're done doing the dishes, come to me under the little shade house." The teacher said, "Come out, and while Regine isn't here, you can come and learn a little bit like zeros and things." And for those three days when Regine was gone, I sat there under the shade house with this teacher. And when Regine came back from the city, I didn't see that she was coming, and so when she got there and I saw her, I got up and ran away.

I went inside. She asked me what I was doing. "You think you need school?"

"No, it wasn't me. It was the teacher who called me."

And so she beat me all up, and she said, "So when you learn to read, what's that going to be useful for you?" And she whipped me with a whip, and she opened my skin, so then I never learned again. I stayed there, and I went through a lot of misery.

And then there was a neighbor that said, "I'm going to get you out of this. I'm going to put you in another neighbor's house." But I said, "No, I don't know where that is. Leave me where I am. Let me go through this with my courage."

And then one day she [the neighbor] started to have an argument about me, and she said, "Oh! You're treating this child like an animal. You're the one that's an animal!" And she said, "You don't even give her your clothes, or the food you cook for your own children you don't give to her."

And so she told the school. The little school had a catechism class, and it was for everyone. And so when the lady invited me to go to catechism class, I said, "No, I can't because Regine is going to beat me." And so the ladies of the neighborhood put a lot of pressure on Regine. They told her if she would beat this little girl, they were going to call the police or burn her house. And then when she saw that, they let me go to the catechism class.

And then when they had tests, I went to the test for my catechism, and I passed it for the First Communion. And she said, "Oh! I'm going to have to give you a communion? And because they pressured me, intimidated me, said they're going to burn my house, I guess I'm going to have to give you a first communion." Then I was eleven years old.

But the day of the communion, she took a dress that had three different kinds of fabric in it, and I wore that to the communion service. All the children had parents. They were so pretty. But I went to church with this dress and barefoot. And all the other children had nice shoes, and I was the only one barefoot.

And when I left church and went home—as soon as I got home, she told me to take that dress off and put that old rag on. And then I did that, and she told me to get the board, which is a calabash, to go and get water in it. And the sun was so hot. And then when I was coming back with the water, there was another child that was in the same communion service. And the mother of that child saw me; she cried, "Oh, what a pity!" That day I remember very well because she said, "Oh! How hard it is for a child that doesn't have a mother!" And then she called me; she gave me a little food of the party food of the other child. And there was some lady that saw that, and she told Regine that I went and that I was eating at somebody else's, and then Regine beat me up. She said that I had gone and gossiped, so they gave me food. I told her, "No. It wasn't me. It was because the lady saw me, and she offered me the food." And I told Regine that, "you know, today I am just little, but I know that there is a God, and one day I know that he'll say something for me."

And so I stayed there. Then all these people that came from Port-au-Prince said they're going to take [me] with them, and I said, "No, I don't know where that is. I can't go there because this is what I know. Even if I stay here and she kills me, I'm going to stay here." All the things that she did to me, I just stayed there. When she would beat me, I would say, "No. You have children. Even though my grandmother left me here with you, it wasn't to beat me like this." And she said, "Oh! So now you're starting to talk back to me? Oh, and you want to take my husband away from me?" I said, "No, I would never do that. Even though I just get a little food here, but you give me a place to sleep. Even when you don't give me the food that you to give to your other children, at least I have a place to sleep here."

And then one day I saw that I just couldn't stand it any longer. There was a woman from town, and I said, "I'm going to go with you because I can't stand it any longer." And so when I came to understand that she [Regine] was offering me her husband, I couldn't stay there any longer.

And I got up and left. So one day when she went out, I took the clothes that she gave me—not the clothes from the Communion—but I got the clothes that she had given me, and I ran away. And so the lady told me where she was going to be waiting for me, and I found her there. I thought it was a good thing that I was doing, but I should have stayed at Regine's house. So I got to the second person; then I was twelve years old.

So I had to get up early because she was doing a lot of commerce, this woman. She had a restaurant; she needed food. So then I had to get up really early because I was the one who cleaned all the pots and the pans for the restaurant, and then I had to get to the marketplace. She used to hire people to work for her, but then since I was there in her house, she didn't have to hire anybody anymore. Then I had to light the fire. Had to do all these things. She was the one that would put oil in the pot, but then I had to do everything else. But to know if there was enough salt, I had to bring her a spoonful so she would taste it to know if it was correct, enough salt. And after she sold all the food, she would tell me that I can scrape the pot to eat.

I left because I was so bad, and now I've gotten worse off. But there was a woman who said, "Now you're old enough. You could probably work for yourself." There was another woman that was living across from this woman I was working for, and she saw the misery I was going through. And she told me that when I was old enough, I can make a living myself, and I said yes because when I need some clothes, I need to be able to buy them myself.

CALLAHAN: She believed that there was anything good about those people?

LAJEUNEESE: I always had the hope that somebody would deliver me. I always had that hope. Because I believe that not everybody can be the same way.

So I spent two years at this woman's house with the restaurant. And so the woman said, now [that] I was fourteen, I can work for myself. And so I asked her to go look for some work for me. This is the other woman has said I can work. And so she found some work for me. And so then I was working for 9 Haitian dollars, at 45 gourdes a month [a little more than one U.S. dollar]. And I would make food, and I would wash clothes, and I'd iron, and I'd carry water, and I did the marketing. The woman I was working for had two children, and I was taking them to school. And then at noon I had to go back and get them. And so I thought it wasn't too bad.

Even though I would feel tired, when I was able to get 45 gourdes, I could buy some sandals or a dress with it. So I stayed there, and I stayed there, and I spent six years there. And so they treated me well because they saw that I liked children, and they really took care me. Even though they gave me forty-five gourdes, sometimes if they saw a brand new pair of panties, they would buy it for me. And so I spent six years there, until I was twenty.

And why did I leave? One day when I went and got one of the kids from school—at that time the child was four—so I was walking the street, holding her hand, and I just passed the priest's house. The child fell down while I was holding her, and so her leg got scraped up. And the woman that I was working for called the police. She said that I scarred her child. "It wasn't my fault, Madame Martine, because while I was holding her hand. and she tripped and she fell. To be spending six years of this, it is not now that I would do something to hurt them." And all the people around said [to Madame Martine], "How is it, after six years, that you would do this? You would make the police come and beat her, too?" And she said, "Oh! I am working so hard for my own children. If my children have a scar, they're not going to be able to do what they want to do. If they want to leave, they can't leave."

And so one day I saw that there was someone that was going back out to the countryside, I decided that I wasn't going to stay there any longer, and I would go with them.

So I went to a place called the town [unintelligible], a place very, very far from the town of Jérémie, that's on the southern peninsula. So then this person took me to this place very far. They weren't my family. So I went there, and so then I bought a machete, and I started making a garden just like a man. When they had coffee and needed to harvest, I'd go out and get coffee. And those places, they would pay you for a day's work in the garden, and they would buy coffee from you. Sometimes they'd pay you for a day's work, but they'd just give you a can of coffee for payment.

I stayed there, and I worked for people, and I just stayed, and then I found a man who loved me. And he wanted to know my family, and I said, "Well, God put me on this earth; I don't have any family." But his parents liked me a lot, and so I stayed with them. And I had a child, and so the parents of the man got mad at me because I had this child. And then I didn't know where I was going to go, and then I was really having lots of misery then. I was just perishing.

And this man had a brother here. When his brother came to visit, I was the one that washed and cleaned for him. And his brother sent word to a brother-in-law of his in Port-au-Prince. At that time, to get a boat from Jérémie, it cost 50 gourdes, and they sent 75 gourdes to me. And they said that they would pay for the boat trip, and then the rest would be for food, and I should come into . . .

CALLAHAN: Who is this?

LAJEUNESSE: Okay, this is the brother of my husband who did this. And so then I went to him, went to his house.

[Translator continues to try to clarify.]

LAJEUNESSE: So he was married. Because I was passing so much misery because I was living with my husband's mother. And it was so bad that his brother saw that and sent for me to come into Port-au-Prince. And he lived in the area called Cite Soleil, and then he went to the area of Matisse, and I stayed with them. And I still live with my brother-in-law, his wife, and his child. And then I had another two children at his house. And then my husband came. They rented a house together like a family, and we had one room in their house.

[This was in] 1994, '95, '96 time. That was the events during Aristide, who... And one night while I was sleeping with my husband and my three children, I heard a knock on my door, but I didn't open it. That should be my husband knocking on the door, but he's with me, so I don't have anybody else. And I saw that they knocked the door in. So these people had black masks over their faces, so you couldn't see their faces. They asked "Oh! You didn't open the door?" And I said, "No, Why should I open the door? I don't know anybody outside. My husband is here with me." There were several that came. There were three that raped me. When they were finished, they took my husband, and to this day I don't know where he went.

And then my brother-in-law left that area, and I left too and went to another place and stayed with people. And then I had a lot of troubles because I had nobody to give me anything to help me. And so then I found a man who was already married, but he said he would take me, but I wouldn't have chosen that, but for my children I did. And then I had a child for him. And we had no problems, really; he helped me when I needed something. And I left with my children. And then there was a woman that went and told the wife of this man, and she brought him to my house. And so that wife ... every day she would come to my house, and she would swear and persecute me, and so she would come every day and scream and holler and give me problems every day.

And so I decided I've already gone through two stages of life. If God's going to give me something, I'll take it. But I can just at least do little job[s], wash somebody's clothes, maybe give me a little food, and I can share with my children. And I'd rather not have anything but have peace with my children. And so the man left. And so I told him that, "Now that I have two children for you, if you remember them, send something for them through another person. I don't need to have anything to do with you anymore." So then I went, and I rented a little room, and I went to Fodasyon,[4] and I was able to get a little loan, so I can do a little commerce. But it's not really anything you would call money. It's only 1,000 gourdes [less than U.S.$25], and every fifteen days you have to pay back part of it. And so sometimes I would go and I would sell a few candles or some juice powder. And so whatever I would sell, I would buy some whatever it was . . . tomatoes or potatoes . . . and give it to my children to eat.

So there was a school close by, a rural school, that I was able to put my children into. But I wasn't able to buy books, and every day they sent them back because I didn't have any books. And so then in 2005, my second daughter was twelve years old. In 2005, when things got heated up politically, so that Aristide was going to be having a coup d'état, I sent my daughter to a friend of hers in Village de Dieux. And while she was at this friend's house in Village de Dieux, there were bandits that came in and raped her, and now she has a child at twelve years old. And now she's taking care of a rape child, and I don't have anything. I don't have any commerce. I don't have anything.

And then now I've found [organization name unintelligible], it was like a delivery when I found them. And so sometimes when I'm not able to go to the meetings, they pool their money together, so I can give something so I can feed my children. So the two children that are in school can't do their final exams, even though it's not their national exams. I don't have the money to pay for it.

[Video ends here.]

3

Case Study

INTERVIEWS FROM A BROTHEL

THE INTERVIEWS COLLECTED IN THIS CASE study represent years of research by Inge Bell, a German investigative journalist whose work focuses on human trafficking and forced prostitution in Europe. She produces magazine articles and television documentaries from the interviews she conducts with the victims and the perpetrators of human trafficking. Her website, www.ex-oriente-lux.org (now inactive), was explicitly designed to allow potential purchasers of sexual services to learn that some women are forced to work in the sex trade. Her commitment to this important work won her the European Woman of the Year Award in 2007 from the European Movement Germany Network. Bell's work is remarkable because she is able to gain the trust of the full cast of characters involved in the trade— the sex workers, the traffickers, the brothel madams, and the clients. The interviews here include the testimonies of an enslaved sex worker, Lena; the brothel madam, Katarina; and the trafficker, Grigorij. Each of their stories corroborates the others, even as each of them speaks from her or his own vantage point.

The first two interviews included here are with young Lena, who first entered the sex trade at fourteen in Italy. She was sold by her cousin to members of the Bulgarian mafia, who then resold her to Macedonian pimps after she escaped from them for a time. She landed in a brothel situated just outside Tetovo (on the border of Kosovo) that largely served the community of soldiers employed in the Kosovo Force (KFOR) beginning in 1999. Lena represents a fairly common case in which a young woman believes that sex work is indeed better than being out of work, starving, homeless, or helpless. She says, "I thought, 'At least I can make some money to survive. . . . I have no choice; I have to take care of myself.' I thought after a while they would let us go. . . . But this didn't happen." Lena's interview can tell us much about the way young women are lured into the sex trade. At first, they think that they will be able to gain some modicum of control over their lives if they become prostitutes. In an unfortunate twist of fate, in far too many cases the young girls lose all control over their lives and become captives of their pimps.

Regardless of whether Lena sought a life as a sex worker, it is clear from the way she responds to Bell's questions that she is still quite a young girl, interested in playing dress-up and having parties. Her choice to pursue sex as a work opportunity led her to the seeming protection of a pimp and a brothel. What she found there was rampant physical abuse, far too many customers to handle, and a system that did not allow her the choice to leave. What she found was slavery.

The brothel "mother," Katarina, whose voice we hear in the next interview, would like Bell to believe that her brothel is a model for the whole country to emulate, decent enough that it could constitute evidence in an argument for legalizing sex work in the region. For better or for worse, however, Katarina's honesty forces her to provide evidence to the contrary, revealing the brutal conditions minors are forced to endure there. If she is able to delude herself, her narrative does not allow the reader any illusions about sex slavery in Macedonia. She admits that only girls younger than sixteen actively turn a profit for the pimps, so that preference determines the age of the girls held captive there. Young women are asked to lie about their ages for the police, but for certain pedophilic customers they are expected to behave and look like the very young girls they are. She also insists that nothing happens in the brothel without condoms, but Lena directly contradicts this claim, saying that many men want to have sex without condoms, and she is forced to do as they say. Even Grigorij says that if a man likes to have sex without a condom, he gets what he wants.

Katarina reminds us of Kevin Bales's comment that modern-day slaves are being treated as if they are "disposable people."[1] Katarina complains, "For those guys, the girls have no value . . . they are like a glass of water. Once you break it, you can buy another one. They treat them like garbage cans." She continues by suggesting that all the pimps think about is, "Does it work, or does it not work?" Even by using the word *it* to refer to the sex worker, Katarina reiterates the inhumane treatment of young women in brothels in Macedonia. If they are not working, they are broken and can be disposed of and replaced.

Bell is an expert journalist. At times, she remains silent, waiting for the speaker to say more. Her frequent silences and those of her interviewees are indicated by ellipses here. Sometimes the silence is to help Lena expand on what she has been describing. More often, however, Bell uses it to urge the brothel mother into divulging more of her own opinions. As a result of Bell's skillful techniques, Katarina ends up confessing to her that many of the young girls are already carrying sexually transmitted diseases when they arrive at the brothel, but they continue to work there anyway. She admits that the young women are likely unable to return to their hometowns after they have been exposed to these diseases and to life in the sex industry. Katarina doesn't know how to avoid talking about these traumatic realities of the brothel.

In one of Katarina's moments of necessary honesty, Bell asks her whether the girls have any choice about whether to perform the sex work or not, and Katarina is forced to respond, "Yes, that's true. Something has to be done for the girls and for the soldier." An astute businesswoman and former commercially exploited teen herself, Katarina recognizes that the situation is one of supply and demand. She cannot imagine that the illegal trade in young girls will be eradicated because she knows that anywhere there is a military complex, there will be a demand for commercial sex. What she envisions instead is a world in which women do not have to be forced into the sex industry, where it can be legal and out in the open, where they can seek medical care, and where soldiers can trust that they are in a hygienic brothel environment—and, more important, where the girls are not held captive. Katarina admits that what she sees in her own brothel is indeed modern-day slavery. She says the girls are simply treated as "flesh." They are bought and sold, and she hates to think of this exchange. She thinks women should have no price. And yet she herself is condemned to and implicated in this life.

Nonetheless, it is difficult to condemn Katarina or her work as a brothel madam because, like the other women in the brothel, she, too, was bought and sold in this system and has been shaped by it. In part, the reason why Katarina needs to be convinced (or to convince herself) of the brothel's propriety is that she is a product of the very same brothel. She was a prostitute in Grigorij's brothel before she became the house madam. She worked

The soldiers whom Lena describes are lonely but concerned about the ethical decisions they are making. She says that they confess to her that they have long-term girlfriends or wives. She wonders why they continue to frequent the brothel. She asks a question that perhaps the military needs to ask itself: Why and how do all of these soldiers end up in brothels? The men are not worried about their visits to the brothels solely because of ethical concerns; they are also afraid because they are officially forbidden from frequenting them. Soldiers nonetheless seem to visit brothels in droves. Despite the ethical, practical, and legal implications of their decisions, they significantly contribute to the clientele at the brothels in the regions where military personnel are stationed. Military officers sometimes apprehend soldier johns, but there are more than enough clients to keep the business lucrative.

Katarina suggests that there should be legalized brothels, where the soldiers can go with official permission and where they can be sure that the women are being treated appropriately. She believes that it is the secrecy that endangers the young women and keeps the soldiers from reporting abuse when they witness it. She declares, "I mean, this is the truth: a soldier has his needs. Every man has." She believes that every soldier needs to engage a prostitute's services during his service career. Grigorij agrees: "That's normal, a human need. Every man wants to go there [to the brothels], and the taxis drive them." In the brothels of Tetovo, near the Kosovo border, people apparently consider it a natural human requirement that men must have sex regularly, a need so innate that they cannot forgo it in times of war, a compulsion so biting that they are willing to take any risk at all—even another person's life and freedom—to meet that need. When this attitude to sex for men is prevalent, it is urgent that the military do more to protect the citizens among whom they live.

In the end, despite all the horrific revelations that come from these narratives, Grigorij is a man of his word. He does help girls return to their hometowns. He bought Lena a bus ticket and drove her to the bus station. Another woman reported that Grigorij dropped her off in front of the embassy so that she could report herself to the International Organization for Migration and get a passport to return home. But both of these women and all the other women whom Grigorij allows to leave his brothel can leave only because they are no longer a saleable product. They have been so devastated by the work of being a sex slave that they are unattractive to potential customers. Only then is Grigorij willing to let go of them, but even then their stories do not turn out well. The woman who was dropped at the embassy was allowed to go home, but her Romanian passport is now marked with a black stamp on it that prohibits her from ever leaving her home country legally again. She married, had children, and made Inge Bell the godmother. Nonetheless, she remains seriously traumatized to this day, unable to take care of herself or her children. She sometimes behaves as if she believes she is only a young child. As for Lena, the last time Inge Bell contacted her, she was eighteen or nineteen years old, had been retrafficked in Bulgaria, refused Bell's help, and, according to Bell, looked like a very old woman.

Bell has altered all of the names in her interviews for legal purposes.

LENA, FORCED SEX WORKER

Origin: Bulgaria   *Trafficked in/to*: Macedonia

Form of enslavement: Forced sex work   *Current status*: Unknown

Source: Interview by journalist Inge Bell, 2001, 2003, Inge Bell Archive, Leipzig; transcript reproduced with permission.

Context: In two interviews with Lena over the course of two years, Inge Bell documented Lena's life while she was a forced sex worker and inquired about her life after she became free. Both interviews are Bell's own translations.

First Interview, 2001, Bulgaria

BELL: How was your life at home?

LENA: I was not in school for four years. My mother is in Turkey, my father is here, but I was with my grandmother. In 1998, I ran away.

BELL: Why?

LENA: My father also lived for four years in Turkey with his new wife, and I was with my granny. But after he came back, he beat me a lot to bring me up, so I ran away. I was hanging around on the street. The mafia picked me up and brought me to Italy. They beat me and sold me to other people. . . .

BELL: Was it the Bulgarian mafia . . . ?

LENA: Yes.

BELL: Did they pick you up on the street?

LENA: No, it was in a dance club. One of my distant relatives sold me to them. But why should I be angry? I cannot change it. In February 1999, I was sold to

Italy. In September 1998, I was still working in Haskovo [in Bulgaria], before they brought me to Italy, where I spent nine months in Milan. I ran away to Bulgaria then. I came home, but I was scared of my father . . . that he would beat me again. Actually, he is a good man, but I am scared of him. So I ran away a second time, and I was caught again by the pimps. This time they brought me to Macedonia.

BELL: How was the way over the border?

LENA: You have to walk through the forest by foot. It takes around five or six hours over the Macedonian border. On the other side, a car picks you up. From Strumica, it goes to Tetovo. There were three of us. The other two are still there. They were older than me—one was sixteen at that time, the other fifteen.

BELL: Where and how did you work?

LENA: In Haskovo in an apartment, but also in trucks and vans.

BELL: And in Italy, where did you work there?

LENA: On the street . . .

BELL: How was it in Italy?

LENA: My boss was quite okay.

BELL: You were illegal there all that time?

LENA: We had forged passports . . .

BELL: Bulgarian?

LENA: Yes . . .

BELL: What was your name there?

LENA: Gergana. I was twenty according to the passport.

BELL: And you liked Italy?

LENA: Italy is beautiful. But there were also Albanian pimps who sometimes beat the girls so brutally that they could die. A friend of mine died that way. She got ripped up. But our pimp was good to us.

BELL: Were there other girls there, too?

LENA: Yes, Italian girls, Brazilian girls, black girls. Most of them were minors. Only a few of them were mature. Adult women can get thrown into jail, so the pimps prefer minors. . . .

BELL: And then you got involved in the raid?

LENA: From the police station, they just put me out in Milan. So I ran away to Bulgaria. I paid a $400 bribe, so the border police let me in and didn't ask me questions. Then I went home.

BELL: How long were you in Macedonia?

LENA: From December until August.

BELL: It was after the war [the Kosovo conflict]?

LENA: Yes.

BELL: Again with a pimp?

LENA: Yes, they sold me again. I worked in a bar where mostly Germans came. Soldiers, you know. Then sometimes English, journalists. . . . First I was just a hostess, later more . . .

BELL: What was the name of the bar? Was it in Tetovo?

LENA: It was in Neproshteno [near Tetovo], the bar of Grigorij, but I don't know the name.

BELL: You were there the whole time?

LENA: Yes. We had a day off one or two times a month, but we weren't allowed to go outside, so the police would not pick us up. But they did catch me at last and deported me to Bulgaria.

BELL: How were you treated in Macedonia?

LENA: My boss was good, but there were other bars where it wasn't good at all. My boss was the Big Boss; he was a Macedonian. But when you got sold to Albanians, this is very bad—they don't give you anything and beat you whenever they can. Some girls have been sold to us from Albanians, and they cried all the time because of all the lashes they got—broken ribs, heads, everything. . . . Thank heavens I was sold to such a guy only once. They took me to the Black Sea to Pomorie for a week. Three strong guys beat me there with a baseball bat and raped me then. I had long hair at that time, but they cut it off. After that, I sat two weeks on the toilet.

BELL: Why did they do that?

LENA: I ran away, but they found me again, and therefore they punished me. But this year I have grown older and have promised myself not to follow this way anymore. Because you get only bad, very bad things from it. I have never stolen, but, as you see, it's better to steal than to do those things where people beat you so much . . .

BELL: Tell me about this bar . . .

LENA: For my clients, I was twenty years old, but I am actually sixteen. Well, when I was in Macedonia, I was even fifteen.

BELL: Now you are in this home for homeless minors [Podem][4] . . .

LENA: I am ill. My father wants to get me out of here. It's really not nice here. But I want to stay in my real home now, not run away anymore. I know this life. I'll wait until I'm eighteen, then I will leave Bulgaria. There is no future here.

BELL: You said you are ill at the moment . . .

LENA: My kidneys hurt very bad . . .

Second Interview, February 2003, Bulgaria

LENA: I got sold by Bulgarians. They brought me to the Macedonian border and sold me to Grigorij.

BELL: How did the traffickers get you to Tetovo?

LENA: We were waiting on the street, on the road to Macedonia, where Grigorij picked us up. First, I came to his hotel in Tetovo. We worked there. We were the first girls who worked for him there. Then others came—from Romania, Bulgaria, and Moldova. I was together with a Turkish girl from Plovdiv. Later more came. All sold. Grigorij bought them all: the one was twenty-two, the other eighteen. I was fifteen [in] those days.

BELL: Did he know that?

LENA: Yes. And we didn't have passports. . . .

BELL: Let's get back to the Bulgarian–Macedonian border. How did the trafficking happen?

LENA: Over in Petritch, we crossed the border during the night. Through the forest. In Macedonia, they left us in Strumica. There, a car came to pick us up. First, it was Bulgarians; then the Macedonians took over. I can't remember it so well, but I think one of the guy's names was Atzo or something. . . . He brought me to a woman. Then Grigorij came, checked us, and took us with him.

BELL: How much did he pay for you?

LENA: I got sold for 2,000 [Bulgarian leva] but had to work off 4,000 [about U.S.$927 and $1,855]. Seventy to thirty—70 percent for him, 30 percent for me. But I never saw money. Then I got caught by the police.

BELL: When did you get out?

LENA: In winter . . . well, in October 2000 . . . no, it was February 1999, now I remember. I was with Grigorij for over a year. They caught me in August 2000. Or was it February 2000, when I came there . . . ? I don't remember that so well . . .

[Pause in conversation.]

BELL: You saw the films we showed you. Was that the brothel you worked in?

LENA: Yes. And I saw my room, too. Grigorij established Katarina as the boss. She took care of us. He came one or two times a week to have a look.

BELL: Tell us about the other girls . . .

LENA: Later many came. There was one who was fourteen years old. I don't remember her name. There was an Elena from Moldova and a Tanya. They arrived with passports. During the raid, they got caught with me and also sent to the Bulgarian border. But there they didn't have their passports anymore. They drove back with them to get the papers. I don't know what happened then. Grigorij had the passports for sure. I did not have any papers. I was a minor. I didn't have anything. One of the two was fourteen or fifteen, the other was mature. . . .

BELL: Was there a Eugenia from Chisinau?

LENA: Yes, she was there with her sister. They got kidnapped. I couldn't talk with them much. And a week later I had already been caught in this raid. But they're still there. There was also a girl called Lia. She was also a minor. She was sixteen, from Bulgaria. From Blagoevgrad. I knew where she lived, so later when I was out of prostitution, I visited her. . . .

BELL: So was the place more of a hotel or a brothel?

LENA: A brothel. The rooms were there for only one reason—[for us] to have sex with men . . . work rooms. . . .

BELL: How did the rooms look?

LENA: A big bed, a cupboard, a shower, and a toilet.

BELL: And you slept and worked there?

LENA: Yes. The windows were locked with grates, so we couldn't get out. It happened a few times that girls escaped . . .

BELL: Could you go outside?

LENA: No. Only together with Grigorij or Katarina. Sometimes we could go to the mall with them.

BELL: Why not alone?

LENA: We were minors. Police could have caught us.

BELL: So they knew 100 percent that you were minors?

LENA: Of course.

BELL: Was there a dog?

LENA: I can't remember a dog there. I only know there was this high iron gate that only they could open. It was always locked with a chain.

BELL: Could you have run away?

LENA: No, I was on the second floor. Only in the little kitchen was there no grate in the window, but that room was locked.

BELL: Did you earn any money during this time?

LENA: I made 7,000 Bulgarian leva [U.S.$3,247]. But when the police came, they took me without the money. Later I called Grigorij, and he said, "Come to Macedonia and pick it up," but I did not want to do this.

BELL: How did you know you had all that money? Or did you have cash under your pillow?

LENA: No, it was all recorded on paper. Katarina also had this kind of record . . .

BELL: But you never saw cash?

LENA: No. Never. Just some tips. But I lost them, too—they stayed there with my clothes, photos, and my jewelry. . . .

BELL: So you were locked away all the time . . .

LENA: Yes. I didn't feel so bad after a while. I got used to it. But once I had a high fever—40 degrees Celsius [104 degrees Fahrenheit]. There was a German soldier in my room. I think he was from Munich. He gave me some tabs against fever and told Grigorij that I was ill. Then Grigorij let me rest for two days.

BELL: The soldier was from Munich?

LENA: I guess . . .

BELL: Could it be Münster?

LENA: I don't know . . .

BELL: What did he look like?

LENA: Very big. Without hair or beard.

BELL: Could you refuse clients?

LENA: No. We had no choice. If the client wanted to do it, we had to go with him.

BELL: When did you work during the day?

LENA: Because of the soldiers, we had to start very early. Around 7:00 P.M. The day was over around 4:00 A.M. From 7:00 P.M. to 10:00 P.M., it was only with the Germans. Later the Albanians and Macedonians.

BELL: Why from 7:00 to 10:00?

LENA: Because they had time off only during that time. . . . They came with taxis, which already waited in front of the military base. One taxi driver was called Niki—he brought them here. He got 10 Deutschmarks [about U.S.$6] for each client.

BELL: Did they come every day?

LENA: Every day. Sometimes more, sometimes less. . . . There were days when more of them came. Always mixing groups . . .

BELL: How many . . . more or less . . . ?

LENA: Fifteen or twenty Germans [each day]. Sometimes more. It depended . . .

BELL: This may be a stupid question, but how did you know they were Germans?

LENA: They were speaking German, and the KFOR in Tetovo is mostly German. Sometimes there were Russians, but very rarely.

BELL: Were there regular clients?

LENA: Yes, but not only here. But this place was nicer; the girls have been nicer. And they also told us about other brothels. And some girls who have been in other places before told us about the other brothels, too. Some of them told us they have also been ordered into the military base to serve there. Grigorij also checked girls in other brothels, in "Dallas" for example. The barman there was called "Milen." "Dallas" was kind of a bar in the center.

BELL: You ever heard about "Hotel Macedonija"?

LENA: No.

BELL: The "Cobra Bar"?

LENA: Yes, I have heard of that. But I was never there.

BELL: When the KFOR soldiers came, what would happen?

LENA: They invited us for a drink. We chatted a little. They asked us how old we were. I told them I was nineteen because Grigorij told me they were not allowed to know how old you are. So I said nineteen.

BELL: Did you have many clients?

LENA: Many, yes . . . so many I can't remember them all.

BELL: And they all had sex with you?

LENA: Yes . . .

BELL: Before your sixteenth birthday?

LENA: Yes. Also on my sixteenth birthday. I couldn't celebrate because I had to work.

BELL: Did the soldiers tell you any stories from home?

LENA: The one from Munich told me about his girlfriend he'd had for six years. Many told us they did not want to cheat on their wives. But I don't know why they slept with us then. . . .

BELL: Did they appear in uniform sometimes?

LENA: Yes. Green uniforms, with dots. And caps with tags. Sometimes I put them on. On the shoulders they had badges showing their rank. Sometimes they had their names on the uniforms, but mostly they took these badges off. They didn't want us to see their family names.

BELL: Were they allowed to go to brothels?

LENA: It was forbidden. They did it secretly. They stayed until 10:00 P.M. Then most of them left again.

BELL: Have there been any real officers?

LENA: Yes, but not in uniform. Once uniformed officers came and chased away the normal soldiers. None of them came again for a whole week. But others came instead.

BELL: Was Grigorij satisfied?

LENA: Yes, he collected the money in another room, or Katarina did it. . . .

BELL: How much money?

LENA: One hundred Deutschmarks [U.S.$60] per hour. Or a whole night if it was an Albanian. Because soldiers could take only one hour.

BELL: How was it with the Germans?

LENA: It was better. The Albanians and Macedonians were bad to us. They often came drugged or wanted odd sex. You couldn't refuse. They often wanted it French[5] without condoms. But the Germans were more humane. More good.

BELL: Did the Germans know you were locked away?

LENA: No. They didn't ask those things, and we were not allowed to tell them. We were scared they would speak against us. Well, they could see the grates on the windows, but they believed we did not live there, but somewhere else. But they were astonished [to see the bars on the windows].

BELL: What did they think about you and the fourteen-year-old girls?

LENA: They did not know we were so young. . . .

BELL: Tell us about the raid.

LENA: I had a friend who was a bodyguard at the prime minister's office. I called him "Diamond" because he had this strange tooth made with a diamond. Maybe he called the police. Or another possibility is that Grigorij wanted to get rid of me but did not want to pay me off as he had said, so he arranged the raid. I don't know. Everybody who didn't want to pay the cops were taken away. I couldn't even take anything from my room with me. They took me, Elena, Tanja, Lia from Blagoevgrad, and one of the Moldovan sisters. Grigorij had already sold the fourteen-year-old girl to Velesta. She was quite disobedient and didn't want to get pimped. . . .

BELL: What happened after the raid?

LENA: Then we spent one night in Tetovo; later they brought us to Strumica—I believe . . . then to Petritch in Bulgaria and then to Sofia. I was very scared of my father, but they sent me directly into the Podem home.

BELL: The German soldiers did not know you were minors and imprisoned. After the change of the contingent in May, were there other soldiers?

LENA: Yes. Until August they always came. . . .

BELL: [Extended pause] . . .

LENA: I thought, "At least I can make some money to survive. I have no choice; I have to take care of myself." But I did not know they would keep us locked away. I thought after a while they would let us go. . . . But this didn't happen. . . . There was a girl who managed to get out. She left with a customer. He bought her.

BELL: Were there minors in other brothels, too?

LENA: I know that there've been minors in other brothels, too. Grigorij bought some there, and they told us that it was so terrible. "Big Star" was the name of one club; I don't know in which city in Macedonia it was. The Albanians torture and beat the girls a lot. If an Albanian doesn't see blood, he's not very happy. . . .

BELL: How did you get things you needed?

LENA: I didn't have any money. When I needed something—shampoo or whatever—then Grigorij cut it from my money. His wife was a sales agent from Oriflame, so we had to buy it from her. We told him what we needed, and Grigorij organized it. We had no idea what the price was. . . .

KATARINA, BROTHEL MADAM

Origin: Macedonia   *Role*: Brothel mother, former forced sex worker

Source: Interview by journalist Inge Bell, 2001, Inge Bell Archive, Leipzig; transcript reproduced with permission.

Context: Inge Bell traveled to the brothel where Lena worked to learn from the brothel "mother" what the conditions were for the girls who worked there. The "mother," Katarina, had been a sex slave in that same brothel as a young woman. The interview is Bell's translation.

BELL: Is prostitution allowed here?

KATARINA: It is indeed not allowed, but the way we work here is different. If everybody would run his club like we do, there would be no problem. Should be like this everywhere. The girls are treated right and not like animals. . . .

BELL: You know of such things . . . ?

KATARINA: Yes, I know about this. Too much. . . . All the stories I hear from my girls—women treated worse than dogs, without place for sleeping, eating. . . . This really touches me. This is heartrending.

BELL: What kind of ideas do all those traffickers and pimps have about women?

KATARINA: I think they see only the money in the woman, nothing else . . . just a job. . . . Wherever you turn, nobody can help you—everybody is just after your money, after the years of your life. When it's about money, it's like that. That's something they understand. Money, just money. The women get abused, just to earn as much money as possible. . . .

BELL: What do you know about the pimps? Where are they from?

KATARINA: Most of the guys running this business here are Albanians, who, in my opinion, are not born of a mother, but of something much worse. They act like they don't have any of their own children or wives at home. They seem never to think that what they do to these girls could happen to their own girls as well. One should think there is a God. The Albanians are the strongest power in this business here in Macedonia.

BELL: You said this club is of a better kind. What do you know about the bad . . . ?

KATARINA: Unfortunately I had girls here, those who've been looking for a second chance, who came here and said that it looks like heaven on earth for them. The things they told me I couldn't believe until I saw it myself. I wish you could see it with your own eyes: fifteen or twenty girls sleeping in one room. Not on beds, but on the floor. Fed from tin cans. Potatoes, beans. Held in custody against their will. All kidnapped, forced to work in the sex business for somebody else's money and really not for their health. What can I say?

BELL: [Extended pause] . . .

KATARINA: I know it from so many stories my girls told me and also from other people, johns, coming here. If you just hear it from one person, you maybe don't believe it, but once you've heard it from dozens of girls and other people—who saw it and sometimes made it. . . . For those guys, the girls have no value . . . they are like a glass of water. Once you break it, you buy another one. They treat them like garbage cans. Does it work, or does it not work? They don't ask themselves: "Did I do right or not?" It seems to me like they are doing this their whole life, since their birth. Maybe they learned from their parents to be like that. This is very bad.

BELL: What do you know about minors?

KATARINA: Of course there are minors here. I can't tell you names and places. I would risk a lot then, and I am still young and want to live. But sure they are here. More than a thousand girls that have not even achieved the age of fifteen or sixteen. They get used to making money. . . .

BELL: Why are minors so important here?

KATARINA: In our business, you can't use a woman who's old or who looks old. You need young women here to make money. Those who are under sixteen. Somebody who is in possession of those girls can have a lot of clients from his own people to use the girls. But also others. But to reach such various clients, he needs young girls who don't know yet what life is about.

BELL: What about the soldiers here?

KATARINA: Well, I think there should be official places where they can easily go in their spare time so they don't need to do it secretly. So they don't need to go to such bad places. They should become more aware of where they are going and with whom they are speaking. If a soldier is aware of the fact that the girl is forced to do it, he should report it to some higher authority. The army should do something for their soldiers and create a safe place where they can spend their time. Where everything is alright, and you can be together with a woman without doubts and fears. Where they can talk with the girls and go to bed with them.

BELL: How is it here?

KATARINA: This is an unusual club. The girls feel like they are at home here. They are not used to such circumstances. I wish there would be dozens of those clubs here.

BELL: What about condoms?

KATARINA: Without condoms, nothing goes on here. Not here. That is the rule for the women . . . hygienic.

BELL: Do the girls respect that?

KATARINA: As far as I know, many girls come here and have no clue what a condom is. They often haven't even heard the word before. And they are already working for months in this business. . . .

BELL: [Extended pause] . . .

KATARINA: It's dangerous for the girl. Also for the client. Mostly for a fifteen- or sixteen-year-old, at the beginning of her life, who maybe thinks to have children one day. This is quite unlikely under such circumstances, after going home again. Well, *if* she goes home again. . . . I don't know what to say. It's difficult to talk about this.

BELL: [Extended pause] . . .

KATARINA: I would like to change this, make things better . . . but we here, in this club, are quite alone. We have no power compared with the others. The others do whatever they can to keep living their way and not to change anything.

BELL: There are many minors here. Why do the soldiers not recognize them?

KATARINA: The way the girls are smartened up and sent on the street, well, I guess only a man with a very big heart could understand it and realize who he's looking at. If someone has a soul, he realizes it in the first second. That depends on the person who comes to such locations.

BELL: Can you see it?

KATARINA: As a woman, yes. And if I would be a kid myself, I could see it. They [the other girls] see it in the first moment.

BELL: And the girls have no choice.

KATARINA: Yes, that's true. Something has to be done for the girls and for the soldiers. I think if someone would really want to help, he could help. I mean there has to be a place where a German soldier who serves his country can come in. Where he feels no danger and does not need to think about tomorrow, if he will catch a disease. Where he can come in with trust. I mean, this is the truth: a soldier has his needs. Every man has. . . .

BELL: But does your boss not keep the girls under arrest?

KATARINA: They all will be sent home again. . . .

BELL: Do the girls have a lot of trust in you?

KATARINA: Oh yes, very much. They have nothing other than trust.

BELL: Is this all modern slavery?

KATARINA: Oh yes, that is true. The women are treated like a piece of flesh: you buy it, you eat it. I think that says everything. Don't know what they cost. I don't want to know it. It is enough that I know that they get bought and sold. For me, a woman has no "price." She's God's gift and should be treated like a doll in a showcase.

BELL: How do you make the girls trust you?

KATARINA: First, they tell me where they come from and what happened to them. I want a new girl to feel like my daughter, and to this day they all really do. That's what I think. . . .

GRIGORIJ, BROTHEL OWNER

Origin: Macedonia   *Role*: Trafficker, pimp

Source: Interviewed by Inge Bell, 2001, Inge Bell Archive, Leipzig; transcript reproduced with permission.

Context: Over time, Inge Bell established a relationship with the owner of the brothel where Lena was enslaved, Grigorij, who allowed her to interview him about his brothel and the role of prostitution in Macedonia in general. The interview is Bell's translation.

BELL: Is prostitution legal here?

GRIGORIJ: Prostitution happens everywhere in the world. In Macedonia, it is not legal, so it always has problems.

BELL: The girls working here in Macedonia are illegally in the country?

GRIGORIJ: The girls here in Macedonia came almost all illegally into the country. Very rarely their status here is legal; very rarely they do the job of their own free will. Most of them have to be forced to do this work. And I don't see a solution. But I hope prostitution will get legalized here.

BELL: Are the circumstances similarly bad everywhere around here?

GRIGORIJ: I think the circumstances in my circles here are rarely good. Rarely do locations have such a good situation like my place.

BELL: Do you plan to let the girls go again?

GRIGORIJ: At the moment, it is difficult for the girls to return home because their status here is illegal. They want to go home for sure, but they can't do it the legal way. And when some of them do it and succeed, it's quite probable that they fall into the hands of those who already got them here once before. And they just land in another place like this. . . .

BELL: How do the girls come here?

GRIGORIJ: The girls come over mountains, over hidden ways, illegally. . . . Here they get sorted—some come here, some go there. . . . The trade in women is fairly typical. Everyone who brings girls has his own interests, his profit, and his provisions. The girls simply get sold here. Then they work, some longer, some not so long, some stay. You can't say one thing about all of them. But I can say that my girls do return home. I help them with it, to arrange the return legally.

BELL: But how about the bad treatment of the girls . . . ?

GRIGORIJ: I think the girls here are quite safe—I treat them like humans, not like prostitutes. I want them to have it good here. But of course it is a hard job.

BELL: What about the others?

GRIGORIJ: Sometimes worse, sometimes better. It depends on the character of the owner, how he behaves toward the girls.

BELL: But every girl has to get forced first before she gets used to it?

GRIGORIJ: Not everyone likes the job. There are cases where girls have to get forced, through rape, beatings, or torture. Once she starts to fear for her life, she gives up the resistance and starts to work.

BELL: What has changed since the beginning of the war?

GRIGORIJ: In the past two years, the prostitution increased here since the UN-PROFOR [United Nations Protection Force] and KFOR soldiers came, who need such establishments. So such places mushroomed up here. Only a very few of them offer a proper environment for such work. It's illegal work. How far anyone knows how to run it or not—well, everyone is doing it his own way; somehow it always works.

BELL: How do the johns find the establishment?

GRIGORIJ: Usually they go to the city and ask the taxi drivers. They [the drivers] know where the right things are. Or the taxi drivers already wait in front of the military bases. The boys just jump into the taxis and ask where the bars and clubs are. That's normal, a human need. Every man wants to go there, and the taxis drive them.

BELL: Is it a good job for the taxi drivers? Do they get provisions?

GRIGORIJ: They can make 60 Deutschmarks [U.S.$35.78] extra for driving the soldiers. . . .

BELL: Do the taxi drivers have special agreements with the club owners?

GRIGORIJ: Here in this region there are more Albanians, so the Albanian taxi drivers drive to Albanian clubs. And the Albanians know each other and also the taxi drivers.

BELL: Are the soldiers the only customers here?

GRIGORIJ: It's not only the KFOR here—every man needs it. You have to make it possible—for the soldiers of the KFOR, for everyone—but in a respectable establishment, with a good environment. No improvised stuff that does not meet the requirements for such a work. If it's not really good . . . you know, diseases, unpleasant things. . . .

BELL: How long do the KFOR soldiers stay here every day?

GRIGORIJ: Two or three hours. They sit down, talk. Those who want to go up to the rooms go; those who don't, don't. . . .

BELL: Tell us about Lena.

GRIGORIJ: She was an extraordinary girl. With a temper, liked the work, was intuitive, devoted. In a good mood and interesting. She had contact with this soldier guy. I don't know details, but I guess this was something serious.

BELL: Do the soldiers know anything about the clubs they are brought to and if the girls are minors?

GRIGORIJ: The soldiers of the KFOR cannot know where the taxi driver is bringing him, and he can't demand the girl's papers to check if she is a minor. These things should be done by the pimp or the owner of the bar. The client you can't tell everything—regardless if he is a native or a KFOR soldier.

BELL: Can't the soldiers recognize a minor?

GRIGORIJ: It's not their fault. Normally they don't know about the age. You can't see it. The girls dress like they were nineteen or twenty, but in fact they are fourteen, fifteen, or sixteen years old. The men don't know it.

BELL: They don't want to know it?

GRIGORIJ: Well, some want to know it explicitly because they have an affection for it [younger girls]. It all depends on the men and their special likings . . .

BELL: Is there sometimes trouble with the soldiers?

GRIGORIJ: I don't think so. Until now I have come to know the KFOR soldiers as very proper people. I know their work here, especially those from the German KFOR contingent. No one who came here ever caused trouble. I appreciate them as people, then as soldiers—but I see the people in them most of the time.

BELL: What about "safe sex" . . . ?

GRIGORIJ: Some people want it without safety. But most of the German KFORs do not want to do it without condoms. They want to do it their way.

BELL: So you like them . . .

GRIGORIJ: They are good guys. And as soldiers they are no shame to the uniforms they wear. I can only talk about the German contingent. About the others, the French and the Americans, I can't talk. I don't work with them.

BELL: But some want it without a condom?

GRIGORIJ: Yes, some want it without, and that will be done then. . . . That's a problem.

BELL: Let's talk again about the selling of the girls. How does the price get figured out?

GRIGORIJ: I don't take much part in that. The price depends on the beauty of the girls, for sure. If she is beautiful, she is more expensive. If she is ugly, she is cheap. Most of the girls get lied to by agencies. Ukrainians, Moldovans. They receive promises of jobs in Greece and Italy. The economic situation of their countries is not so good, so they struggle for their lives. Some end up in Greece, some in Italy, in Macedonia or Serbia, each with her luck. I try to help all that work for me to get home again. I have mercy. None of them came here of her own free will to do this kind of work.

BELL: How many girls are now here?

GRIGORIJ: I have heard a figure. Around two thousand or three thousand girls just in this region. In other parts of Macedonia, it's rather rare. Most of it happens here in the western part of Macedonia, down to Struga and Ohrid.

BELL: So everyone here knows what's going on . . .

GRIGORIJ: Nothing is wrong about that truth. It's a normal process. When there is a demand, the job gets done. Like here now, since the KFOR arrived. Suddenly more stores opened because there is this demand for girls, dancing girls, strippers, go-go girls, whatever we call them. . . . It's not good yet because it's illegal. Everyone is sinning here. It would be best to legalize it all.

4

Painful Defiance and Contested Freedom

UNTIL SHE WAS SIX YEARS OLD, young Harriet Jacobs was oblivious to the fact that she was the child of an enslaved woman and therefore a slave herself.[1] Born in Edenton, North Carolina in 1813, she was allowed the freedom to enjoy her childhood in the care of her generous grandmother until the day her mother died. It was then that she was told that she would be the property of her mother's mistress. Unfortunately, her mother's gentle mistress died when Jacobs was only twelve, and Jacobs was soon dispatched to the home of a Dr. James Norcom, who continually abused Jacobs for more than a decade thereafter. Norcom was known to force-feed a cook when he didn't like a meal, to separate and sell children away from their horrified mothers on New Year's Day, and to whip a young slave woman until the cowhide dripped with blood. However, Norcom's abuse of Jacobs was not precisely physical (it is possible that he may have raped her, though she never confessed to that in her autobiography). She writes that with her Norcom "did not resort to corporal punishment, but to all the petty, tyrannical ways that human ingenuity could devise."[2] Norcom psychologically tormented Jacobs for the entire time she lived under his roof. He sent her perverse and sexually explicit notes, he threatened to take her children away from her, and he refused to sell her to her white lover and the father of her children despite all her protests. Norcom's wife also resorted to psychological abuse when she learned of her husband's desire for Jacobs; she whispered in Jacobs's ears late at night to encourage confession of an affair and forced her to go without shoes on errands in the snow.

Harriet Jacobs had no desire to remain in slavery. However, for quite some time she could not imagine a way to escape because Norcom's power over her seemed all encompassing. She knew that if she escaped, he would have complete control over her children. He might capture her and treat her worse than he did before. He might retaliate for her escape by punishing her beloved grandmother or brother. His continual refusal to sell her revealed to her that he would do anything to keep her in his possession, and she knew that if she escaped, he would use every means available to him to bring her back. Though she could plot a route to freedom, Norcom was always simultaneously preparing roadblocks.

For so many people who are enslaved in the twentieth and twenty-first centuries, this story might sound quite familiar. Though they may be held captive in rooms with unlocked doors, though they may know their captors quite intimately, though they may have the ability to go to the store or on errands without accompaniment, though they may come in contact with kind strangers and even police during their daily lives, they are just as enslaved as a black woman on an antebellum plantation in North Carolina.

In the nineteenth-century American South, the law maintained that the status of black people was that of slave, and, as a result, the slaveholder's power extended far beyond the boundaries of his plantation, even into the North after 1850 because of the Fugitive Slave Act. Today, however, slavery is illegal in every single country on the planet. No human being is legally subject to enslavement, and there are no laws that protect the slaveholders' rights to human property. Nonetheless, many people are enslaved and find it just as difficult to walk away from slavery as Harriet Jacobs did.

Many people who first learn of modern-day slavery and the kinds of stories that are included in this chapter wonder why enslaved people do not simply escape. It is easy to read the story of a woman who has been deceived into prostitution, for instance, and imagine her quickly deciding to sneak out of the brothel or call a friend or inform a client or complain to the police. This way of thinking about the situation overestimates the generosity of strangers and the people associated with slavery, and it underestimates the tools that traffickers have at their disposal to maintain power over their victims.

The first story in this chapter exhibits how a simple lack of documents, an inability to prove one's own identity, can make escape nearly impossible for a person who has been trafficked. Marsha's Russian passport was hidden behind the bar where she worked and guarded at all times. She was unable to speak German, so she could not report her status to the authorities. Surveillance cameras ensured that she could not escape. She knew that girls who tried to escape were beaten. Marsha tried to avoid her sexual exploitation by dressing modestly for work in an attempt to turn off potential clients. That resistance went unnoticed, and clients forced her to have sex with them nonetheless. When police finally raided her workplace, she justifiably complained, "I was not given a chance to explain what had happened to me—that I never wanted to be there, that I was tricked, threatened, and intimidated into staying." Instead, she was charged as a prostitute, jailed, and deported. Her traffickers were not charged, however, and there was no investigation into the trafficking network that made her enslavement in Germany possible.

Marsha was without a passport, without the ability to speak the local language, and without a receptive audience for her concerns, so her identity and experience were essentially illegible. People could not recognize her as an enslaved person. Traffickers all over the world know how to make that happen. Passport theft is one of the most common tools of the trafficker. Natalya admitted to investigative journalist Inge Bell that not having a passport made her totally "dependent" on her traffickers. This is doubtless by design. She said frustratedly, "What should I think? I don't want to do this kind of work, but what can I do? Nothing. All the women just wanted to go to Italy to work there, but they landed here. None of them wants to do this, but what can you do if you have no passport?" The trafficker created a situation in which he was the only person the women could turn to. Escape seemed impossible.

Though all useful definitions of slavery involve forced labor, the question of escape is central to our ability to recognize what it means to be enslaved. A person can work in a public space and come in contact with hundreds of people every day, but if he or she cannot walk away from that job, we are talking about a person who is enslaved. When workers are warned that if they leave their place of employment, they will be beaten or their family members will be killed, or their citizenship will be revoked, or they will be arrested, they do not have the freedom that most people enjoy. If a person does not have the right to change jobs or to switch employers, she is enslaved. Freedom entails the right to walk away from an exploitative situation, even if it means choosing a life of poverty or hardship.

The women who tell their stories in this chapter help us to understand the psychological bondage of slavery. Like Natalya, many people who are enslaved today have had all avenues of escape blocked, and they cannot imagine a way in which freedom can be theirs. Because this kind of freedom is something we often take for granted, we don't always realize what an extraordinary amount of imagination it can take to conceptualize one's own freedom once it has been taken away. Traffickers attempt to squelch the imagination for freedom through torture and deception so that their captives find defiance too painful and resistance too futile.

VP wanted to escape as well, but she could not get past the barriers erected by her boyfriend-turned-trafficker. She ran away, but she realized immediately that she was in an unknown country, could not find her way around, and was unable communicate. She writes, "The roads of Athens are the property of my trafficker or his friends. How can a person escape from them?" Though she had left him, she knew that the bounds of his power extended far beyond the walls of his home. In Athens, her powerlessness left her vulnerable to him, and she eventually had to return to him to save herself from freezing on the street. When she returned, he beat her so badly that she couldn't move for more than two weeks. This torture ensured that she could not physically run away and erased her mental image of a successful escape from his grasp.

Harriet Jacobs did not lose her ability to imagine a successful escape. She retreated to the rafters of her grandmother's house, where she waited for the opportunity to free herself and protect her children. Though she created a kind of escape for herself, she was still not free, and she still was forced to live her life in Norcom's presence, unable to leave his grasp entirely so long as he kept possession of her children. Finally, after seven years in hiding in a cramped attic space and after she had managed quietly to manipulate Norcom into selling her children to their father, who set them free and sent them to the North, Jacobs left the attic and moved to the North herself. There, she was able to educate herself and her children and to publish an autobiography that would expose the uniquely inhumane treatment to which she, as an enslaved woman, was subjected.

Even then she did not count herself as a free person. In a chapter she titled "Free at Last," Jacobs describes the continued terror she felt while living in New England under the Fugitive Slave Law of 1850. Even after Dr. Norcom died, she was still haunted by his specter because, as she writes, "[h]is departure from this world did not diminish my danger. He had threatened my grandmother that his heirs should hold me in slavery after he was gone; that I never should be free so long as a child of his survived."[3] Norcom's power over Jacobs extended even beyond the grave because she could be treated as property as long as he and his heirs had the legal power to do so. Though a friend of Jacobs eventually bought her freedom from Norcom, Jacobs was never completely satisfied with that conclusion to her enslavement because it still meant that she was understood as an object that could be bought and sold. Long after Jacobs declared herself free, her freedom was contested, and her ability to live freely was constricted. Freedom was not merely a status for Jacobs, but an understanding of herself as an independent and self-determining citizen.

The stories in this collection similarly reveal that the psychological weight of slavery can come to dominate a person even after he or she has physically left the scene of bondage. VP did eventually manage to escape her trafficker, but she never escaped the damage he had done to her. She admits that she returned to sex work despite her desire for a different life. She remains exploited in this new life by a man who still gives her only half of her profits. As discussed in chapter 1, the global economy offers little else for so many women who want to provide for themselves and their families. VP longs for a new life but continues to live in the cycle of exploitation that many survivors of modern-day slavery experience. Once they are out of slavery, few alternatives are available to them other than exploitative labor, and so they end up enslaved or exploited once again. Such persistent exploitation makes it difficult for people to imagine themselves as free.

Inez's experience of enslavement was much like that of many other modern-day slaves. In search of a better life for herself and her family, she agreed to leave her home in Mexico for restaurant work in the United States. When she arrived in the States, however, she learned that she had been deceived, that she had been illegally smuggled into the country, and that she would have to work as a sex slave in order to pay off her debts to the trafficker. She was forced to have intercourse with more than thirty men in a day, and she was beaten when her boss even *thought* that she was attempting to run away. Her life and her family members' lives were threatened by her traffickers. A year after she escaped, Inez still reported being haunted by the experience. In a testimony she provided to the Protection Project, she lamented: "Although it has been more than a year since all of this occurred,

I cannot seem to get past the ordeal. I am dating a young man now, and I try to act like a normal girl, but it is not always easy. I also have a steady job and will soon be promoted, but I lack confidence and never feel secure. Once in a while I still have anxiety attacks. I still remember the horrible beatings, the constant threats, and the drunk and pushy customers. I am trying hard to be the person I was before I came to the United States."[4]

Inez's understanding of herself was completely altered by the experience of enslavement. The timeline of her life is now divided between the time before she was enslaved and the time after it. She longs to be the unchanged, "normal" person she was before she came to the United States, but she is emotionally haunted by the memory of what happened to her and what she saw happen to others in Florida. Furthermore, as she states in her testimony before the U.S. Senate Committee on Foreign Relations included here, her life and her family's lives are always in danger because her captor's family is still living in her hometown and threaten her family's well-being. Her liberation is undermined by the continued presence of her enslavement in her free life.

Elena feels similarly haunted by her enslavement. She confessed that being with customers makes her feel "like a rag, like a doll or a toy." After being treated in this way for so long, she has come to justify this inhumane treatment in economic terms, saying, "And you know in their way they are right: they paid, they want something for their money." Though many sex workers embrace the potential to capitalize on their bodies, for Elena the commercial aspect of the work undermined her own sense of herself as more than a simple commodity. Through being forced to perform sex work, she came to define herself by the attitude that her johns had toward her. She is also haunted by the idea that if she could have been tricked into sex slavery once, it might happen again. She fears the cycle of enslavement, and she fears all that she cannot predict. "Of course I am scared . . . that . . . I . . . I don't know where the evil might come from the next time." Though she may no longer be a sex slave, she is not free of the fear that the experience inflicted upon her.

Each of the women in this chapter resisted her enslavement. They devised ways to escape the pain of their captors. Many of them managed to escape their traffickers and start a new life. But freedom is a fragile concept. Simply leaving the site of enslavement does not necessarily free a person from the slaveholder's power. Some traffickers continue to terrorize their victims for years after they have gone free. Many people fear traffickers and their henchmen even after their victimizers have been put into jail. Some survivors never associate their own name with the story of their lives for fear of retribution from their slaveholders. Even once physical freedom is secured, so many people live with the trauma of their experience. They live in fear of violence, slavery, and the unexpected. They are unable to trust themselves and the world around them. They are ashamed of the life they led while they were enslaved. They are shunned in their own communities for having been enslaved. Though they are able to leave the scene of enslavement, they are never truly free of its repercussions. The narratives collected here tell us about the long reach of slavery into freedom.

MARSHA

Origin: Russia   *Trafficked in/to*: Germany

Form of enslavement: Forced sex work   *Current status*: Free

Source: Testimony, *Hearing on the Trafficking of Women and Children to the Subcommittee of Near Eastern Affairs of the Foreign Relations Committee*, U.S. Senate, 106th Congress, 2nd sess., April 4, 2000, 146 Cong. Rec., Serial No. 63-986 cc, 88–90 [2000].

Context: Marsha provided her testimony as evidence in front of the U.S. Senate Foreign Relations Committee in 2000, responding to the call by Senator Sam Brownback (R–Kans.) and former senator Paul Wellstone (D–Minn.) for strict federal legislation against trafficking. These testimonies were crucial in the drafting and passing of the Trafficking Victims Protection Act. Laura Lederer, founder and director of the Protection Project for ten years and current vice president for policy and planning at Global Centurion, helped to locate and prepare Marsha for this testimony. In this testimony, the names of traffickers have been changed for legal reasons.

My name is Marsha, and I am from southern Russia. In 1996, when I was twenty-four, I visited St. Petersburg. I was preparing to return home to my village, waiting at the train station one day, when a woman approached me. She started talking with me about life problems, encouraging me to share mine with her. We had a nice talk, and the woman suggested that she could help me to get work somewhere abroad. She told me she had an acquaintance in Germany, a woman who could connect me with a family for whom I could be a housemaid.

I was issued a tourist visa to Spain and left on a bus tour of Europe in February 1997. I was supposed to get off the bus in Germany. There I was met by a woman named Julia, who had a flat in Hamburg. She took me to an apartment there, where I met about twenty other girls who had come from Russia and Poland. Most of them were younger than me. After a few days, Julia told me she could not find a family who would hire me as a housemaid. She said I owed her 2,000 German marks [about U.S.$1,150] and said that I would earn that money by providing sexual services to men. I was shocked.

I was afraid to say no because she had taken my passport, and I didn't know any German. She and her husband, who was a drug dealer, threatened to beat me if I tried to leave and said if I went to the police, I would be deported. They said no one would care what happened to me and no one would help. Girls who would not cooperate were taken down to the basement of the bar, where they were beaten across their backs, where it would not show but would still be painful, possibly causing damage to their kidneys. I was afraid they would use drugs and alcohol to force me to prostitute myself—I had seen other girls given cocaine and beaten into submission. Julia tried to tell me that it didn't happen, but her husband threatened that I would suffer the same if I did not go along with it.

Downstairs from our apartment, there was a bar where we were to find clients for sex. I tried not to attract attention by dressing modestly and sitting by myself. The girls who had come to Germany knowing they would be prostitutes were regularly beaten. Our passports were kept behind the bar, but we were afraid to take them because big guards supervised us all the time. The place had surveillance cameras on the bar and on the road so they could see clients or police coming.

I was kept there for two months and never made much profit. I had only a tourist visa, good for one month, but Julia told me she could prepare documents that would say I was married to a German man. She would do this so I would have to stay longer and work for her. I refused, so instead she sold me to a Greek pimp who was operating in Germany.

Shortly after that, the police raided the bar, and I was taken, along with the other girls, to the station. I was not given a chance to explain what had happened to me—that I never wanted to be there, that I was tricked, threatened, and intimidated into staying. Instead, I was charged with prostitution and held in a jail cell. I was issued an order to leave Germany or face deportation. The Greek pimp then gave me money for a ticket back to Russia. Some would say that he took pity on me, but in reality this helped him to avoid being arrested and charged with pimping. He was never charged, and the German police never attempted to do anything about the network of people who had trafficked me—from the woman who recruited me to the agent who got me the visa to the Russian woman pimp and her husband.

NATALYA

Origin: Moldova   *Trafficked in/to*: Macedonia

Form of enslavement: Forced sex work   *Current status*: Enslaved (at time of interview)

Source: Interview by journalist Inge Bell, 2001, Inge Bell Archive, Leipzig; transcript reproduced with permission.

Context: Inge Bell did extensive research on the trafficking situation in Macedonia, during which she collected many first-person interviews with the women who were working in the brothels. "Natalya" is a pseudonym to protect the interviewee. Bell transcribed and translated this interview for use on her website, discussed at more length in chapter 3.

BELL: How long have you been here so far?

NATALYA: I've been here for two months now. I came over Romania and Yugoslavia.

BELL: How did it happen?

NATALYA: I have a friend here. I wanted to go with her to Italy, but we came here. . . .

BELL: With a pimp?

NATALYA: Yes, with an Albanian.

BELL: How old are you?

NATALYA: I am twenty-two. I have a child; it's two and a half.

BELL: Where do you work here?

NATALYA: In a cafe in Tetovo, in the center. It's the Cobra Bar. I'm already a little known here, so people call for me. They ask for Natasha or Natalya.

BELL: Soldiers, too?

NATALYA: Yeah, they come, too. Eight or nine customers from the KFOR. One of them is my regular.

BELL: Tell us how you got here from Moldova.

NATALYA: We got sold from Moldova to Romania. Then to Yugoslavia, driven by bus, by car, or by foot, whatever. . . . From Romania, we had to walk illegally through a river. In a bus they drove through Yugoslavia. There we got sold again. The pimp brought us to Macedonia. We are staying here illegally as well.

BELL: How did you get sold?

NATALYA: For money, what else?

BELL: Describe the way through the river.

NATALYA: There was a boat.

BELL: How many people were there?

NATALYA: Eight girls. Me and another girl got here. I don't know where the others have been brought. One was just fifteen. I don't know where they are.

BELL: Do you like it here?

NATALYA: So-so. It's not so bad; it's not very good. I am homesick. . . . Of course, I want to go back.

BELL: How is your daily life?

NATALYA: It's boring. And they pay bad. I have a claim to keep 30 percent from a customer. Thirty Deutsch marks [about U.S.$17]. But I don't see much of it. It's not enough for anything. You can't earn much when there is Ramadan.

BELL: How many Germans are among your customers?

NATALYA: Not many, not few . . . they go also in other brothels.

BELL: How do you live?

NATALYA: There is one room for all the girls. There are seven girls in one room. I can't go out of the room during the daytime.

BELL: Are there minors, too?

NATALYA: Of course. Well, I heard that. I haven't seen it.

BELL: What nationalities?

NATALYA: All kinds . . . Albanians rarely work here. More Ukrainians. Many got robbed from home. This fifteen-year-old girl ran away from home. I really felt pity for her.

BELL: Why?

NATALYA: Why? Don't know . . .

BELL: What was your first reason to go abroad?

NATALYA: Life in Moldova or Ukraine is bad. Even if you live a bit better than most there, it's still quite bad. There's hardly any work there.

BELL: So how did it happen, when you were trafficked? First you were in Romania . . .

NATALYA: In Romania, we were three weeks in Iasi, locked in a room. We didn't work there. Just waited for the next journey. Then we continued with a bus and with a car to the Danube. Some guys waited there. We were in Yugoslavia for two days only. Then we marched by foot over to Macedonia.

BELL: How can you get back now?

NATALYA: To get back, I need a passport and a ticket. I don't have any money for a ticket or passport. I am totally dependent on the pimp. That's bad, but what can you do?

BELL: Do you have a place where you can go?

NATALYA: I want to go home and then to Moscow. Relatives of my husband are there.

BELL: What do you think about all this?

NATALYA: What should I think? I don't want to do this kind of work, but what can I do? Nothing. All the women just wanted to go to Italy to work there, but they landed here. None of them wants to do this, but what can you do if you have no passport?

BELL: What do you do when you have any problems?

NATALYA: When there are problems, I tell the pimp.

BELL: Tell us about the men from the KFOR.

NATALYA: I can't keep their names. It always had to be quick because they never have much time. Just one hour or so. And then I can't speak German. They are friendly and never make trouble.

BELL: What about condoms?

NATALYA: I don't want to do it without.

BELL: You said you have child?

NATALYA: Yes, with my parent at home. But there's not enough money.

BELL: What does it look like where you stay now?

NATALYA: A big room with a toilet and a tub. Normal. One bed. Whoever's not on the bed, sleeps on the ground. Sometimes there is water to wash, sometimes not.

BELL: Do you ever get paid directly?

NATALYA: Just tips, but even that the pimp takes away.

VP

Origin: Albania   *Trafficked in/to*: Greece

Form of enslavement: Forced sex work

Current status: Free, but remains an exploited sex worker

Source: Narrative collected and translated by the Association of Albanian Girls and Women, 2005; reproduced with permission.

Context: See O's testimony in chapter 1 for details on the association's collection of client narratives. VP's story was very long, so the association abbreviated it to conform to the limitations of Internet publication. We do not have access to the longer version at this time.

My story started because of the deep poverty in my house. We were living on my mother's pension payment since my father was unemployed. When I was sixteen, I had to go to Athens and work there for my living. There I was introduced to a guy from Fier, who first promised to marry me but very soon cheated me and made me a prostitute.

I was unlucky, living with a cruel person who treated me as a slave. I stayed with him for more than two years. During that time, I was working ten to twelve hours a day, and he got all my profits. The first thing I experienced in the morning was beating and torture by him. He would hit me with his belt and tie me up with rope for twenty-four hours at a time without anything to eat. I hate him and sometimes think that his bad life made him criminal.

I wanted to escape but had no other place to go. I did escape once and spent the night at the train station on a bench. As I was tired and exhausted, I fell asleep, but I got up immediately because it was so cold. Where could I go? The roads of Athens are the property of my trafficker or his friends. How can a person escape from them? When my trafficker found me, he thought that I had been working and asked me for the money. I told him I didn't work that night because I was sick, and he didn't wait until I even finished my sentence; he caught my hair and hit me on the sidewalk. He beat me so much that night that I couldn't move from the bed for fifteen days. So it is hard to get away from traffickers.

Finally, after two years, I escaped and came back to my city in Albania to get a job, but it didn't work well. I left Albania again, this time by a speedboat to go to Italy. There I met a guy from Vlora who, even though he exploited me as a prostitute, treated me better by giving to me half my profits.

If I had a good job, I would never begin the profession of a prostitute. I would even be a street cleaner, but there were no other jobs, especially for a young Albanian girl like me. You may ask how is this thing possible in Italy and Greece? I couldn't get any other jobs. What do you think, that once you get to Italy or Greece, they present you a long list of jobs and then ask you which one you like the best? I am telling you: there is only one job there for young girls, the most difficult one, the most humiliating thing for a girl. I have always faced two paths: to sell my youth or to turn back to Albania. But I thought, "Where can I go in Albania, and what will I do there?" My family was so poor that we were never full and satisfied.

You might think it is embarrassing to be a prostitute, but to me it is embarrassing to live on somebody's shoulders, and that somebody is my paralyzed mother, who gets only 3,000 leke [about U.S.$32] a month. My situation and the situation of many other Albanian girls like me should make the Albanian government think and create jobs in order to employ Albanian young people in Albania. Why did they make us sell our honor abroad? And they say that Albania is going to Europe . . . but I saw Europe. We Albanians are going to the gap of poverty. If there was an agreement between the Albanian government and other foreign governments on immigration issues, we Albanian girls wouldn't have become prostitutes. We sell our honor to make money because we cannot live on 2,000 to 3,000 leke [about U.S.$20 to $32] a month. I am feeling that this profession is making me sick.

Every Albanian girl has her own mind. I don't want to make statements, but I want to tell you that this profession of the prostitute is the dirtiest of every other profession, and every girl understands what I mean. I would never wish my fortune on anybody else.

INEZ

Origin: Mexico   *Trafficked in/to*: United States

Form of enslavement: Forced sex work   *Current status*: Free

Source: Testimony, *Hearing on the International Trafficking of Women and Children to the Subcommittee of Near Eastern Affairs of the Foreign Relations Committee*, U.S. Senate, 106th Cong., 2nd sess., February 22, 2000, 146, Cong. Rec. Serial No. 106-705, 26–29 [2000].

Context: Like Marsha, Inez (a pseudonym) provided this testimony to the U.S. Senate Committee on Foreign Relations as part of the proceedings that led to the drafting and passing of the Trafficking Victims Protection Act (TVPA) of 2000. When Inez testified, she wore a scarf and sunglasses as a disguise to protect herself from her traffickers, who had been convicted but were nonetheless a threat to her and her family. She was introduced to the Senate hearings by Laura Lederer of the Protection Project. Inez was assisted in her testimony by Virginia Coto of the Florida Advocacy Immigrant Center, who acted as both attorney in the case and translator for this testimony. Ms. Coto read this prewritten transcript into the record as Inez told her story. After she testified, Senators Brownback and Wellstone reinforced the importance of her testimony in shaping the TVPA and in ensuring that people who are trafficked into the United States receive protections from continued terror by their captors. The surname of Inez's trafficker and his family has been changed in this transcript for legal purposes.

INEZ: Good morning. I would like to thank the Foreign Relations Committee for the opportunity to speak to you on behalf of trafficking survivors. My name is Inez. I am in disguise today because I am in fear that my captors would recognize me and thus place my life and that of my family in danger.

My story begins in the fall of 1997 in Veracruz, Mexico. A friend and neighbor approached me and told me about the opportunities for work in the United States. She told me she worked in the United States at a restaurant and had made good money. At the time, I was working with my family harvesting lemons. I was eager to assist my family financially, so I decided to learn more about this job opportunity.

My friend set up a meeting with two men, who confirmed the job openings for women like myself at American restaurants. They told me they would take care of my immigration papers and that I would be free to change jobs if I did not like working at the restaurant.

I decided to accept the offer. I was eighteen on September of 1997, when I was brought into the United States through Brownsville, Texas. My friend who told me about the job traveled with me. We were transported to Houston, Texas, where a man named Roberto Martinez picked us up and transported us to a trailer in Avon Park, Florida. This is when I was told my fate. I would not be working in a restaurant. Instead, I was told I owed a smuggling fee of $2,500 and had to pay it off selling my body to men.

I was horrified. I asked my friend what this was all about. She said she had already worked in the brothels, and it did me no good to complain. I was told that if I did not pay, the bosses would go after my family in Mexico since they knew where they lived. I was also told that it did me no good to try to escape because I would be found and beaten.

Next, I was given tight clothes to wear and was told what I must do. There would be an armed man selling tickets to customers in the trailer. Tickets were condoms. Each ticket would be sold for $22 to $25 each. The client would then point at the girl he wanted, and the girl would take him to one of the bedrooms. At the end of the night I was to turn in the condom wrappers. Each wrapper represented a deduction to my smuggling fee. After fifteen days, I would be transported to another trailer in a nearby city. This was to give the customers a variety of girls, and so we never knew where we were in case we tried to escape.

I could not believe this was happening to me, but even worse was that some of the girls were as young as fourteen years old. There were up to four girls in each trailer at one time. We were constantly guarded and abused. If any one of us refused to be with a customer, we were beaten. Most of the customers were drunk or high. This was very frightening to us because they often would beat us as well. Sometimes we would tell them about our situation and plead with them to help us escape. The men would agree to help us, but we had to perform certain sex acts which were not part of the regular fee. They did not care about us. They wanted their money's worth.

On other occasions, if we declined a customer ourselves, the bosses would beat us severely or show us a lesson by raping us. One of the girls was even locked in a closet for fifteen days. We worked six days a week and twelve-hour days. We mostly had to serve thirty-two to thirty-five clients a day. Weekends were even worse. Our bodies were utterly sore and swollen. The bosses did not care. Often, when our work night was over, it was the boss's turn with us. If anyone got pregnant, we were forced to have abortions. The cost of the abortion was then added to our smuggling debt.

The brothels would always be in very isolated areas. We were transported every two weeks to different brothels in order to give the clients a variety. We never really knew where we were. We were not allowed to go outside of the trailer. We were only allowed to use the telephone once a week to call our families in Mexico. However, the bosses stood next to us to ensure that we never revealed the truth about our situation.

On other occasions, we were taken to bars for the purpose of recruiting customers. At the bars, the bosses forced us to perform sex acts with customers in their cars.

I was enslaved for several months. Other women were enslaved for up to a year. The INS [Immigration and Naturalization Service], FBI, and local law enforcement raided the brothels and rescued us from the horrible ordeal. We were not sure what was happening on the day of the raids. Our captors had told us over and over never to tell the police of our conditions. They told us that if we told, we would find ourselves in prison for the rest of our lives. They told us that the INS would rape us and kill us, but we learned to trust the INS and FBI and assisted them in the prosecution of our enslavers.

Unfortunately, this was difficult. After the INS and FBI freed us from the brothels, we were put in a detention center for many months. Our captors were correct. We thought we would be in prison for the rest of our lives. Later, our attorneys were able to get us released to a women's domestic violence center, where we received comprehensive medical attention, including gynecological exams and mental health counseling.

Thanks to the United States government, some of our captors were brought to justice and were sent to prison, unfortunately not all. Some of them are living in Mexico in our hometown of Veracruz. They have threatened some of our families. They have even threatened to bring our younger sisters to the United States for them to work in brothels as well.

I would have never, ever have done this work. No one I know would have done this work. I am speaking out today because I never want this to happen to anyone else. However, in order to accomplish this goal, women like me need your help. We need the law to protect us from this horror. We need the immigration law to provide victims of this horror with permanent legal residence.

We came to the United States to find a better future, not to be prostitutes. If anyone thinks that providing protection to trafficking survivors by affording them permanent residency status is a magnet for other immigrants like myself, they are wrong. No woman or child would want to be a sex slave and endure the evil that I have gone through. I am in fear of my life more than ever. I helped to put these evil men in jail. Please help me. Please help us. Please do not let this happen to anyone else.

Thank you.

SENATOR BROWNBACK: Thank you for coming forward and being willing to have your testimony stated so that we can hear and we can shine that light on what takes place in so many horrifying situations. Is she willing to answer any questions?

INEZ: Sure.

SENATOR BROWNBACK: First, we are deeply grateful to you for being willing to subject yourself to this and the fear that goes with what you have been through, and God bless you for doing that because you are speaking out for millions of women around the world that this has happened to them as well. How did they sneak you across the border? How did that occur?

INEZ: In a van they brought me to the border. I was brought across the border and then transported in another van to Houston and then Florida.

SENATOR BROWNBACK: Was it an organized operation, an organized group?

INEZ: Yes.

SENATOR BROWNBACK: And the name of that group has been brought forward and prosecuted already. Can you say the name of the group that did the organization in bringing you across the border?

INEZ: It is the family, the Martinez family, of which Roberto Martinez has been prosecuted in the United States and is in prison. Maria is in Veracruz, Mexico, as are other family members and other ring members.

SENATOR BROWNBACK: Do you know other women . . . do you know personally other women who have been tricked into the sex traffic in the United States as well?

INEZ: Yes.

SENATOR BROWNBACK: Many?

INEZ: Yes.

MS. COTO: If I may, I represent fourteen of the women. In the Martinez family that were prosecuted in Florida, after the sixteen indicted, seven were prosecuted and imprisoned, and the rest are still at large, living in her same hometown, in Veracruz. Maria [Martinez], I believe, was finally detained in Mexico. I am not sure of the status at this point. But there are actually seventeen in this case. They know of at least twenty-five women, some are in Mexico, and I represent fourteen, but there are some still in the United States as well.

SENATOR BROWNBACK: Is this a growing activity from Mexico into the United States from the organized rings of bringing people in and then tricking them into the sex trade? Does she know, or do you?

MS. COTO: I do not know. I think Dr. Lederer[5] might respond to that.

SENATOR BROWNBACK: I have asked more questions than I should have. . . . Paul . . .

SENATOR WELLSTONE: I think, Senator Brownback, there are a couple of things, that this is less a question of—I think, Ms. Inez, you have given us some very important direction. There are several things you have said that are very important to take note of. One is that when women are put in this situation, as happened to you, they are not going to be able to step forward if what they have to worry about is either being deported or put in detention camp, and that is one thing we have to make sure that does not happen.

Instead, what we should be getting to women is the medical services and counseling and help. The second thing, and I think in the bill that I have this is perhaps a weakness we need to look at, which is, we talk about these protections for women and also women being able to stay in our country, but that is if they cooperate with the prosecution, but some women may not be able to do that because literally their loved ones could be murdered back in the countries they come from, and so I think we have to sort of come up with another standard to provide protection, if that makes sense to those of you who are in this room.

And then finally, I just would like to thank you again because I think quite often we think this all happens in other countries and not here in the United States, but it does happen here. Thank you again for your courage.

ELENA

Origin: Bulgaria   *Trafficked in/to*: Greece

Form of enslavement: Forced sex work   *Current status*: Free

Source: Interview by journalist Inge Bell, 2001, Inge Bell Archive, Leipzig; transcript reproduced with permission.

Context: Inge Bell, the journalist whose interviews constitute all of chapter 3, investigated the brothels of eastern Europe and spent extensive time talking with the women who were held captive there as well as those who escaped. Elena was one of the lucky women who managed to escape, even though that meant having to spend time in jail before being freed. Bell transcribed and translated this interview.

BELL: Tell us how it all started . . .

ELENA: I was a waitress in a dance club in Tutrakan. My boyfriend came one evening and told me my mother asked me to see my father in Sofia. I was happy about the idea of seeing my father. Two other guys were there with him [the boyfriend]. I'd never seen them before, but my boyfriend said they were his friends, that they were from abroad. After work in the evening, I drove with them from Ruse to Sofia. One of the guys accompanied me. In the evening, I was talking with him and wanted to know his name.

BELL: When did you find out the truth?

ELENA: After we arrived in Sofia, he told me it made no sense to lie to me anymore—"I better tell you straight: you're going to Greece. Your boyfriend sold you." I couldn't believe what was happening. I was standing around, looking stupid, couldn't get away. He brought me in his apartment, locked me in, and told me he would come the next morning. The next day he came and told me that things were postponed a few days. In the evening, he came again, put me in a car, and we drove to Sandanski. On our way, we changed cars. In Sandanski, there was another man who didn't allow me to speak, to ask him anything. I stayed there for two days.

BELL: How was the trip to Greece then?

ELENA: On the evening of the 17th of February, they told me we had to go. They brought me to a house close to Kulata. I spent half an hour there—then we left. Outside we waited for the guard change on the border—to bring me over. The guy who was there all the time in Sandanski talked with the guide—he told him to keep an eye on me. There were also two Kurds with us. I asked one guide a few things. He said: "You stay close to me and do not say anything." I asked him about his name. "Ivantsho," he said.

On the border itself, suddenly one of the border guards came! He opened a gap in the fence, and we sneaked through: the two Kurds, the guide, and me. We followed the path to a river. We crossed the river. It was not as difficult as I later heard it was from other girls. After arriving in Greece, a car was waiting. A Greek guide took over. The other guide just walked back to Bulgaria. The two Kurds went to a construction site to work. I was brought to my Greek boss. They brought me into the apartment where I spent all my time since then.

BELL: Tell us about your boss.

ELENA: She explained to me how much money I had to work off and how I had to behave. The next day I had to start to work. I asked her why, but she just said that there is another girl working, too, and she can't handle it all alone.

BELL: What was the work like?

ELENA: Before we left, she said, "Take a sweater and jeans. Only dark stuff and take some water with you." It was thirteen kilometers away, through forests and rivers. The first day was very hard because I was the new girl and all the clients wanted me. I had twelve customers this first day, and I was still so tired from the journey over the border the day before. But they woke me up in the early morning and made me work night and day. I didn't even have time to go home between the customers. Some came to our place, but mostly we visited them. Or we went to a hotel with them. Also the boss-woman worked.

BELL: Were you under strong observation?

ELENA: She was always there when I worked. She always waited until I finished the client. Except if she had an appointment herself. Then I had to go alone.

BELL: Did you not want to run away?

ELENA: But how . . . ? I was in a foreign country. I didn't know what the police were like or if I could trust them.

BELL: So you were scared of the police as well?

ELENA: Yes.

BELL: How were the clients?

ELENA: Only Greek, but those who have companies in Bulgaria or some other connections to the country.

BELL: How did they treat you?

ELENA: They believe, "If I pay, I can do with you whatever I want during the time I paid for." In their hands, you feel like a worthless rag, and you know in their way they are right: they paid; they want something for their money.

BELL: Could you refuse clients?

ELENA: No, rejection was not possible. They wanted to get what they paid for.

BELL: There seems to be women from many different countries working here.

ELENA: I don't understand this . . . Romanians, Russians, but also Bulgarians. Most wanted are the Bulgarians. It happens sometimes that girls don't return from clients. . . .

BELL: What happens?

ELENA: They simply get stolen. Sold to another place or country. I was scared of that because it can happen anytime. You have no safety—with each customer you can disappear.

BELL: How did you feel all that time?

ELENA: How did I feel? Like a rag, like a doll or a toy. I also didn't receive any money for the work. The boss bought me cigarettes and gave me 5,000 Drachmae [about U.S.$20] for three days.

BELL: But you had to work off your price.

ELENA: Yes. I had to work off 2,000 Deutschmarks [about U.S.$1,150]. I know my boss got 15,000 or 20,000 Drachmae [about U.S.$60 to $80] from the clients— I didn't know how it was calculated. Working off would mean you had to get booked 5,000 Drachmae from each job.

BELL: How did you get all the things you needed?

ELENA: She [the boss-woman] bought it. Cosmetics, personal things, cigarettes . . .

BELL: What about your parents?

ELENA: They didn't know anything. First, I called her [my mother] from Sofia. She had doubts. I called her a week later but didn't tell her I was in Greece. Then I talked with her a week before I got caught. I told her I was in Greece. She tried to ask me a lot of things.

BELL: How do you feel now?

ELENA: Like a nothing . . . [starts crying].

BELL: When you meet your mother . . . are you going to tell her everything?

ELENA: I will tell her everything because I never had secrets from her.

BELL: Can you ever forget this?

ELENA: I want to try to forget, but whether I can . . . I don't know . . .

BELL: Are you scared it can happen again?

ELENA: Of course I am scared . . . that I don't know where the evil might come from the next time. Possibly now when I come home, I am scared he will get me stolen again. That they will bring me back to Greece. I told the police everything.

BELL: Did you not know that there are traffickers and that there is forced prostitution?

ELENA: I knew it from magazines and TV. But I never thought that this could happen to me. Even in Greece I still couldn't believe it.

BELL: You were arrested in Greece.

ELENA: When I was in this Greek jail, in Thesaloniki, I talked with a Russian woman. She was seventeen or eighteen. She was just working as a waitress, but her bosses kidnapped her. They were mafia. They sold her to Bulgaria, then to Greece. She was also forced into prostitution—got no money. And they beat her, and they put out cigarettes on her skin. She had scars on her belly from the cigarettes. One day, she climbed on a high wall to create some attention. When people saw her then and called the police, she got arrested for ten days and sent back to exactly the same place. She got trapped by the same people, sold to Bulgaria and Greece, and tortured again. They wanted to kill her, so she climbed out again! "I am three months here in the jail," she told me. "And I'd rather stay here my whole life than to go out again. Back to Russia, where they will just kill me."

BELL: How long were you in jail?

ELENA: I was there twenty days. She remained there. I didn't have any papers, and I am a minor. They check you there, send faxes around to the embassy, then to Bulgaria, then to Silistra, and wait for their confirmations.

BELL: How was the jail?

ELENA: Jail was a great misery . . . fifty women in one cell. Two days before I left, there was a Georgian woman brought in who was sixty-two years old. There was also a Serbian woman with a three-year-old child. Babies and grannies . . . pregnant women, too. In the beginning, there was only this one cell, made for thirty women, but there were fifty of us in there. There was no room in there; everyone was sleeping on each other and on the floor. There were no bed linens or anything . . . nothing, just a few mats. There was another cell too—so altogether we must have been around one hundred women.

BELL: What nationalities were there?

ELENA: Well, let's say 10 percent of the women are Romanians, 30 percent are Bulgarians, 50 percent are Russian, and the rest come from other countries. Most of them were in because they had outdated papers. But some of them were trafficked, Romanian women who worked in a bar. Anka went instead to a client of the police. Together with the police, she drove to pick up the other girl. They spent forty days in jail! The Romanian administration works very slow. They came to Greece as waitresses in a bar. In the beginning, they really even got some money.

BELL: Were there many minors?

ELENA: In the other cell, there was a sixteen-year-old. Most of them were nineteen years old. There was a fourteen-year-old Romanian girl and two from Poland—one was nineteen and pregnant. They come from the whole world—all to Greece. Many go to Crete because of the tourists. The others told me that. Clients also come from everywhere—Greeks, tourists, Americans. There are many on Crete. There were also two Bulgarian women there, a little older. Just doing honest work in the coffee fields. But they got betrayed by envious colleagues and got picked up directly from work.

BELL: Were there conflicts in jail?

ELENA: No, we didn't fight there in the big cell. . . .

BELL: Did it cost money to be there?

ELENA: Yes, around 1,000 Drachmae a day: 350 for a sandwich, 750 for cigarettes [U.S.$4 a day: $1.50 and $3.22].

5

Community Response and Resistance

IN THE PREVIOUS CHAPTER, survivors of slavery lamented the difficulties they encountered in imagining and inventing an escape from slavery. Escape takes an imagination of one's own right to freedom, and it takes an unusual opportunity. Even after people have escaped their captors, it takes enormous strength and years of psychological rehabilitation to find something that feels like complete freedom from enslavement.

For the two contributors to this chapter, escape was similarly difficult to imagine and no more than a distant hope for some time before they fought their way to freedom. Both of them struggled to comprehend the conditions and contours of their servitude. Both wondered whether their treatment was appropriate. Both struggled with a new culture and different norms for labor standards and employer behavior. Both were manipulated by false contracts and negotiations for their labor. Both were prevented from resisting by threats to and fear for their vulnerable families back home.

And both of them were enslaved in the United States.

Miguel is an agricultural laborer from Mexico. He came to the United States in search of work that would pay him enough to afford the medications his son needed to treat cancer. Like 175,000 other Mexican people who cross into the United States each year in search of a reasonable wage, Miguel sought work that would support his family and ailing son. He crossed the Mexico–U.S. border with a trafficker (often called a "coyote") who promised to find him work in Florida that would help him to pay off the cost of his journey. By the time Miguel arrived in Florida several weeks later, an imaginary but enormous debt had accumulated, which he was willing to pay, but he was so severely underpaid for his backbreaking labor that his supposed wages simply disappeared before he ever got a paycheck. As a result, Miguel was forced to subsist on less than he had been making in Mexico and had nothing extra to send home to his family. Though it was clearly not a worthwhile situation for him, Miguel dared not leave his job—he had seen other people beaten, and his employers threatened him with death if he left.

Given Kachepa was a young orphan in Zambia when he was recruited to join an a cappella choir directed by a minister from the United States. He leaped at the chance to travel to the United States because he was told that his work in the choir would support his brothers and sisters back home and would help to build a school where he could study when he returned to Zambia. When he arrived in Texas, however, he found that his situation was not at all as described it would be. Kachepa and the other boys in the choir, all of them preteens and early teens, endured a grueling performance schedule, singing in several shows a day. The boys also served as the crew for the show—they were expected to construct and deconstruct the sets. They were never allowed play time, were refused an education, and were not allowed to attend church. When the boys were not singing, they were required to do manual labor. These ten- to fifteen-year-old boys actually dug the hole for a swimming pool with shovels alone. The minister and his family who ran the business did not pay the boys a wage, nor did they build the promised school in Zambia. All of the donations collected during the concerts went straight into the minister's pocket. When Kachepa and his friends realized that they were being inappropriately treated, they did not chance resisting because their boss threatened to deport them and would withhold food and water when they disobeyed his orders.

We might wonder how it is possible that something like this could happen in the United States. The U.S. government estimates that between 14,500 and 17,500 people are trafficked into the United States each year as forced laborers.[1] In the case of agricultural workers, this trafficking is particularly difficult to regulate because U.S. laws do not protect farmers (or domestic workers) in the same way they do other laborers. Until 1966, farmworkers were not even included in the minimum-wage laws. Today, farmworkers are not guaranteed overtime compensation, have no right to a union or to collective bargaining, and are not even guaranteed minimum wage on small farms.[2] Furthermore, traffickers abuse the Guest Worker

Program, which might have some positive potential for migrant workers if it were properly regulated, because there are not sufficient resources to monitor the farms that use guest-worker visas. Guest workers are promised a wage and a route to citizenship if they participate in the program. However, the *2011 Trafficking in Persons Report* shows for the United States that rampant visa violations and employer abuses characterize the system as it functions today.[3] Both Miguel and Kachepa were denied their rights as workers and as immigrants—whether documented or undocumented—when they were forced into bondage and had their lives threatened for attempting to quit their jobs.

Given the history of labor standards in the United States, it doesn't take much of a stretch of the imagination to understand that domestic and farm laborers often go unpaid and are held as slaves, as Miguel was. However, who among us would pay careful attention to the labor practices of a Christian boys choir? Many of the people who saw Kachepa and his choir perform were suspicious of the pastor and his business practices. Some of them had even made claims to the authorities about the organization. But the trafficker had covered his bases. He had legally taken the boys out of Zambia, though it took some political maneuvering to get all of their visas in line. In the United States, he avoided suspicion through his cover as a preacher as well as by monitoring the boys' movement and communications. He kept the boys working or traveling constantly. He assuaged any concerns the audiences might have had by telling them tales of how successful the choir's work had been in providing for people in Zambia. Slavery walked right into many churches and community organizations in the United States, but few people at the time could recognize the signs.

Everything changed for both Miguel and Kachepa in a simple moment of collective recognition. For Miguel, the moment came when he and his friends realized that the traffickers were actually planning to kill another worker who had tried to run away. For Kachepa, the moment came when he and his friends realized that his captors had tried to deport several young boys for misbehaving and would not answer inquiries about them. In both cases, when these enslaved laborers saw that one of their companions had been threatened, they looked to their fellow workers, discussed the situation they were living in, and decided there needed to be a change.

In the narratives these two men tell of their enslavement, this moment of collective recognition is a turning point in their existence as forced

laborers. Like Frederick Douglass, who experienced an existential transformation when he won a fistfight against his overseer, Miguel and Kachepa
experienced a moment of transformation, but their transformations were
not characterized by the individual change that occurred in Douglass. For
Miguel and Kachepa, the transformation came in the recognition of the
power of the collective to enact change.

At first, Miguel and Kachepa tell their own personal narratives of how
they found themselves enslaved. In both the narratives, however, the narrator's voice quietly shifts from the singular to the plural at the moment of
recognition. In an unexpected turn, both begin to tell the collective story
of all of the workers at once. Miguel states,

> So we were talking about, well, maybe we can get out somehow. But we
> thought, "Well, we can't do it too early. We can't do it in the middle of the
> night [or] even in the morning because even if it's in the morning, that's
> when they start to get up really early to start working, and they could easily
> find us down the road. And if they find us, they're sure to kill us."
>
> So we were thinking that we wanted to leave some one of these days, but
> we thought, "How could we do it? Because if we leave, even in the night,
> they get up so early in the morning, that's when they get up to go to work;
> they're sure to find us. If we have to run down the road, they're sure to find
> us in the car, and when they find us, they're sure to kill us.

One of the most compelling aspects of this narrative is the way Miguel's
discussions with his fellow workers are relayed in one unified narrative
voice. Their discussions no longer come from different individual positions
or from different people—they collectively "think" through the process by
which they can gain their freedom together. This unified voice is of course
primarily a means to narrate a complicated conversation, but this way of
telling his story continues for more than a page afterward, and it represents
the way the men came together to help one another escape their bondage
by the violent traffickers. As Miguel put it, men in Mexico like to work
and move together because "it's a lot more courageous . . . or we have more
courage to go, five or six together. And always in Mexico, we are going
out together, five or six of us, and always in a larger group we have more
strength to say, 'Yeah we're gonna do this.'" It is this collective voice, the
collective spirit, that allows Miguel and his friends to resist the family who
has enslaved them.

Similarly, when Kachepa and his friends realized that one of them had disappeared, they became angry and afraid together. Just as in Miguel's case, the boys began a collective thought process that helped them to gain the courage they needed to stand up to their captors in a unified front. Kachepa writes, "We thought we were tired of being abused to raise this money. We had a meeting that night; we all had agreed to resign from singing." Kachepa and his friends feared being deported more than anything because it would bring shame on them and on their families. They decided their biggest bargaining power came from saying that they would only leave the country together as a group. Kachepa and the boys allowed that collective power to speak for them and to aid them in escaping the choir: "to protect our friends, as we'd done many times (to protect our group), the whole choir demanded to be deported." A group resignation, a demand for collective deportation even, was the sign of unity that allowed them a route to freedom.

These small groups of daring survivors connected with others outside their group for support as well. In both cases, they found the courage to reach out to organizers and police for help. Miguel was approached by the nonprofit group Coalition of Imokalee Workers (CIW), who offered to assist him if he was engaged in an exploitative labor situation. Kachepa was approached by U.S. Immigration and Naturalization Service (INS) officers, who had been investigating the Zambian boys choir directors for some time. Both men had misgivings about enlisting the services of others because they feared for their safety and were concerned about their status in the United States. In both cases, however, their escapes were eventually aided by the efforts of nonprofit organizations and the government. When Miguel ran away, he called Laura Germino and Lucas Benitez of CIW, who came to rescue him and his friends. When Kachepa resigned, Salvador Orrantia of the INS arranged safe places for the boys to live while their claims were investigated. Coalitions between organizations, the government, and workers can often save lives; however, for immigrants to this country, interactions with the state can often appear to be an untenable alternative even to slavery.

What we gain from reading Miguel and Kachepa's pieces together is a sense of the impact that collective communication has in helping people to recognize their situations as forced laborers and how a connection with fellow sufferers can empower people to liberate themselves from living as slaves. It also helps us to understand why so many of the traffickers described throughout this book cut victims off from their families, from people who speak their language, from people who might be sympathetic to their pain. Isolation allows fear to paralyze, but a sense of community can transform that fear into collective action.

MIGUEL

Origin: Mexico	*Trafficked in/to*: United States
Form of enslavement: Forced agricultural labor	*Current status*: Free

Source: Interview for the Free the Slaves' documentary *Dreams Die Hard*, dir. Peggy Callahan (2005); transcript reproduced with permission.

Context: This interview was conducted by Free the Slaves through its connection with the Coalition of Immokalee Workers, a community-based nonprofit organization that provides services for the immigrant labor population in Southwest Florida. Miguel chose not to use his real name for this interview. All of the traffickers' names have been changed in this testimony to protect Miguel. This transcript is drawn from the simultaneous translation during the interview.

CALLAHAN: How did you come to the United States?

MIGUEL: Well, I come from Mexico. So I was thinking to come, from Mexico, come here to the United States, because I was thinking to come here to work. We had some problems with sickness at home. So I decided to come, and I gathered together some money and even borrowed money, lent money, and I came here with some friends.

Then first I got together with one friend who had been here once before, and so we had gone together. And we first went to Arizona; we went there to Arizona, walking. We really had no idea where we were going or how to get there. We were just kind of walking in the direction of the house of the guy who gives a ride.

Well, I have one son, and he has cancer, and it costs a lot for the medicine and treatment. And the government helps out, but they can only give so much treatment, and it still costs a lot. I came because, I mean, the wages there are so low, and I'm not earning enough there. They only pay maybe $70 a week. Yeah. The wage is very low there; it's maybe $46 to $60 for a whole week of work. So that's when I thought if I could go to the United States and maybe earn $6 or $7 an hour, well then maybe in a whole day I can earn $48, $50 dollars. And with that, I could be earning in three or four days what I could earn . . . more than I can earn in a whole week, and then I can be sending that home to my family. That will help sustain the family and help pay for his sickness.

But it's a really tough decision to think, to come to the United States, because you have to cross the desert, and I heard that they kill people there, people could even die. And it's really difficult, but I can't be like some guy who just doesn't have enough money. And I have to come over to the United States and earn some money, earn enough to send to my family, and so for that reason I decided to go.

So I decided among friends, we decided together that we'd go, five or six of us because . . . it's a lot more courageous . . . or we have more courage to go five or six together. And always in Mexico, we are going out together, five or six of us, and always in a larger group we have more strength to say, "Yeah, we're gonna do this."

So I decided with a little bit of money that I had that I would go, and I went to the border of Mexico and the United States. So I asked to borrow money in order just to get to the border, and I figured that when I would come here into the United States, I would work and pay off the debt. So, in the desert we spent about eight days there looking for the house of the guy who would give us a ride because the guide we had, he just left us, and it took eight days to get to the guy's house with the ride. It wasn't really much money that I borrowed, maybe 3,000 pesos; that here is maybe not much money—$300.

CALLAHAN: How long did it take to get to the border?

MIGUEL: Four days.

CALLAHAN: Was it a coyote or a bus that dropped [you] off at the border?

MIGUEL: There's no problem to get there to the border. We all went with friends, and we took a bus.

CALLAHAN: Did you have to pay anyone to help you cross the border?

MIGUEL: Yeah, I had to pay, but I didn't have any money to pay. So that's why we looked for a boss who might be from here who could send the money to the guy who would drive us, and then we could pay him back by working.

CALLAHAN: Did he have a name?

MIGUEL: The name was Juan Rodriguez, who is the one who sent the money and arranged for us to come here, a whole group of us. Really, we didn't know of him, but we just looked around and asked around for somebody who would give us a ride across and who we could work for, someone who could pay for our ride, and then we could pay them back. So supposedly you can find these people, and if you just ask around, people will know them, and so that's what we did.

Well, really, it wasn't a direct way to get to Florida, to get here. It wasn't a quick way. We had to stop and wait, and there were places where we were just waiting, and then we had to get moving again and change.

Well, first, when we crossed over the border we had to wait around for ten days there in the desert of Arizona, to find someone to take us over. From the 21st of February to the 14th of March, which was the day that I arrived here in Florida. That was the time that it took to leave from Mexico, to get to the border, to cross the border, to wait around in Arizona, to get a ride, and then to come here.

When I arrived, I really didn't think of anything. I didn't expect anything, and we all came, the same, same situation. We were traveling for three days, and we hadn't eaten for three days, so we were hungry of three days, and we just came here like that.

So when we arrived, we were in front of a shop. It was just a normal shop, and there was a big tree out front, and that's where we arrived, fourteen of us. When we arrived, the driver, he said, "You wait here, I'm gonna look for the boss." And he went off, and he went to look for a boss, but it seemed like he didn't find it, but he came back, and he said, "Don't move, you just stay here, but there's no problem with any immigration or any border patrol. You just wait here." And I was thinking, well, this is the first time I was here in the United States, and all the time we're afraid of immigration and being caught. And so I didn't know. I was afraid, and we're just thinking to wait here and fear for the immigration.

So this guy was still looking for a boss, and I wanted to find some boss, and so I went to look for him, and I saw he's always on the phone. Hard to get in touch with, talk to this guy 'cause he was always on the phone. Well, then he, then this guy came, and we saw that he was one of us, but we didn't know him. It was a different guy, and I saw this guy in the group, and he was talking to the guy on the telephone, but I know he was part of us, the fourteen of us who came. And because of that, I didn't think much of it; I thought, "He's one of us, so okay."

So this guy, he started talking to us, and he started coming right up to us and said, "Okay, okay, so we're all here to work, right? You're all here to work."

And so we said, "Yeah, yeah, we've all come here to work."

"So do you know how to? Are you ready to get to work?"

"Yeah, we don't really have anything."

"Did you pay for your ride to get here?"

"No, we didn't have anything to pay for the ride here, so we're ready to work."

CALLAHAN: Where did the man say he'd take you to work?

MIGUEL: This was a boss guy. So that man telling us about the jobs, he was a brother of the Ramos family. That man who was talking to us about the jobs, he was of the Ramos family. So this guy said, "Well, [unintelligible] know any of you who got here? Do you have any money to pay me? And if so, here's the telephone, you call them, you call the family members and tell them to pay me for the ride." Well, so I knew I didn't have any family here, and no one else had family here, and I thought, "Well, even still, I came here, and I have to work."

"If I had family here," I said, "I would have come with them; I wouldn't have taken your ride with you, and I wouldn't have had to owe any money. I wouldn't have any money to be having to pay you. If I had family here, I would have come with them."

So that's when he gave the first threat to us. He said, "Look, if you want to work here, you're gonna work here, and it's hard work. You gotta work hard, you gotta be motivated, and you gotta cut oranges, and you have to harvest those oranges; you gotta use a big, heavy knife." And he said to us that "if any of you want to work but not pay back the ride, if you, any of you, try to escape . . . ." That's when he said, "If any of you assholes try to leave without paying back your ride, that's when I'm gonna really fuck you up."

CALLAHAN: Then what happened? Did he get a place to live? What happened?

MIGUEL: So it was one of the Rodriguezes, and he said that we can now take something to eat, but whatever we took we would have to pay for that, too. That's when Juan Rodriguez came, and he said, "Well, you can go and take stuff to eat but don't take much and hurry up because we gotta get to work tomorrow." That's when we took some stuff, and that's when he took us to a little ranch. I don't know . . . it was like an apartment or so.

So that's when we started to hear more threats. I was with a friend from the place where I came from, and he and I were together, and we were going to stay in a room together, and that's when he asked about a television. He complained, "Well, there's no TV here," and that's when Rodriguez, he said, "Well, shut up and don't talk about any TV. This isn't a place to watch TV. This is a place to work. And if you're going to complain about it, we're gonna throw your ass into the pond, where you'll be dead."

So then we were starting to think we had to work, but we didn't have any social security card. We didn't have any insurance or anything, so we weren't really sure what this was going to be like to work.

CALLAHAN: So what was the work that you were doing? What were you actually doing? And what kind of hours were you working?

MIGUEL: We didn't work for pay by the hour. We worked by the bucket. We had to cut oranges, and that's how they paid us—per bucket.

CALLAHAN: What size bucket were you filling up?

MIGUEL: It was something really big actually [shows with his hand]. It wasn't really a bucket.

CALLAHAN: How many? Was it hard work? Did he work a lot of hours? Was it terrible?

MIGUEL: I had to fill up this container, and then we had to carry that over to this bath. It's a large bin, and they would pour those [containers] into it. And every time we had to fill up one of these bathtub-size things at least ten times. And to fill up one of those, it took at least an hour. But then we had to fill up so much because there were so many, so many oranges, and we had to, of course, pick up only the really nice oranges. I was working from the morning to night. And because he took us to fields where there were trees, but there weren't many oranges, and there wasn't much to pick, we were in the field all from really early in the morning to really late at night. And for working for the price of about $7, and we could only fill maybe three or four tubs, and that would get us maybe $28.

And it was such a problem because they were taking from us not just the [payment for the] ride, but we had to pay rent and some taxes . . . or I don't know . . . but they were taking it from our check. They charged us money for cashing the check. And it was all the same movement: to take us to the same shop, and we cashed the check there, and he charged us, and he could never take us to another bank. It was all the same thing.

For a while it was fine. There was nobody threatening us or trying to beat us or anything. But then there was this time where there was this guy, he was just talking about going. And we saw him go toward the Cash and Carry Supermarket there, and they saw him, and now you heard [one of them] outside of our apartment talking on the telephone, saying, "Oh, we're gonna get that motherfucker. We're gonna get him. We're gonna grab him, and we're gonna throw him into the pond with the alligators and kill him."

So I was inside the house, and my friend, he was just laying there drinking, and when I heard that, when I heard them say that outside, that's when I went up to listen and hear, and I said, "Whoa! Wow! He's talking so tough."

So we were about eight of us and, you know, in a group in a house, and we were talking about this. And we said, "Oh, those words are serious. And he means what he says. And who was that guy? Who was saying that? Was it the boss? No. It wasn't the boss. It was another guy. It was a guy who's watching us. And you know, I noticed that they have cell phones." And this is what we discussed. And we decide that we knew that when these guys talk about throwing someone out or catching them and killing them, we know those words are serious because that's how they work.

So we talked about it. There was one guy who drives a little tractor, and we asked him about it, if he knows anything. And he said he overheard about one guy who was threatened, saying [things] like, "We're gonna really fuck up your mother." And that means that those words and the words themselves have the meaning that we know that they can really, like, hit us hard. They can kill us. They can shoot us with a gun. Hit us with a bullet. All these things.

So we started talking to each other: "What can we do?" And we decided we are right now not earning anything. It's a misery wage, what we're earning—450 pesos [about U.S.$35] is what it would be in Mexico, is what we're earning here. It's the same wage, and it's a misery.

So we thought we put it together. We are earning this low wage, and then we always had these threats and all around us. We heard it wasn't just this one guy. We heard with the cellular phone—there were more of them, and they were everywhere, and they were watching us. There were something like forty guys who were working for Ramos, and they were there watching us.

So there's a group of four of us, and we tend to be working in the same place in the fields. And so we started to take notice of this one tractor driver here. And so there was this one guy who came in. We noticed he was new, and he came in some fifteen days after we arrived. So we called him "new," but he was actually an older guy, maybe forty-seven years old. But he came later than us, and he seemed to be threatened more. He was always tired, and he was always threatened by them.

And so that guy, he said he wanted to rest, sit down and take a rest, and he asked one of the guys watching if he could just take one day off and just take one rest. He was so tired, and he [the man watching] says, "Hey, we don't want any fucking assholes to be resting here. This is a place of work, and if you want to go rest you can get the hell out of here." So that really made me feel so sad to see this old man: he's so tired, and he just wants to rest, and he's being forced to work.

And it was around that time when there were a couple of people—they arrived, they came in. And one was a Mexican; his name was Lucas Benitez. The other was an American; her name was Laura Germino. And so when they came in, they asked us, "Well, how are y'all doing here? What's the situation like here?" And none of us wanted to say because what we thought was that maybe they're spies of the same boss. So what I thought is . . . 'cause, well first of all, you know, I've walked in the city. I know the streets. And so what I thought was maybe I'm not gonna see them. Then maybe they're not working for the boss. Maybe they're somebody else. And so I know that if I react right away too tough, maybe that would get me into trouble, maybe that would get me more threats, but I know to think of things differently and check out the situation. So in Mexico there is always someone like this who learns what the, like, the parental education, what you learn from your parents, and so you know to kind of lay low and assess the situation because otherwise maybe you end up dead.

And so there was another group, a group apart from us; they were there from before we arrived. Anyway, we started to talk out to them. They started to tell us, "We're here working. We're here getting these threats. They're not paying us these wages. We don't have any papers, and we're here working, and all these conditions . . . . " So they started to open up to them [Benitez and Germino]. They were saying things like, "I've been here for six months," or "They've been paying me, but it's not even enough to pay for the ride that I have to pay for, and I've been working here for years."

So when they were here, I didn't say anything to them. I didn't say anything to Lucas. I didn't say anything to Laura. I didn't say anything to them because I didn't really trust them. But I did say one thing, and I said, "Well, you can give me your card."

Okay, so I was the only one who took the card. And I had it, and the other guys with me, the four companions, they were saying, "Oh, well, maybe we should go. We should go to them." And I said, "No, why don't you calm down?" and "We can't. We can't just do that."

So I said the problem was that, you know, we're working here. We don't even have a minute to rest. These guys here who are so bad, the ones who are watching us so we were not able to rest, not even a single moment, from the 14th of March to the 14th of April. So from the 14th of March to the 14th of April, since we've been working here, we haven't had a single day of rest. And even when it's raining, we have to work. We have to work every Saturday, every Sunday. We don't have a day off. And even though we were waiting for the rains,

us. And if it wasn't for that, who knows what would've happened? Maybe we would have been killed. Or maybe we would have been left there and stranded and away from our families because we were stuck there. We had to pay for the ride, we had to pay for the rent, we had to pay for all those things, and we weren't making anything.

Well, I felt like a slave from the moment that I arrived because we couldn't pay for the ride and because we had to pay for that, and then they started to threaten us.

It was horrible. We were piled in the dorm of three beds piled on top of each other, six in a room, and for the person on top, they had to jump over all of us just to get to the floor. Well, they do it for business 'cause you know these guys have to work for them, and they're not just going to have people to not work for them. They do it, well, they do it for a business. They can't just have people who aren't going to be working for them.

Well, my dream was to work like work in Mexico, but not with the same wage that I get in Mexico. But when you work, if you don't like working with this guy, if I work with this guy, and you don't like it, you can change and say, "I'm going to work with him [that other guy] because he'll pay me better." So that's what I came here with that thought, thinking that I could just change jobs if I didn't like it. So maybe I could earn 1,000 pesos [about U.S.$75]— well, maybe 1,000 pesos really isn't that much money—if I could earn a little bit more somewhere else, I can do that, and so I came here thinking that.

Well now things are much different now. I'm working eight hours a day, but I'm working for a boss, he pays me, and I get to work eight hours—no more, no less. And now I'm working for my own will. I'm working. I know if I want a day off, that he's going to give me a day off, and I know that if I want to work ten hours, I can work ten hours. But it's not because I'm being forced to. Yeah, my wage right now—it's really satisfying, but I want to go back to something.

Yeah, he's doing really well now; he's, my son, is doing really well now. He's getting his medicines, and I send what I can. And well, you know, it's still not a lot because the medicines cost a lot, but I send him what I can.

Well, what I thought was not really not much; I was thinking like a human being, you know, because I didn't think badly of them [the traffickers]. But, you know, then I thought of my family, and I thought, well, I was thinking about my family, and I didn't like what happened to me, but I thought they're also people too, and they have their families. But at the same time, maybe they're not thinking in their families like I'm thinking of my family. And I also thought with my reason, and I thought, "Well, whatever the law says, that's the law and that's that, and that's what should happen."

Yeah, yeah, I'm still afraid. And I'm afraid for my family, too, because, you know, here things happen, but you know I don't speak English, so I don't know the news. I can't follow. And in ten years my passing maybe in Mexico something can still happen, and I'm still afraid for my family. And ten years, maybe they're out of prison. Something can happen with all of the hate and all of the negative feelings they have for what happened.

I had to pay taxes, to change the check, I had to pay for the food, and, you know, it was like we had to take food from the shop, and then they would take money out of that as well from the check. And the wage, it was a misery wage. It was only like 100, 120 bucks for working the whole week. So it was almost nothing that was left after they took out everything. One day it was only 20 bucks. And what am I supposed to do with 20 bucks? How can I send that to someone when they charge money to send the money? So with that I don't have anything.

I think the world should know that these things happen and that it's really horrible. But it has to realize that these things are happening.

Well, what I really hope for is to see my family and to be with my family. And you know, it's been four years since I've seen them, and I'm still here. But, you know, America is beautiful, but it's not with my family. And it's a scary thing, too, if you come here illegally, and then if you try to work, you could end up in the same situation as a slave. I have permission to work. That means I have permission to be here.

GIVEN KACHEPA

Origin: Zambia   *Trafficked in/to*: United States

Form of enslavement: Forced child labor   *Current status*: Free

Source: Given Kachepa's application for a nonimmigrant T-visa in 2002, with parts of speeches he gave, prepared with the assistance of Sandy Shepherd; reproduced with permission.

Context: Large parts of this narrative come from Kachepa's application for a nonimmigrant T-visa. In order to protect the identities of people involved in this case, some parts of the visa narrative had to be redacted, and names have been changed. In order to provide continuity, Kachepa (with the assistance of his host mother, Sandy Shepherd) has interwoven into that narrative some elements of speeches he has given in support of the antitrafficking movement. The legal context of the narrative is especially evident when Kachepa resorts to the legal definition of slavery, describing his work as "induced by force, fraud, or coercion for the purpose of subjecting [him] to involuntary servitude, peonage, debt bondage, or slavery."

I'm here today as one of the 27 million victims of human trafficking. I'm excited to share my story with you and hope that you will learn something new about human trafficking, commonly called "modern-day slavery."

OVERVIEW

I applied for the T-visa in 2002 as a result of being a victim of trafficking for the purpose of labor or services induced by force, fraud, or coercion for the purpose of subjecting me to involuntary servitude, peonage, debt bondage, or slavery. From May 8, 1998, until January 19, 2000, I was associated with TTT (Teachers Teaching Teachers), Partners in Education. I was brought to the United States under the impression that I was going to sing to help raise funds for schools in Zambia with the understanding that this was a Christian organization. My family was supposed to receive a small amount of money while I was here. I was also promised education while touring. There were many promises made to me. I was not aware that I was going to be exploited and used for reasons to only benefit TTT and put money into their own pockets. Promises were made about school, salary, the tour schedule, and I found myself suffering with methods used to coerce me into constant performing to raise more money. I was eleven years old and expected to cook, clean, and take care of my own laundry when at the home base. Mental, emotional, physical, and spiritual abuse were a part of my experience with TTT.

I am twenty-five years old and come from Zambia, which is located in South-Central Africa. I grew up in Kalingalinga, a compound of about twenty-three thousand people [and], as you would expect, very poor.

I have three brothers and two sisters, and I'm an orphan. My mom died when I was seven and my dad when I was nine. We six kids moved in with my aunt Margaret, who had six children of her own. So we had twelve kids and two parents living in a two-room house. The house I lived in was made from muddy bricks and had no electricity or running water.

My journey to America began after losing both my parents and long suffering from poverty.

Like many Zambian recruits, I fell for the dream to help my community, my ailing Zambian family, and looked ahead for a brighter future for myself. I wanted to buy shoes for my little sister and help my family with food. Often I would help ladies coming off the minibus by carrying their bags

[and] helped crush rocks or sell paraffin in the community to help make a little extra money.

Unfortunately, my dreams were shattered as I became a slave, singing four to seven concerts a day, asking for love offerings, selling CDs, and having no control over my life. My passport was withheld from me. I was made to believe [that] if I escaped, I would be caught and deported because no one would have interest in helping me.

BROKEN PROMISES

When I joined the Zambian A Cappella Boys Choir in 1997, I was looking for a new direction. At church, I made new friends and found spiritual joy that overshadowed my physical suffering and devastating loss of my parents and older sister. In 1998, my dream came true, when a nonprofit American Christian organization (TTT, Partners in Education), based in Whitesboro, Texas, came to select another choir to go to the United States.

There were many promises made to those of us who made the cut. The first promise made was about clothing. No choir member was to bring any clothes along with him except what they were wearing to the United States. TTT promised they had two bags full of clothes waiting for each choir member. Upon the arrival here, TTT made us throw away our Zambian clothes. They gave us one pair of boxer shorts and one under T-shirt that we wore around for a week. A week had gone by, when TTT started buying us new clothes. We knew then they had lied about two bags full of clothes for each choir member, considering they didn't know our shoe or clothing sizes. During the first week here, they measured each group member's size. After all the measurements of sizes and heights were done, the following week they bought performance clothes. Included were two [pair of] black pants, two white and two blue shirts, a tie, two [pair of] black socks, and one pair dress shoes. Casual clothes included were: one pair tennis shoes, two pair jean pants, three pair white socks, and two TTT T-shirts. TTT never purchased any other clothes for me during the eighteen months I worked for them. I was expected to keep these clothes clean and ready for performance at all times. I was eleven years of age.

TTT promised us that a school would be built in Livingston, Zambia, with contributions from people supporting our music during our two-year tour. The same school had also been promised to previous choirs before my choir ever came to the United States. Being able to attend that school was supposed to be part of the reward for my hard work while on tour. I toured with the group for eighteen months. Many families contributed toward this academy, and it was never built then and still has never been built for any of the returned choir members in Zambia. This promise was never kept.

Financially, TTT never promised me any certain amount of money, but they said there would be a "great reward" at the end of the tour. They never said what the reward would be. Till this day, I still don't know because there never was any kind of reward, only broken promises. There was never any kind of reward.

Most of my choir was attending school in Zambia when we left. TTT promised we would continue with our schooling here. After we had been here for three months and no school was provided, I got curious and asked why school was not provided. I had never asked this before because I thought it was a matter of TTT making arrangements for this. TTT told me to focus on singing and that school would be provided after I got back to Zambia in Livingston. Kevin, Betty, and Greg [agents of TTT] really got mad at me whenever I asked about going to school. I knew they were lying, telling us two different things. After being here for one year, nothing had been built in Livingston, where TTT promised they would build a school. TTT had been renting a house in Kalingalinga, which they declared as a school. Of the forty-five choir members that had been here, who were promised school after they returned to Zambia, only two received any schooling. These two, as TTT said, fulfilled the promise that schooling would be available. I learned later that TTT paid them to go to Livingston so it could look like they had a school. TTT told us that other choir members just didn't want to go to school. The truth was there was never a school built with all of the money that was raised by our singing, though they collected a lot of money and continued to advertise this academy. I was not allowed to have any education while on tour until the United States Labor Department became involved and TTT was told they had to provide schooling.

In Zambia, it is easy to convince people with hopes of a better life and future. Who would not want to come to America? When you live on less than a dollar per day, America is heaven. Sometimes even when people know there are sacrifices ahead, they are enticed to go because of the promises.

To parents, the hopes of a better life far outweigh the risks, and so they let their children go when the promises sound so good. In addition, traffickers prey on the lack of education [and on] language and communication barriers. Contractual agreements are confusing and futile. They were written in English, and no one could really read them.

When I later obtained a copy of the "Proposal and Contract for Choir Members," I was shocked at the force of language and how much I had to agree to when presented with the rules. The scriptures [the contract] referred to rebellion, being obedient, discipline, fear, the love of money, being a servant— From a professing Christian man, why did all of the "Words of Wisdom" refer to these subjects? In my opinion, Keith and TTT were just looking for ways to deceive us to think that this was the word of God, and it was really a way for TTT to make me feel like I was not a Christian if I did not follow these scriptures. While the "Proposal and Contract" packet looked complete, it was a way to only make promises. But they had all of the control to say they were doing their part of the agreement. No one could question their decisions. It was written to appear to be an honest, forthright organization. But in reality the words looked good on paper, but that's not the way it all worked.

While TTT created contracts for choir members to sign, the choir members signed, but it made no difference. Greg, Betty, and Kevin only did what they wanted to do as far as upholding their side of any agreement that was signed. They did only what they wanted to do. No one ever got a copy of the contract that they signed.

Several of us, including myself, received salvation in Zambia and made our profession of faith. Kevin promised us that we could be baptized when we got to the States. We believed him because he was a pastor, but there was never time to do the baptism. I felt very disappointed because it was a very important decision that I had made in my life, and it was another promise that was broken.

WHAT HAPPENED AFTER I CAME TO AMERICA

I came to America on May 8, 1998, when I was eleven years old. (So it said on my passport. TTT changed my age to make it appear I was younger than my real age.) The organization known as "TTT, PARTNERS IN EDUCA-TION" brought me here to raise funds through singing at churches [and] schools, in malls, and on the streets. They advertised that they were building schools for children in Zambia. Kevin Gray, a white, respected, trusted pastor came to Kalingalinga to select more singers.

I never had any professional musical training. All of the songs and tunes came from within the group. To qualify for the choir, I got selected out of sixty-five members who were trying out for the choir to tour the United States. The total number of guys they needed was twelve, and I was selected for the final group. The selection was based on the quality of voice, behavior, honesty, personality, and physical toughness. I practiced with the group for two years prior to coming to America.

For our tours, we traveled in a fifteen-passenger van. With twelve choir members, we were crowded for long trips. There was no comfortable way to sleep or rest. The van had no air conditioning. Tours were anywhere from a week to six weeks. Mostly we sang in churches, schools, and malls. We sang an estimate of twenty concerts a week. We had to set up our microphones and speakers, test the equipment, and then take it down for each concert. Remember, I was eleven years old working this kind of full schedule. Singing for the Lord slowly became a job instead of a joy.

The only time TTT bought food was when we traveled from one place to another or if we were staying in a motel. While on tour, we ate lunches at places we performed. Breakfast and dinner were provided by the host families where we stayed at night. After we returned to the home base in Whitesboro, Texas, from the tour, we might stay there two days to a week, but we still would go to perform around Sherman. There was no time off from work. We thought our Christian teachings would also be continued, but there was no time because we had to perform so many hours a week.

Many times when we were at home base, we would have performed and returned late at night, and still I was expected to get up very early, sometimes at 4:00 or 4:30 A.M., to be ready to travel from home base to the performance site. You had to be ready and dressed, so sometimes I just slept in my clothes because I was too tired and knew I had to be ready to go so early in the morning. I was still expected to smile and be friendly when I arrived to set up to sing at each performance. At the home base, we cooked and did laundry regardless of how excruciating our schedule was. Our suffering was both psychological and physical.

Before going on tour, our bags were searched by TTT to make sure we did not have anything that TTT didn't buy or did not belong to them. After we returned to the home base, they made us stay in the van; they called each individual one by one and searched our bags. If we had anything that was not purchased by them, it got taken away. A negative mark was put on your record. After some months, they began to store my clothes in a box in the storage area.

The toiletries were paid for by TTT. TTT bought the same products for each person, so if we didn't like the product or were allergic to it, we bought our own from gift money that we would try to hide if it was given to us.

While traveling, there was no recreational time allowed. The only time we did anything was if we had a concert in the morning and the next concert was early afternoon; TTT would take me to the mall to just look around.

At the home base, no recreational time was given. The only recreational activity was watching TV, going for walks, playing basketball outside, and soccer if we were not rehearsing. The home base was fifteen to twenty miles away from the city, so we had no choice of going any place other than what TTT arranged.

In the heat of the Texas summer, we were asked if we wanted a swimming pool. Who would have said no? So we were handed picks and shovels and told to hand dig the pool. It was July, and each day we had to dig before choir practice. The pool was never finished.

TOUR RULES AND THREATS

Almost as soon as I arrived to sing, problems began for me. I heard after arriving that other groups had experienced the same difficulties with the extreme rules and busy work schedule. While staying with host families, I was not allowed to talk about any problems I was dealing with. If I felt sick or had a toothache, I was only to tell the road manager.

No communication was allowed after we left the host families, except from TTT. If host families were to give us phone numbers or addresses, they had to be through the road manager. They [the TTT agents] told the host families not to give us phone numbers or addresses. Each host family received guidelines known as "Zambian A Cappella Host Family Questionnaire" to reflect my behavior while with host families. Included were questions such as if I asked to watch TV, used the telephone, my eating habits, my overall behavior, or if I requested anything. To reflect my behavior, host families had to check in the category of excellent, good, fair, or poor and make specific comments as needed. This may have been a good idea for them, but shame came out of it because no group member was ever given a bad comment.

I remember the first host family we stayed with. They gave me their phone number and address. In the morning, our road manager sat the group down, asking if phone numbers or address was given to us. No one answered. Then they threatened to go through our bags, and if any phone number or address were found, that choir member would be returned to Zambia. I got scared, so I gave them the phone number and address.

No clothes or money were permitted to be given to me. Looking back, [I remember] a church that gave the group sweatshirts. Greg got mad at the pastor, saying we had enough clothes, and instead he was going to sell the sweatshirts and contribute the money toward the ministry. Whenever Kevin introduced the group, he made a very emotional plea that involved conversation about the poverty and conditions from which I came. He introduced us and our ages, but he had lied about the age I was on my original passport, so people felt more compassion for "these young boys" and thus would give more money to TTT.

I remember the first two weeks I was here. Four of us had used the gel in the bathroom. Since the gel was in the group bathroom, we thought it was for us to use. Unintentionally, we made a mistake by using the gel. The gel wasn't for our group; it was for the other group. Our group leader talked to Betty about the incident, and Betty said that if I continued with these kinds of acts, I would be sent back to Zambia.

Kevin and Greg both had very short, hot tempers. When they yelled at me or spoke to me in a voice that was mad, I felt scared and humiliated. I personally experienced Kevin's hot temper during a very long performance day. We had already sung about eight performances and still had more to go. I was very, very tired and sat down to rest. Mr. Gray came over to me and told me to stand and get ready to sing. I told him I was very tired. He grabbed me by the shirt, stood me up, and said loudly in my face, "I said get up and sing, boy. Unless you want to go home, you will sing." I was scared and intimidated and forced myself to just keep going. I felt like I was his puppet on a string being moved around, just doing only what he wanted me to do regardless of how tired I was.

MIND GAMES

Coming to America at eleven years old was a very difficult experience. Being with TTT for two years, I had to mature very early. I had come from an extended family. Aunt Margaret, my guardian since my parents died, cooked my food and made my decisions. She washed my clothes and saw that I got to school. As I reflect back, I cannot believe that at eleven years of age any organization could require that I cook my own food at home base, wash and iron my own clothes, and work so hard singing without earning any money for my work.

I learned quickly that the promises made about my well-being were a lie. My parents never gave me false promises. I did not know whom to trust anymore and had no option of discussing this with my "mom," Aunt Margaret, back in Zambia. So many things had been promised by TTT, and they did not come true, and I felt stuck in my circumstances, unable to make any changes except to keep working and singing as required. There were many times that I felt held in bondage, unable to escape or seek other guidance and counsel.

Whenever mail was sent to the office for me, it was always opened before I received it. Sometimes, I learned later, my family or friends had written to me, and I never was given my mail. We knew that pictures, money, and phone cards had been taken. I thought that first-class mail was to only be opened by the receiver in the United States.

We continued to sing and raise a lot of money. We never knew how much money was raised, but anyone could see that there was a lot of money in the offering plates taken up for us at churches.

People have since asked, "How could you not know about what would happen? Other choir members had already returned to the community." Mr. Grimes was very clever. He told the 1996–98 choir, "The good choir is coming to replace you," and he told us in Zambia, "Don't have anything to do with the big choir. They have been disrespectful and disobedient." He drew an invisible line in the ground, and we did not talk to those guys in the community.

A CHANGE IN DIRECTION

In the spring of 1999, Mr. Kevin Gray of TTT passed away, and his daughter, Betty, and son-in-law, Greg Mann, carried on the "ministry." Fearing deportation and embarrassing our families, we sang in sadness for nine more months until the ministry decided to carry out TTT's plan and deport four choir boys considered untrustworthy and disobedient. They were considered disrespectful because they continued to ask about the education and funds promised to us and our families. But without conclusive evidence of disobedience, to protect our friends, as we'd done many times (to protect our group), the whole choir demanded to be deported. Through this quarrelsome process, the Sherman Police Department was alerted, but the nature of [the] case was unusual for them, so they contacted the U.S Citizenship and Naturalization Services (INS) to handle the case. Then an INS agent was dispatched to Sherman to enforce the deportation of the four members. The first day two boys were picked up in handcuffs, and the next day two more boys were removed.

Besides losing my parents, seeing my friends in handcuffs being harassed was one of the most uncertain and scariest moments of my life. I was scared because I didn't know if my fate would be the same. Only a few days after the four boys had been picked up, the remaining seven of us decided to stay in the United States. It was better to keep hope than face the scrutiny and shame of returning to Zambia without anything. After about nine more months of continued singing, we were tired and confused as we learned our choir mates had not been deported but were living in host homes and going to school. We felt deceived knowing that our friends had new found freedom.

THE TIME AFTER THE DEPARTURE OF THE FOUR GUYS

One night we called Mophat and Martin [two of the other choir members who had been threatened with deportation] and asked what had taken place after they were taken away. They told us every detail. They said the government was involved and that the INS was investigating the case. We admired what he said; we thought we were tired of being abused to raise this money. We had a meeting that night; we all had agreed to resign from singing. It was difficult because there was constant pressure to continue performing the schedule.

The United States Labor Department got involved in the fall of 1999. There was a lawsuit filed on behalf of sixty-seven choir members who had been robbed of their earnings. The Labor Department told TTT to start paying us for our labor. TTT then designed a way which allowed time for us to go to school and still perform. We were paid $570 per person every month. However, TTT devised a way to take back our money. TTT Partners in Education then furnished a monthly income but retained most of our money for our expenses, such as house rent, school, electricity, food, and my airline ticket home. I had about $40 per month left.

After I saw this budget, I had many questions inside my head. If this budget had been the same for the previous year, where was the extra money such as medical, clothes, entertainment, personal care, and pocket money used for the previous years? Airline tickets from here to Zambia one-way cost $1,000 each. If TTT had been saving the air tickets money the previous year, why did we have to start saving for that now? TTT was supposed to be a nonprofit group organization, and it took in many dollars. Where had the excess money gone?

Why did I have to save if they already had the money put away for my ticket? If this same budget applied to the previous groups, just for the airline tickets, it seems that a lot of money was undisclosed.

About six months later in Houston, we asked the road manager to call the office because we wanted to have a meeting with Barbara right way. Betty came right away, and we had a meeting. We told her we were resigning singing. We demanded the money that had been promised to us. TTT refused to pay us, and even though we were scared, we demanded that the INS agent that had picked up our friends nine months previously come and get us.

Since she knew the government and the INS were involved, she did not deny our request. We drove back to the home base that night and stayed there for a week. Somehow the INS agent heard we resigned. He came and picked up every choir member and arranged to have us taken to a safe place rather than put us in holding cells. He took us to First Baptist Colleyville, and I was very confused and scared. First Baptist Colleyville members had many experiences with TTT and knew they were not an honest organization. TTT had many problems that had been noted by many previous groups. They also were known in Zambia for their deceit and exploitation. TTT had made many promises, raised a lot of money, and no one knows where the money had gone. Previous choir members had not been paid for their work or received their promised education long before my group arrived in May of 1998.

LIFE AFTER INS PICKED ME UP

So many great things have happened since we departed from TTT. We arrived in Colleyville, Texas, at Colleyville First Baptist Church in January of 2000. Sandy Shepherd of First Baptist Church Colleyville [FBCC] helped me and my choir mates look for a host family. While in Colleyville, we stayed with temporary host families while looking for new places. Members from FBCC had been involved with TTT from 1996 to 1998. When INS called the church to say they needed help with seven Zambians who needed a place to stay rather than be put in holding cells, FBCC members graciously responded and took us into their care. During that time, the INS agent had all of us fill out a deposition. I cooperated with INS in every way they asked. I was given many injections at the health clinic and got my Social Security card. I also received my work permit, for which I have been very grateful.

By God's grace, every group member ended up finding a new host family that was willing to love and care for them. I went to Childress, Texas. There I was enrolled in seventh grade. I participated in boy's athletics at school. I was there for three months; sadly, I had to leave due to my host family's health problems. I came back to Colleyville and ended up in the house with the Shepherd family. They have three daughters, now all married, and eight grandchildren. There were three people living in the house, Mr. and Mrs. Shepherd and myself. They loved me and cared a lot about me, and I am very blessed and honored to be living with them. In the spring of 2002, the Shepherds went to court and obtained legal custody of me. They are now my legal guardians. I am now fully covered with insurance.

My T-visa was granted in August 2003. This allowed me to stay in the United States after proving I was a human-trafficking victim. I will always be grateful to INS, First Baptist Church Colleyville, the Shepherds, and church members who helped me and my choir mates gain our freedom.

I enjoyed my time in middle school and high school, participating in soccer, cross country, theater, and choir. In eighth grade, I attended Colleyville Middle School, and at the end of the year I received a "CMS Colt Award." My class of approximately three hundred gave me a standing ovation—the only one of the award ceremony. Our soccer team at Grapevine High School set the highest record for JV [junior varsity] in GHS history. I was blessed to have several jobs, including cashier, landscape work, washing windows, and courtesy clerk at local grocery stores. I enjoyed working at Skate Town and driving for the Cotton Bowl Association.

FREE AT LAST

Finally, I received my green card in June 2009. Having that gift from the U.S. government assured my freedom in the United States. There was never any prosecution of TTT since Mr. Kevin Gray had died, and we had been rescued in January 2000. The federal Trafficking Victim Protection Act was not put in effect until October 2000; prosecution was not retroactive, and Betty and Greg were not the primary traffickers.

Now in 2012 I have finished high school and college at the University of North Texas, and I am currently a D2 Student at Baylor Dental College in Dallas, Texas.

A way we consumers can help fight modern-day slavery is to buy slave-free produced goods. The symbol that says "Fair Trade" is a logo that ensures that that item has been made by people who have been paid for their work. For example, you can find this trademark on some brands of tea, chocolate, rice, spices, sports balls, and coffee. I encourage you to look at a Fair Trade website to obtain more information.

Losing my mom at age seven and dad at age nine caused me to doubt God's love for me. Why were my parents taken when I was just a kid? Why was I used and exploited? While everything I endured was bad, I learned how to forgive. My faith in God is my guiding rod.

Through this process I've learned so much. I'm a better person because I decided to become a survivor and make the best of my bad experience. Speaking about and helping educate others about this global atrocity helped me understand that my voice could make a difference. Maybe my voice can free just one victim that can also reclaim their life and achieve their dreams.

My perspective on life is that it's important to value each and every human being because we are all special in one way or another. You know I believe we all have a calling, we were all born for a reason, and that God did not put us on earth for our own pleasures.

6

Case Study

IN THE SMALL INDIAN VILLAGE of Azad Nagar, strong, sinewy men carry heavy loads of rock to an open space, where they hammer boulders into gravel and sand. Their skin has been darkened by a lifetime of laboring in the sun, but their eyes are bright and clear. Unlike in nearby villages, in Azad Nagar you won't see children chipping away at the rocks next to their mothers; instead, they are in a small open-air school, learning to read and write. Many of the women are able to stay at home to care for their small children instead of toiling in the quarry, where women had previously carried enormous loads of sand to be counted by the mine owner against an ever-increasing and unknown debt. They have time to create self-help groups that give microcredit to villagers who want to buy a goat or start a small business. Though the men and many of the women of this village do still endure the backbreaking work of quarry mining, they do it with hope and enthusiasm because, unlike most quarry workers in India, they are free. Not only are they free, but they collectively own their own mine and thus their own lives and livelihoods.

Azad Nagar means "Land of the Free," a name the villagers gave this area when they gained the rights to the mine lease and emancipated themselves from lives of slavery. But it hasn't always been a land of the free. In this particular region of Uttar Pradesh, the system in which quarry miners work descends from the feudal system that characterized Indian land ownership before independence in 1947, and it has inherited some of its more insidious aspects, including a laboring class that is forced to work for mine contractors who lease the land from local leaders.

In 1999, the villagers who now live in Azad Nagar lived in a town called Sonbarsa, where they labored breaking rocks for a mine owner who maintained his control over the workers by providing them with high-interest loans when they needed medicine, funeral expenses, or food for their children. Paid only in grains and then only enough to avoid starvation, the villagers were regularly compelled to ask for loans when emergencies arose. The mine contractor never allowed them to know the real amount of their principal or the interest that had accrued, and so they toiled perpetually in the hopes that one day the mine owner would announce that they had finally worked off their debts. In some rare cases, a small windfall or inheritance made it possible for someone to pay off his or her debt, but soon enough an emergency would strike, and the worker would find that he or she needed to be financed once again by the mine contractor. Small though the sums might have been—sometimes amounting only to about $25 or $50—whole families could be bound by the debt, and some even found themselves paying back the debts of their fathers and grandfathers. In this way, generations of quarry laborers were kept in debt bondage—a form of slavery that can either be inherited (as chattel slavery was in the United States) or originate with a simple need for health care or seeds to start a farm. Although this system can only be described in the past tense in Azad Nagar, for many people all over India's Uttar Pradesh region, this life-long, transgenerational debt bondage is a very present reality.

As far as Indian law is concerned, this system is illegal. As discussed in the introduction, slavery is illegal in every country in the world. In India, this form of debt bondage is explicitly illegal, to the point that even the act of paying a lender for an illicit debt may be technically illegal as well. Though the law requires that labor not be used to pay off debts, the laborers themselves are typically unaware of that protection. What's worse, most local authorities know about this epidemic of enslavement, but they do nothing to stop it. The quarry workers in Sonbarsa never thought that they had any other option but to pay off the vicious mine owners.

In Sonbarsa, the work was particularly grueling because the land owners were cruel and unpredictable. Contractors regularly beat workers if they did not perform as expected and sometimes even for no reason at all. On a few occasions, they burned down the house of a worker without warning. Some women in the village were sexually abused while the men were away at work. Workers were not able to seek out other work opportunities or to travel to other villages if they wanted. Ramphal puts it eloquently in his interview:

> When I say I was a slave or that my parents were slaves, I want you to understand what I'm talking about. You know, at that point of time, even if there was a road and I had a cycle, and I wanted to move on that road with my cycle, the moment I stepped onto my cycle and moved on the road, I had it. I would be stopped and thrashed. The reason? I didn't get the contractor's or the slave owner's permission to use the road.
>
> If I would move in[to] my house or out of my house, if I want to sit somewhere, get up, if I want to eat, if I want to drink, any single action, at any point of time, anything that I wanted to do, I required permission.
>
> That's what I mean when I say I was a slave. Freedom of movement was something I didn't know existed, I was not aware of.
>
> And it was not just me. My mother, my father, my grandparents had to live through this generation after generation. It was deep in my psyche.

The adults in Sonbarsa were treated as if they were the children of the mine owners—not insomuch as they were treated like family, but in that they were under the thumb of the contractors at all times, forced even to ask permission to move about the town. Any dream of refusing to work was delayed by a family's pressing needs for food, security, and health. Any notion that they might simply revolt was checked by the violence the owner utilized to punish them for the slightest infraction. The notion that they might escape was perpetually thwarted by the reality that they had nowhere to go and no money with which to sustain themselves. Like some of the contributors in chapter 4, the quarry workers in Sonbarsa worked within an economy that refused them any imagination for freedom.

In a hideous reversal of the way that it is almost impossible for many of us to imagine—really imagine—ourselves as slaves, constantly and entirely under the control of another human being, the quarry workers in the mines of Sonbarsa found it impossible to imagine themselves as free. Freedom is an idea that is difficult to imagine, and, once imagined, it can seem to be an ideal impossible to attain. People in Sonbarsa had been forced laborers for generations. How were they to imagine that they might have the right to break free of that bondage?

In 2000, everything changed. A local Indian nonprofit organization, Sankalp, had been visiting the village to provide for the villagers' health needs and child care. Some adults were even learning to read at night. Meanwhile, in a nearby village, quarry workers asked Sankalp to help them do something revolutionary—buy a mine lease for themselves. Instead of relying on the job skills workshops that help most freed slaves find a new life and new work after being emancipated, these quarry miners thought they would do what they knew best—run a mine. By pawning everything they had and putting it in a savings program, the miners were able to free themselves from their abusive bosses and run their own mine with the skills and knowledge they already possessed. When Sankalp saw the success of this village near Sonbarsa, where productivity rose as soon as the villagers were working for themselves and where their profits were helping them pay for their children's education and for small non-quarry-oriented enterprises, it began to spread the word to Sonbarsa.

Because the villagers in Sonbarsa were certain that they were compelled to pay off their debts and remain slaves for the rest of their lives, they originally balked at the notion of freedom. With some reflection, however, they slowly began to understand what it might mean to be free. Sankalp told them that freedom was not going to come if they fought head to head individually with the mine owners—what they needed was unity. Through collective action, the villagers could gain a lease to a mine of their own and turn their backs on both their imaginary debts and the people who held them hostage. Choti, a former bonded laborer whose interview is included here, remembers,

> Earlier when we had initial meetings with the local authorities and with the Sankalp members, they told us to cooperate and coordinate with each other. That didn't mean too much to us at that point in time.
>
> But slowly when we had a couple of meetings here and a couple of meetings there, things began to sink in, and we came to realize we are doing all the work. We are the ones who are cutting the stones, we are the ones loading the lorries, we are the ones working in the house every single day and not getting any assistance or any monetary benefit from it.
>
> That's when we all decided, sat down in motorcars and lorries, moved, met other people, met the Sankalp members, and took action in our hands.

A collective drive slowly came to motivate the village, a collective voice that told them that they could survive on their own so long as they were unified and helped one another.

Ramphal even uses the collective voice that we discovered in Given Kachepa and Miguel's narratives in the previous chapter, through which the narrators explore the way the thoughts of the individuals in their exploited groups began to come together as a community. This voice reveals the way the narrative of slavery, at least in this modern context, is often a collective one, told through a first-person plural "we" narration that reveals the way enslaved people can come to think of themselves and their actions as necessarily connected to the lives and actions of other enslaved people. In his interview, Ramphal recalls, "We met them [the Sankalp representatives], and they went away, but somehow something sunk in at some level. Because on their departure about ten-odd families, ten people, ten families among us, got together and started talking. There was this thought process about how we should get together and form this organization, this informal committee, and once our thought processes got conceptualized and formalized, the entire village joined in unanimously." A unanimous thought process was the source of strength that allowed the villagers in Sonbarsa to hold a protest against their enslavement. In retaliation, the mine owners burned every single thing that the workers owned. But even that did not stop the workers—in fact, it brought them closer together. And today they no longer work in Sonbarsa. They work in Azad Nagar, the land of the free, where they are free to make their own gravel, their own profits, and their own life stories.

The life stories told in this chapter present a case study for understanding both enslavement and collective liberation strategies. Part of that liberatory life story is about owning the means of production, as Marx would put it—owning the mine and taking control of the skills and knowledge the people of Azad Nagar possess. Yet another part of the life story the villagers want to tell is about creating a different life for their own children and for other villages in the area. Children do not work in Azad Nagar; they attend school. The women who are interviewed in this chapter describe how important it is to them that their children do not replicate the backbreaking labor that they had been forced to do for most of their lives. Even Ramphal hopes that both his children and he himself will be able to travel to the cities and do some more personally fulfilling work. Ramphal has already begun doing just that by joining Sankalp and working in other mining villages to help them become aware of their potential freedom. Again, the story they tell is one of unity and collective action, of each individual helping the other, of one generation freeing the next.

Ramphal has an enormous job ahead of him because 10 million of the 27 million slaves in the world today live in India. It is organizations such as Sankalp that address the specific needs, interests, skills, and desires of people living in slavery and make it possible that those 10 million people someday will be emancipated. Following the stories of three people who are now free in Azad Nagar, the narratives of those people who work for Sankalp, who have dedicated their life to this goal, are also included. However, the last piece in this case study introduces one of those 10 million who may never get to see a free day in her life. Munni Devi is too sick to work in the quarry anymore, and the mine owner is threatening to throw her out of her house if she doesn't get back to breaking rocks. She is one of the millions of Indians living on the edge of survival, and her story reminds us that the work there is not complete.

As Ramphal insists, the village that is unified cannot be destroyed. He says that the motto of the village is, "Just like we are able to break this hard, hard rock with the hammer, the chisel, whatever, any enemy is going to be shattered because of the unity that we now have." In India, perhaps unity will be the hammer that will set Munni Devi and others like her free.

For more information on Sankalp, Azad Nagar, and Indian rock quarry mining, read *Ending Slavery* by Kevin Bales and watch the Free the Slaves documentary film *The Silent Revolution: Sankalp and the Quarry Slaves.*[1] All of the interviews given here were conducted by Free the Slaves with the aid of a local translator. The transcriptions are of the simultaneous translation. Callahan sometimes asks questions in the third-person because she is asking the translator to ask the question of the interviewee. At times, the translator also asks questions. All of the interviews were intended for the documentary, so at times Peggy Callahan, the documentary maker and interviewer, suggests that the speaker repeat him- or herself so that segments useful for the film would be clear. These interviews, in abbreviated and condensed forms, were also included in the collected volume *To Plead Our Own Cause*, edited by Kevin Bales and Zoe Trodd.[2]

RAMPHAL, VILLAGE ORGANIZER, FORMER BONDED LABORER

Origin: India	*Trafficked in/to*: Sonbarsa, Uttar Pradesh
Form of enslavement: Bonded labor	*Current status*: Free, mine organizer

Source: Interview conducted for the Free the Slaves documentary film *The Silent Revolution: Sankalp and the Quarry Slaves*, dir. Peggy Callahan (2008); translated transcript reproduced with permission.

Azad Nagar, Uttar Pradesh, November 1, 2004

CALLAHAN: First off, can he introduce himself to us and tell us how old he is?

RAMPHAL: My name is Ramphal. And I would say I am approximately twenty-seven to twenty-eight, actually twenty-eight years old.

CALLAHAN: Can he tell us . . . go way back, tell us what his family has worked, what kind of living they've made?

RAMPHAL: I remember my earliest childhood days. I'm sorry I don't quite remember what my grandparents were doing; I didn't get to see them. But I do remember my parents. I remember my father and my mother in my earliest childhood memories. Way back in my memories, I remember we were farmers. And at that point in time, in a month we would get something like five *pau*. When I say "*pau*," it's about 1.25 kilograms. So that's the amount of grain, no matter [what], we would get. And within that we would be happy; we would survive. We would get our food, our clothing, our shelter. Whatever we needed was managed within that amount of money.

CALLAHAN: Were they bonded laborers?

RAMPHAL: I guess you could call it bonded labor. At that point in time, we were working in the field, and, yes, I would say it was bonded labor. And that was what was happening.

In fact, even now we were all working under the contractor. And for all the stones that we would load them onto the truck, we would get the measly sum of rupees 250 or 300 [about U.S.$5 to $6], and he would pocket away all the rest of the money. So at no time were we free to do what we wanted to do or to have our own choices. So we were agricultural bonded laborers, and then we came to the stone quarry and became bonded laborers there yet again.

CALLAHAN: Can we ask him if, to him, bonded labor and slavery is the same? And if it is, I'm going to have you redo it [the translation] to say bonded labor is slavery. I just want to make sure he sees it that way before I change it.

RAMPHAL: Earlier on, I would say we were all bonded laborers. And then we moved on, and we became slaves. But, you know, when I think about it, there actually is no difference between being a bonded laborer or being a slave. It was the same thing.

All I do know is, later on, it was only when we thought about it and we became aware, we realized that we were slaves. The realization came when we looked at the contractor, and we saw we did all the hard work—we were responsible for loading the trucks. We would take the stones, load the trucks, [the contents of] which he would sell for about 1,500 rupees [about U.S.$30]. Out of the 1,500, we would only get a share of about 250 or 300 and not more than that. That's when we realized that, yeah, we were slaves.

CALLAHAN: So would he say that his grandfather was a slave? His dad was slave? And he was born a slave? And were his children born slaves?

RAMPHAL: I agree. I was born a bonded laborer. And earlier on people were all bonded laborers, but that's no longer true.

Now, if you see, the situation has changed remarkably. What has happened is that people got together as an awareness group. Because of the awareness group, we were able to then go to meetings and come back from there. And these to-and-fro meetings of people coming from outside, talking to us, the awareness growing, committees forming, made the contractors jittery. And because of this jitteriness, they began labeling us as rebel leaders and politicians, and that was what happened.

But I would say now all my children are being born free. They are no longer bonded laborers; they are free men.

CALLAHAN: Okay. Let's go back again. I'm going to ask it again. What actually I want to hear is: "As far back as I can remember, my grandparents were slaves, my father was a slave, or my parents were slaves, I was born a slave. . . . " And one of his children was born a slave, I think, and then one was not born a slave.[3] That is what I'm trying to hear.

[Translator discusses how Ramphal forgets to answer the question and moves directly to talking about the Sankalp movement.]

Tell him we're trying to get the big-story change. It went from really bad to really good. But we're on the really bad part.

RAMPHAL: As far as I can remember, my grandparents, when they were born, they were bonded laborers. My parents, when they were born, they were bonded laborers, or actually I could call them slaves. There is no difference. When I was born, I was born as a slave, and even now the situation really didn't change because about five to six years ago when my son was born, he was born as a slave. It was only when I went to prison, my daughter was born, but even at that point in time, we were still under the control of the contractors or the slave owners. As a result of which, she herself was technically a slave.

When I say I was a slave or my parents were slaves, I want you to understand what I'm talking about. You know, at that point of time, even if there was a road and I had a cycle, and I wanted to move on that road with my cycle, the moment I stepped onto my cycle and moved on the road, I had it. I would be stopped and thrashed. The reason? I didn't get the contractor's or the slave owner's permission to use the road.

If I would move in[to] my house or out of my house, if I want to sit somewhere, get up, if I want to eat, if I want to drink, any single action, at any point of time, anything that I wanted to do, I required permission.

That's what I mean when I say I was a slave. Freedom of movement was something I didn't know existed, I was not aware of.

And this was not just me. My mother, my father, my grandparents had lived through this generation after generation. It was deep in my psyche.

CALLAHAN: That's great. Thank you. Can you tell us about life in that other village? What was happening in that other village?

RAMPHAL: Each time I think back and look at the life that I led in that village, my heart is filled with grief and with sadness. There's deep regret each time I'm made to reflect. At that point of time, there was just no relationship between the slave owner and us. It was a matter of their mood, of their fancy. They could just pick up anyone moving on the road, moving on the cycles, someone's brother, someone's son, myself, my husband, anyone. Any single individual at any point in time could be just picked up and beaten, no rhyme or reason. Just . . . just . . . my mother, my sister, somebody else's mother, sister, wife, daughter, made no difference to them. There was no feeling within them that "this is my employee; this person works for me." It was almost akin to the English school, this master and the rest of the population. Almost like you weren't human. That's the level of torture or indignity that we suffered from.

CALLAHAN: Tell us how things began to change.

RAMPHAL: Like I was mentioning earlier, what began to happen was that the level of torture and harassment was just escalating. There was no end; it kept going on and on.

It was amid this environment of increased harassment that we had people from the municipality coming in and talking to us about forming a committee, about getting together, forming an organization. It didn't quite [unintelligible], though, even though we met them a couple of times. Then people from Sankalp came. There was this lady who would come once or twice, and we met her a couple of times. They would come. In fact, you know, the contractors even harassed them and beat them up a couple of times.

We met them, and they went away, but somehow something sunk in at some level. Because on their departure about ten-odd families, ten people, ten families among us, got together and started talking. There was this thought process about how we should get together and form this organization, this informal committee, and once our thought processes got conceptualized and formalized, the entire village joined in unanimously.

CALLAHAN: And when he says there was increased violence, was that when the women were harassed? Was that when the little girl was killed? Could he give us some kind of time frame for it?

RAMPHAL: The level of violence against the females was always, always very high. There would always be situations when we, the men, would go off to work. We would go to load the lorries; we would go to mine. We would basically go off for work. In these circumstances, very often the contractors or the slave owners would just come inside and do as they pleased with the females first. There was nothing you could do.

We weren't individuals. You have to understand that.

Whatever they wanted to do, they could do. We were completely in total fear of them.

An incident happened in a close-by district, not very far from here. An eight-year-old girl was sitting in a house, and these landlords came, and they just set fire to the house. The girl died.

Even at that point of time, it was just that they do what they wanted to do. As simple as that. The level of fear, the level of constant control that we were under was so high that we were just shaking and quivering each time they would approach us. And that's the environment that we were residing in.

CALLAHAN: Did he ever think . . . did he ever even dream of a day that it would be different than that?

RAMPHAL: Earlier on? No, there was just no dream. It was like a vision I couldn't begin to think of; it was an impossibility. But that began to change, that change sooner or later where people of Sankalp came in and they shared.

And actually what happened, there was a rally organized in this place called Apna. And a lot of us went there, almost the entire village got together and went there. And in the rally there was a lot of struggle, a lot of issues were raised, there were voices, people were taking part. We had a tough time. It wasn't an easy rally. As a result of that rally, there was this feeling that was spreading among the people, that, yes, something was happening, something was possible. These ripples were crossing over everyone.

So once we came back, [the] people of Sankalp would come in [to the village] repeatedly. They would talk to us; awareness spread. And on the basis of what they told us and what we thought among ourselves, we started walking around the path. So a path was not shown, but a direction was shown, and [we were] moving along that or toward that. Till there was another meeting that took place at a place called Ramgarh.

TRANSLATOR: What happened there?

RAMPHAL: In Ramgarh, there was a huge meeting that was organized. When I say huge, I mean in terms of people. A large number of people from the villages adjoining our village had flocked together to meet at a particular destination. This meeting was coming at a time when the ripples of revolt were escalating, so there was expectation in the air that something's going to give, something's going to happen. And that was the feeling that was prevalent among everyone.

The contractors or the slave owners, in turn, also knew that the meeting was going to happen, so they, in turn, were prepared. They were prepared to come and hit people, and violence was what they had on their agenda.

We had the inkling that they knew, so we were going with expectation that something was going to happen. There was electricity in the air, but exactly [for] what we weren't aware. So, anyway, we all went, all together, to this particular meeting point.

We all assembled together. I would say all in all we were four or five thousand villagers who had come together on that particular day.[4] Before we arrived at that particular point of time, there were about five . . . I would say approximately four to five slave owners who had come and inspected the place. They came on their bikes, and they just surveyed the field, and they went away. So once they went away, there was no fear, there was no threat, and we had a meeting peacefully.

As soon as the meeting was coming to some kind of conclusion and was about to terminate, what we did notice was about ten of them now . . . nine to ten I would say, approximately. Slave owners had come back, and they were circling around the entire congregation.

The meeting began to disperse. As the people were moving away from the meeting, some people went to nearby shops and were generally hanging around, buying stuff, provisions, there. The slave owners came to these particular shops, and they used their bare hands, their shoes, their slippers, and just randomly started beating up the shop owners and the people who were buying the provisions. There was uproar; people were screaming and shouting. And we were just getting dispersed, and we heard that. So we all turned around and came back to check what was happening.

Even then, at that point in time, violence did not erupt. People inquired and said, "What's up? What's happening? What have we done wrong? Why are you physically beating us up?" And they were trying to tell us what was happening.

Once we reached the slave owners who were beating up the shopkeepers and the customers over there, we went, we spoke to them, and we reached a reconciliation. And said, "Relax. There's no need. This violence is not required" They agreed to the same, so we started walking away.

The moment we started walking away—we reached some distance—again they just picked up their shoes, picked up their slippers, used their hands, and beat up the shopkeepers and everybody again. Again there was an uproar, and this time every single one of us turned around and came back. So the entire flock of five thousand people turned around and came back toward this commotion.

Well, the situation was almost like déjà vu. We came back. Now there are five thousand people. They've come back. There are ten slave owners here. The mob is still in control.

A discussion erupts between the elders of the mob and the slave owners, and they [the elders] said, "What? We reached a settlement; we came to an agreement; it was peace. Why are we having violence again?" The slave owners refused to respond. And as a response, they took pistols and shot them in the air.

When the mob heard these shots in the air, that's when all control broke loose. Because now they were scared, scared for their life. And also angry. Angry because a temporary peace had been made and been rejected. At that point in time, the mob lost its cool and completely surrounded these ten people. Think of it, think of it yourself: five thousand people, ten slave owners. Where could they go? How could they escape?

So ten of them, they were surrounded. Now the villagers have lost their cool, and they're beating them up. Within the beating-up process, there were sticks being used, there was blows being thrown around, and basically violence erupted.

TRANSLATOR: What happened to the slave owners?

RAMPHAL: When the violence erupted, in the chaos and confusion that took place, the chief of the slave owners, he died. And about four others were wounded. The moment the mob, in its frenzy, realized that the death of someone had taken place, calmness resumed its place.

We then all congregated once again and moved slowly toward the police station [in] Bara. But we were over five thousand of us, and we were on foot. We were walking around the mountain, which is a longer winding path, so by the time we reached the police station, the slave owners who had vehicles had already reached there. And since their version of the story had reached the police first, they [the police] refused to lodge an FIR [First Information Report], that's a complaint in the Indian scenario, accepting our story.

When we went to the police and the police refused to register our complaint, there was a silent protest that we did. We just sat. We just sat on the doorstep of the police station and refused to move, hoping that this demonstration would compel them to register our complaint. However, in the meantime, the slave owners who had been injured had been rushed to the Allahabad Hospital. And over there, in front of a doctor, they gave this testimony. And within the testimony, they named about eight, ten villagers they could think of or who were popular famous as the people responsible for the mob attack. This we weren't aware of at that point in time.

On the basis of the testimony that the police got from the Indian slave owners, they took about eight of us, and they seated us in the Naini jail. In the Naini jail, we were sitting for about five to six months. While my family, my small kids, the families of my fellow inmates were left high and dry. There was no one to look after them.

It was in this scenario that members of Sankalp and the members of the fellow help group came and looked after them. Come to think of it, I was at least safe. I was in prison; there was no fear of any landowner, any slave owner. There was no forces I was under, but at the same time all of the fellow mob members were troubled increasingly, severely harassed by the slave owners. They were under constant pressure.

After six months, I was released from the prison. And even at that point of time, I came to a village called Katra. The slave owners had barred my entry into my own village.

CALLAHAN: Can you tell us about when the village that was burned . . . when did that happen?

RAMPHAL: Do you remember I mentioned a girl that was burned in a house? Well, all these incidents are connected, and there's so much to tell that I don't know how to squeeze it all in.

But anyway, right about that time, the girl belonging to some other village was burned alive by the landlord for no rhyme or reason. Around that time, the Ramgarh meeting happened. So they're all connected, these incidents that took place one after the other, and, as a result of that, the houses were burned by the landlord.

CALLAHAN: Can he tell us what happened? Were there people in the village then? Walk us through that. It sounds scary.

RAMPHAL: You understand the fact that everyone was under their control. The slave owners had complete authority. There was not a moment when they [the villagers] would [not] think, "Oh my God, look who's sitting there," and they would be scared of that person. So there was this complete total control they were under.

CALLAHAN: So it seems so sad to me that people who were already enslaved and didn't have much anyway had to watch everything they had burned....

RAMPHAL: The day our houses were burned, it was approximately right now, this particular time of the day, five in the evening.

[Video and translation get interrupted.]

CALLAHAN: Can you tell us a little bit about how you felt about the fire? After your house had been burned?

RAMPHAL: When the looting happened, you understand that about eight, nine of us men were in the jail. So their houses were looted; they weren't protected; the men weren't there. So not only were their houses looted and looted completely, but also the houses where the men were present were completely looted. When I say looted, every household item that you can think of—clothes, suitcases, food, rations, water. Everything was completely destroyed, burned, just taken away, looted. To the extent that among all our houses, about forty-odd houses, not one needle and thread could be found. Gone, all gone.

And worst is, when there was nothing left ... and you know what? That was a bumper year. There was a great amount of crops that we had. Every house, no matter how poor, had about ten or twenty quintals of rice, wheat, all stocked up. Even if that year the crops had failed for the next two years, we would have survived. All of that, every single speck of grain was gone. Guess what, you think we should have complained to the police, we should have done something, taken some legal action. But you know, forgive my language, the idiots here ... the world is so hopeless. They have taken so much money and even so many bribes that they were standing while the houses were looted, as mere spectators, just standing and watching. They had the audacity to look at it. Imagine that.

CALLAHAN: So can you ask him how he got out of jail? And then we got to go back ...

RAMPHAL: My release from jail was a combined effort of a lot of people—the members of Sankalp, my self-help group, fellow villagers, [people] from other villages. They all tried very hard, did a lot of effort, moved a lot of people, spoke to a lot of officials. In fact, Judge Amar Singh, somebody who sits in Allahabad, was also instrumental in assisting my release.

Six months later when I was released from prison, we all moved to land just close to my former village, where we lived for one year. During this one year, again there was a lot of effort made for us to get a lease, and a fresh lease was then granted. Even once we got the lease, there was some talk going on about getting a license. We were waiting until the license was obtained before we could move on to our new village.

CALLAHAN: When he talks about his life before, it seems dark and kind of hopeless. How would he describe it?

RAMPHAL: I'm just so happy with this new life that I've got, and it gives me so much joy—the fact that I can control my own mind, my own thoughts, my own movements—that I can't even look back at my earlier existence.

I told you what it was like earlier. Each time I had to go somewhere, go meet a relative, go out for some work, I had to go and ask permission, seek somebody else's consent. And if the consent was no, that's it—no, I can't go, no matter how important or how urgent the requirement was.

But now that's not the scene. Now we are in control, to do what we want, when we want, how we want. This new self-belief is so strong among all of us, this feeling of brotherhood that we now share, that we all actually formed this entire village just by ourselves, and it's a village that we've named Azad Nagar, the land which is free.

This means so much to us, the fact that it's self-proclaimed, that we all led a march one day. Look a little farther down, if you just stretch your eyes over there, you might catch a look at it. . . .

[Video recording of interview ends abruptly.]

Azad Nagar, Uttar Pradesh, November 2, 2004

CALLAHAN: Ramphal, now I see you in your new village. And your life has changed a whole lot. Tell us about your life today.

RAMPHAL: Today? You want me to talk about today? You know the very fact that I am sitting here and I've been able to take time from a hectic day's work speaks about today. I can do what I want to do. I am free. Today I am free to not only live as I want to live, but hope for a better tomorrow. And I dream that tomorrow we'll be able to continue the unity we have built up. And take this unity toward a more progressive future for us and for everyone in my village

[Interview moves to new location.]

CALLAHAN: Does he know the original debt that held him in slavery?

RAMPHAL: I had personally taken a loan of about 5,000 rupees [about U.S.$100]. Initially my parents had also taken a loan, but when I was a child, we sold some gold to the moneylender, and in that deal that loan had got wiped off. I personally had taken a loan of 5,000, but in the entire tussle that happened between me and the landholders, even that has basically been forgotten, so today I'm a debt-free man.

CALLAHAN: What special thing does he think Sankalp did for his village?

RAMPHAL: Sankalp has done a whole lot for us. The more and more I congratulate them, the less it seems. Sankalp has already got us freedom, but when I was in Naini prison, they moved every single rock to get me freedom. People who didn't even know me, complete strangers, got together to free me. They went to court; they approached authorities; they got together money for my bail application. When I was in prison, I had no hope that I would see the earth again, that I would be free. It's only because of the striveless [tireless] effort of the Sankalp staff, Mr. Ramphal, the other volunteers, fellow members of my village, that today I am sitting in front of you. The more I say, the less it seems. They've just done so very much, worked so hard.

There's one person or one thing I forgot to mention. There's Justice Amar Singh. Now he's a judge; earlier he was a lawyer. Mr. Amar Saran, he also helped me a lot in obtaining my freedom.

CALLAHAN: Now we're almost done. What does he hope and dream and pray for?

RAMPHAL: My dream is now to start some kind of business. You see, the lease is already working, and mining operations are on. But I now want to move away from that and start some business so there's running income, the business goes on. This will be better for me because I'll have earnings, some savings, for myself and for a better future for my children. So that new business, to start something, is nowadays my plan.

CALLAHAN: What does he hope and dream and pray for for his children?

RAMPHAL: The dream is very big. I don't want to talk about it too much because it's such a big dream. I'm a little scared that it just might not come true. I want my child to study, to become big, to do something, to be successful in all that he does. But, you know, right now I don't want to talk about it; it seems so grand, so big a dream.

CALLAHAN: You said "he." Doesn't he have three kids? Doesn't he have a little girl? Just checking.

RAMPHAL: I have four kids: two boys, two girls.

CALLAHAN: So he has high dreams for all of them, you think?

RAMPHAL: Yes, of course.

CALLAHAN: He does some of the same hard work he always did. What's the difference? It's still backbreaking, hard work.

RAMPHAL: I agree the work is the same, but there's a fundamental difference. Earlier I could not control the hours I wanted to work, when I wanted to work, how I wanted to work. Now I can. I would work days, earlier, and nights. If the vehicle would come, I would load it right there and then, no matter what I was doing.

Now I can go and work in the mountains and work for as long as I want. If I don't want to work, I can come back and rest. I can move up, down, go outside the village, go meet someone, talk to someone. I'm the master of my own mind, my own destiny. That's the big difference.

CALLAHAN: There's all kinds of different slaves in the world, doing different kinds of work. What would he say to them if he could?

RAMPHAL: Not really a message, but there's one hope and thought I have for anybody and everybody who's a slave. Ever since we have obtained our freedom, we've talked to the other people who are still bonded laborers or slaves. We keep telling them and thinking that all we want is for them to live an independent life like we do, and that's what we want for anyone and everyone who's under slavery.

CALLAHAN: What does he think about the people in Sonbarsa who remain enslaved?

RAMPHAL: We are trying. I am trying, and all the fellow volunteers of Sankalp are also trying very hard to get them out of bondage.

When I was a slave, I never dreamed I could go to Delhi, and now I have. I've not only gone to Delhi, I've also gone to Lucknow, three . . . four . . . a number of times. In fact, I've been put in charge of all the running around that has to be done between the big cities. Whenever I go to these places, I learn, I become aware, and I come back, and I impart this awareness to my fellow villagers and also to the other people who are still in bondage.

But what can I do? We all go, we meet them, we talk to them, and they listen. It's not like they don't. They do. But then they forget, or they're too scared of the landowners, and again they forget.

But that doesn't matter. We're still trying. We keep telling them, showing them our life, the life we lead now, and they're keen, they're keen to get out of bondage, so it'll happen. It's just a question of time.

CALLAHAN: People who live in other countries, they're doing fine. Why should they care about people in this area?

RAMPHAL: Well, I guess you're right. They don't care. [Talk off camera.] I guess you're right. But the people living in these cities or countries where there is no bonded labor, they're so aware, they just know so much, there's so much wisdom. They have so much knowledge about their rights, the amenities, what is correct, what's not. Each time I go to any of these places . . . I go to Delhi and didn't think I would go there. I learn so much, and that's when I can come back and teach my fellow villagers. So when people come back here and teach and talk to us, we get to know. So it's their responsibility to tell us about these things, and that's what I feel. But there's so much to learn everywhere that they have to show us the way.

CALLAHAN: It seems that in the past his life was very dark and very hopeless and now his life seems very bright . . .

RAMPHAL: You are right. My present life today is so much better, just so much better, that all I can think of is that coming generations live a life even better than mine.

CALLAHAN: Anything else you'd like to add?

RAMPHAL: No, what to say, what not to say. So much has been said, so much has been done. That's it. That pretty much sums up my life.

CALLAHAN: What can he say should be different? What does he hope will be different about the village?

RAMPHAL: Well, something will change. Definitely something or other will change. In fact, Supriya, the volunteer here, came a couple of months ago, and I asked her to come more frequently. Each time when people like her come, our enthusiasm and motivation get increased even more. So I don't know [what] exactly will change, but yes, there will be a change.

[The interview continues later in a new location, while Ramphal breaks rock.]

RAMPHAL: You know what our motto for the village is? Just like we are able to break this hard, hard rock with the hammer, the chisel, whatever, any enemy is going to be shattered because of the unity that we now have. Anyone who comes and messes with us is going to get it right back.

Not only for our children, even for myself. I don't want to do this any more. Not for long, at least. Our desire is to start something new, something afresh. That's it, that's the wish, that's the hope.

CHOTI, FORMER BONDED LABORER

Origin: India   *Trafficked in/to*: Sonbarsa, Uttar Pradesh
Form of enslavement: Bonded labor   *Current status*: Free
Source: Interview conducted for the Free the Slaves' film *The Silent Revolution*; translated
transcript reproduced with permission.

CHOTI: My name is Choti. I think I'm about twenty years old. No, actually I'm thirty.

CALLAHAN: Can she tell us how she used to live in the past when they lived in the other village?

CHOTI: Life back in the earlier village was very tough. I was made to work in the field the whole day, whether my children were crying or not crying or anyone was sick, I was not allowed to go home. Every single day, long hours, I was expected to be working very, very hard. For all my hard work, I would only be given about five kilos of grain. Within that, I had to manage myself, my family. You want to tell me, if I had to work that very hard, with that much money, whether I [could] look after my kids, my husband? Save? Spend? What would I do?

Not only were we made to work in the field, we were also made to work in the stone quarry. We were made to beat up the stones and break them into tiny pieces. For all that effort, we were hardly paid. Once the breaking of the stones was over, we were also forced to lift them up and load them onto the trucks. Even that would not stop a day's work. For all that effort, we weren't given clothes; we weren't given food; we weren't given shelter. Every day, life was a struggle, and we hardly got any money.

CALLAHAN: Was she afraid?

CHOTI: Yes, I was very scared.

CALLAHAN: What were you scared of?

CHOTI: From the contractors, the slave owners.

CALLAHAN: What would they do?

CHOTI: The reason I was scared was because they would issue directions every day. "Go, go and work here. Go, go to my land. Go break the stones." You could not refuse because if you would refuse, the next step was there. "Go . . . or else I'll just burn your house. Go, go, go, I'll burn your house." That's it, every day. The threat was so strong, and I knew they could carry it out; therefore, we had no choice. We had to go and work.

CALLAHAN: Does she know why she was originally bonded? How did she end up working for the contractor so long?

CHOTI: When I was getting married, I took a loan from these slave owners. At that point in time, because I had taken this sum of money for my marriage purposes, I ended up becoming a bonded laborer.

TRANSLATOR: So were you free during childhood?

CHOTI: Yes, before my marriage I was not a slave. I was free. I would work even then, I would work in the fields, but I was a free worker.

CALLAHAN: How much money did she take for her marriage?

CHOTI: I think I got about 5,000 rupees [about U.S.$100]. This was taken for the marriage ceremonies, the guests—you know, the miscellaneous expenses that are there during my marriage. But I took 5,000, and I repaid 10,000 rupees worth.

CALLAHAN: And how long was she a slave for that 5,000?

CHOTI: For a long, long time—from the time that my kids were tiny to the time that my kids could work. That's the amount of time I was a bonded laborer. Each time I would go back and ask them, "Is the debt over? Have I repaid it all?" They would say, "No, no, now it's increased. It was earlier 10,000. Now it's 20,000. No, no, it is not 20,000 anymore; now it is 30,000."

I was not earning anything. I was barely earning some grain, some rice. How was I to repay? I had no idea. It just carried on and carried on and carried on.

CALLAHAN: We've heard that the contractors were especially horrible to the women. Is that true?

CHOTI: Yes, the females were especially harassed. The men would go off to work, either in the field or in the stone quarry, and even then though the male had gone to work, the contractors or the slave owners would come to our house, show us huge brandish knives, and compel us to work.

If you would refuse, saying the males had already gone, they would just drag us by our hair across this rocky terrain and compel us to work. Things got so bad that there was a point of time when the slave owners came to a woman's house. I think she refused. He had a huge knife, and he just killed her. We never knew when the car would come or a tractor would come and just drive on us and kill us.

In the night, the contractor came once to a woman's house. The man [her husband] had gone away for some work for the contractor. He came, and he raped her. Just no rhyme, nothing.

CALLAHAN: We've heard that women were really key, and maybe the most important key, to slaves starting to free themselves. Is that true . . . [about the] women . . . ?

CHOTI: Yes, I think the females did play a very big role in getting revolution. Earlier when we had initial meetings with the local authorities and with the Sankalp members, they told us to cooperate and coordinate with each other. That didn't mean too much to us at that point in time.

But slowly when we had a couple of meetings here and a couple of meetings there, things began to sink in, and we then came to realize we are doing all the work. We are the ones who are cutting the stones, we are the ones loading the lorries, we are the ones working in the house every single day and not getting any assistance or any monetary benefit from it.

That's when we all decided, sat down in motorcars and lorries, moved, met other people, met the Sankalp members, and took action in our hands.

CALLAHAN: What exactly did Sankalp say to these women or help these women do?

CHOTI: The Sankalp people, when they came initially, said, "Look, you have food that you grow yourself, you have labor that you do by yourself." They made us aware of the fact that it was possible for us to be self-sufficient, for us to be able to sell and buy our own food grains, for us to be able to educate our own children. They made us realize that we were exploited and that we were under the control of the contractors or the slave owners. We knew that, of course. We were aware that there was this evil person who would come and beat us up, this evil person whose permission we had to get, but they made us aware there was something we could do about it. That it was possible for us to get together, move toward the cities and the towns, and then bring about a revolution. That initial seed of thought was what really got to us.

Initially when the Sankalp volunteers would come down to the villages and interact with us, the contractors did not like the idea. The slave owners would come and regularly abuse us. "You motherfuckers" is what they would scream at us. "What are you doing?" So on and so forth. Seeing the retaliation, it just got our enthusiasm more aroused, and that's when we started communicating and taking them a little bit more seriously.

CALLAHAN: Could you tell us about the night they burned down the village? [Choti hesitates] . . . If she's not comfortable with that question, she doesn't have to answer it. [Translator asks her a question, gets Choti's assent, and says, "She's ready to talk," followed by lots of talk among the women gathered.]

TRANSLATOR: [Repeating] Please tell me about that night when they burned down the houses.

CHOTI: A girl had gone to work in the fields. And while she had come back, the contractor came and wanted to misbehave with her. She tried running away, and as she was running away, the contractor burned down her house.

TRANSLATOR: So did he just burn down one house, or was the entire village burned down?

CHOTI: No, he burned down a lot of houses. And in the process of the house burning, the girl was burned right inside that house.

TRANSLATOR: What happened then?

CHOTI: They burned down our house, our food, our clothes—everything was burned down. We had to run away. Not a thing was left; everything was just gone, completely evaporated. Because of that, we had to all just come out and move to a village called Fulva.

TRANSLATOR: And then?

[As Choti tells this story, there is lots of talk among the women. The translator doesn't translate this discussion.]

CALLAHAN: It sounded so horrible, so terrible. What was happening to her?

CHOTI: The night it happened, we were all just crying and wailing. It was sheer agony.

Once the houses were burned down, we were left to live below plastic sheets. That's what we had boiled down to. The basic utensils weren't there . . . the utensil on which we cook *chapatis* weren't there. Nothing.

[The] Sankalp people helped us then a lot. They came together, they gave us a vessel on which to cook our food, they gave us little medical help and assistance for our children. We were just living below [a] plastic sheet: there was no walls, there was no roof, nothing.

CALLAHAN: And where was her husband?

CHOTI: In prison.

CALLAHAN: That must have been really difficult for her, to survive without her husband.

CHOTI: It was very tough. Not only was my husband in prison, even my son—approximately that high [gestures with hand above her head]—died during that time.

CALLAHAN: Did she ever think it would be any better?

CHOTI: You know, I did think things would get better. The reason was because at that point of time the interaction with Sankalp had begun. So I knew there was a ray of hope. There was some expectation that something would give, and there would be some change that would come about.

Life below the slave owners was complete hell. It was certain that they would lock us inside the house, and they would burn us down. They almost did. Grain, sackfulls of them, were burned down, clothes—everything was just completely destroyed.

My husband was in jail, my children were homeless, and there was nothing that I could possibly think would happen. But even then, because of my interactions with the Sankalp people, there was something. Something that was going to happen. I knew that.

CALLAHAN: Can she compare her life today with the way it used to be?

CHOTI: I love my life now. I just simply love it. My children are going to school. I have food in my stomach. Ever since I've held the hand of Sankalp, I love my life. There is just so much happening in it now, so many good things. I've got a lease, there's school, I'm free, there's education, my children are happy. I'm happy.

CALLAHAN: What hope does she have for her children now compared to the way it used to be?

CHOTI: My dream for my children is that they grow up, they become big people—people who can read, who can write, who can live in the cities, and have a job. They shouldn't be like us, any of us. They should not be working to break stones, they should not be dying like we do, day in and day out, under the hot, scorching sun. They should be people who live a life in the cities, big people. That's my dream.

CALLAHAN: How many children does she have?

CHOTI: I have five kids.

CALLAHAN: Does she do the same work that she used to, but she feels different about the work she does?

CHOTI: No, no, no, my work is completely different. I don't work now. Before, when my children woke up, they would be rubbing their eyes, and I would be far, far away in some field, working under the contractors and slave owners. Now I don't work. I get up, I feed my kids, I send them to school. They come back. I relax in the afternoon. In the evening I make sure they're okay. You know, a regular wife. That's what I do now. That's my work.

CALLAHAN: Is there anything [else] that she'd like to say?

[Another woman talks to Choti.]

CHOTI: No, nothing really much to say excepting I really want that nobody takes away my lease, so I can work here, I can eat here, and be happy here. [I hope] that one lease is not taken away from me now.

CALLAHAN: Is there anything she could say to other bonded laborers or slaves who are still in bondage or slavery? Can she tell them anything that can show them a different way of life?

CHOTI: All I want is that nobody remains bonded any more. That every child is free: free to study, free to learn, everybody's free to live their own life.

[Conversation among women.]

What can I tell you? Life was just so traumatic. The night that my houses burned down, not only were my eyes weeping, my very soul was torn, shattered. It was almost like I was ripped apart. Each time I look back, there is something inside me that is unbelievable.

SHYAMKALI, FORMER BONDED LABORER

Origin: India	*Trafficked in/to*: Sonbarsa, Uttar Pradesh
Form of enslavement: Bonded labor	*Current status*: Free

Source: Interview conducted for the Free the Slaves' film *The Silent Revolution*; translated transcript reproduced with permission.

SHYAMKALI: My name is Shyamkali, and I am about thirty years old.

CALLAHAN: How many children does she have?

SHYAMKALI: Three.

CALLAHAN: What can she tell us about her life before and her life now?

SHYAMKALI: I can tell you the whole story, from beginning to the end, about what happened to me. Every single incident.

CALLAHAN: Can you tell me a bit about the days when you were working as a slave?

SHYAMKALI: Earlier on, my husband would work very hard, and so would I. For all the hard work, we would only get about five grains of food to eat the whole month through. Within that, I had to run my household, try to save some for a bleak day, and that's how I would lead my life. It was extremely hard, and there was no freedom at any point of time.

We were made to do two forms of labor: (*a*) we had to work in the fields, and (*b*) we had to break stones. For all this hard work, we were barely paid, sometimes 300 rupees, sometimes 400 rupees [about U.S.$6 or $8].

Early on in this environment, the people of Sankalp came in, and they told us that unity is our strength. If you all unite together, there is nobody who could do any form of exploitation against us. The deputy told us that the individual by himself is going to be weak; he's not going to be able to defend himself against the slave owner. But if we all form our organization, get together and form a self-help group, then we'll be able to defeat the pressure that was going to be put [on us] by the contractors or the slave owners.

CALLAHAN: Does she know why she was bonded or enslaved in the first place?

SHYAMKALI: The reason I became a slave was because I took a loan. I took one loan; he [the contractor] wrote two loans. I was illiterate, so the documentation was something I could not read. He probably messed up with it and made it to suit his own purposes, and because of that loan I became a bonded laborer.

TRANSLATOR: Do you know how much the loan was for?

CALLAHAN: And for what was it?

[Much discussion between the translator and the women in the group to clarify the story.]

SHYAMKALI: I never took a loan myself because of which I became a slave. It was actually my in-laws, my husband's parents, who were taking the initial loan. The only loan that I would take would be in time of duress, in emergency, when my son needed medicine or I needed—the roof had fallen down, I needed some money—I took little bit, little bit.

   And each time I would go back to the moneylender, the amount of loan had always increased. The last I heard, my family owed him 10,000 rupees [about U.S.$200].

CALLAHAN: So compare that in the past with today.

SHYAMKALI: Very different. There's a huge, huge difference. Earlier we were slaves, either agricultural slaves working in the fields, or we were slaves working in the stone quarries.

   But now we are free. Free to work if we want to, not work if we don't want to. And this freedom is the biggest difference.

CALLAHAN: Does she have different hopes for her children now?

SHYAMKALI: I now want my children to study. I want my girl child to study. I want her to be able to read, to write, to do a job somewhere as well as to manage a house. I want her to be able to do both of them together.

CALLAHAN: Do the children ever come home and teach their parents what they learn?

SHYAMKALI: When I ask them what happened in school and how the day went, they tell me about the events of the day. In fact, recently, she could count from one to ten, and all by herself she came up to me and wrote out the numbers on her slate.

CALLAHAN: Does her mom know how to write the numbers? Can the children teach the parents how to do it?

SHYAMKALI: No, I don't know how to write.

TRANSLATOR: Do your children ever teach you?

SHYAMKALI: I never went to school, you see, so never in my life did I have a chance. So I haven't been able to learn.

TRANSLATOR: Do your children ever teach you, or you would like to learn from the children?

SHYAMKALI: [Smiling, pretends to write] Yes, my children do come and teach me, but they lose patience very soon. They come, and I write an alphabet, sometimes I mess it up, and I can only write half. And then they say, "Tsk, enough already," and they walk away. So little by little I am getting there.

CALLAHAN: Is there anything she'd like to add?

SHYAMKALI: Earlier on when I was a slave, I had no dreams and no ambitions.

Later on, when we started forming the committees, there was hope. The hope was shattered when they died and the burning incident happened, and everybody went to jail. There was again this sadness that was creeping in. But the unity that we had among us had kept going, and I believe in this unity. And this is giving me joy and happiness now. This has become a life trait.

CALLAHAN: What's the next step? The group did all kinds of great stuff. We heard today that they're pretty unhappy about some things. What's the next step?

SHYAMKALI: The next step for all of us is to ensure that the cooperation and coordination, the unity, remain strong and move from strength to strength. Ensuring that unity remains, we now want to get a government hospital built somewhere close by. We also want to improve the conditions of our school and make it more safe. That's what the next project is all about.

CALLAHAN: Why are women so important in the move to free slaves?

SHYAMKALI: We have a huge role to play.

TRANSLATOR: Can you tell us a bit more about that?

SHYAMKALI: We play a very important role because we're also bread earners. Since we earn, we also have [an] equal role to play in fighting for our freedom. Freedom for me means economic independence as much as it means freedom of movement.

SEEYAWATI, SANKALP ORGANIZER

SEEYAWATI: My name is Seeyawati. I'm twenty-eight years old, and I work for Sankalp. Sankalp is an organization that aids and assists people who were former slaves to attain freedom. And at the same time, [it] informs [them] about sanitation, medical awareness, how to get the medical program from the government to the villages, education for the children, and such like.

CALLAHAN: Can she start off by telling us when Sankalp comes into a village, what do they do? And what did she do with this village she worked with?

SEEYAWATI: Initially when I came to this village, everybody over here were bonded laborers or slaves. It was very difficult to come, to let us even talk to them because initially nobody had the freedom to communicate with anybody at all.

We would come to the villages and try to organize a meeting, but there would be zero attendance—the reason being that they were very scared of slave owners, and if they would leave their work and come to talk to us, they would be paid less.

We then had to start a campaign where we spoke to every individual, one by one. They had to know a little bit about Sankalp, [so we wanted to] introduce ourselves, create a little awareness of what we wanted to do, and what our mission was. Slowly and steadily people started coming to our meeting. And once we got a congregation of eight to ten people, we were able to elaborately tell them about freedom, about exploitation, about the fact that they were slaves, the meaning of freedom, education, and the benefits that Sankalp could provide to them.

CALLAHAN: How long did this take?

SEEYAWATI: It's almost took us five years to get it going from scratch to formation of our self-help group. Since May 2000—the incident that everyone has spoken of took place somewhere around that time—ever since that incident or that meeting, the entire freedom movement has kick-started and increased in space.

CALLAHAN: Why was this village any different? Was this village different because of the people, the villagers? Or because the slave owners were so bizarre? What makes this different?

SEEYAWATI: The reason we chose Sonbarsa was because this particular village was more severely exploited by the slave owners than the others. The wages they were paid were less; the work they did was more.

There was in 2000—since the incident began, the frequency of our meetings with the villagers increased—a relationship with the villages [that] was built up over a period of time, and a bond developed. They were willing to listen to us, progress began, and the movement was able to take on a pace unprecedented compared to any other village. That's the reason Sonbarsa is called our biggest success story.

CALLAHAN: What did she come in and say to them? What do villagers need to hear to make a change?

SEEYAWATI: There were two things we told the villagers when we started coming here. We gave them a live example of another village where we'd been able to get some progress done. We also made them aware of the fact that how long, how long could they live this life of a slave? How long could they let the women be exploited? How long could they possibly tolerate the fact that they were the people working all day long, and the slave owner was taking away more than 75 percent of the wages?

This awareness was what we tried to stress to them—the fact that they were doing all the hard work, that somebody else was living off them. On the basis of this message, we were able to create a feeling of community and create the group, a "self-help group" as we like to call it, among these people. It was within this time period when the entire message was just about being circulated to the villagers that the Ramgarh meeting happened. That happened during the time when elections were near, and that's when the incident took place, postwhich, like I've told you, things just escalated.

CALLAHAN: When she came in, was she meeting with women's groups? How important were women to this movement?

SEEYAWATI: We would come in and speak not only to the women, but also to the men. The rationale was that we knew, and we also made them also realize, that the men and the females had to work together in order to get about the revolution to be successful. That's why we have consulted the importance of both the groups. When we came in and made them realize about the entire importance of self-help groups, that's when the meeting took place.

Postwhich, whenever the meeting happened, the slave owners would come and constantly threaten them, saying, "How dare you have a meeting?" Abuse them, beat them up. But they [the villagers] were adamant. They had reached a stage where they were adamant; they would hold a meeting at whatever cost. That's when they had the Ramgarh meeting at which this incident took place.

CALLAHAN: It seems to me like she's in a pretty dangerous business.

SEEYAWATI: Danger does exist. In fact, there was a point of time when me along with two of my other assistants were supposed to come and conduct a meeting. The slave owners had a preconceived idea that that was the day they were going to come and beat us up. However, news had come to the other villagers, and the villagers informed us that "something was not right. We suspected that something was up and some plan in the air. It would be better if the meeting for today was postponed and you would return to your villages."

We were on the way out from the village and were circulating out toward the road when we saw the slave owners on motorcycles approaching us. The plan in their heads was to kidnap one of us, take us somewhere, and probably misbehave—or I don't know what actually—with us and then release us.

So yes, there is danger, but you learn to handle it.

CALLAHAN: Sankalp offers a lot of things to the villagers and tries to help them see things for themselves. But they also ask the villagers to promise Sankalp something. What do they ask?

SEEYAWATI: We at Sankalp make no promises when we start our work. Yet at no point of time [do we] promise them that we will ensure you get a school, we will ensure that you get a hospital, we will ensure that you get a lease.

What we do do, our modus operandi essentially, is to hear from them their problems and aid them in solving them how we can, based on a consensus that we receive from them. So they highlight a problem, work among themselves to try and figure out what is the best solution, and then we help them work toward the solution.

TRANSLATOR: But what does Sankalp get from the villagers in turn? Do they promise to Sankalp something?

CALLAHAN: There are five promises . . . ?

SEEYAWATI: Yes, I have a hazy idea about them. When we get them a lease, we basically get about five promises. Then the nature of the fact [is] that [they promise the following]: "We will get education for ourselves, we will ensure that our children go to school and are educated, we will assist in the reforestation of the area, and therefore we will not only plant saplings but also look after them."

These are the promises we get from the villagers.

CALLAHAN: When she says Sankalp goes to villages and asks them what they need and helps them formulate a plan. What typically do villages need? What is usually the issue?

SEEYAWATI: One of the problems that is faced by the villages is the fact that where they reside, the land is not their own. So because they are residing on someone else's land, they're threatened very often [by] the fact that they will be thrown out and made homeless again.

TRANSLATOR: What are the other problems?

SEEYAWATI: Some of the other problems are to do with leases. There could be a situation where the lease could belong to A person but B person has occupied the area, and it uses A person to conduct mining operations.

Another problem that is faced is that if they're living on A person's land, and A person only agrees to give them a sum of 300 or 400 rupees [for work, about $6 or $8], they have no option but to work for 300 or 400 rupees. If they refuse, they're threatened to be thrown out from A person's land. Problems like these are often what we encounter.

CALLAHAN: What difference does she see between the villagers here before they get their lease and after they get their lease?

SEEYAWATI: The big difference is that they are free. They are no longer slaves. What that means in real time is that, earlier on, very often, the children were taken with the females to the stone quarry or to the field, or they were made to create [unintelligible]; there was some work they were doing. Education was not a priority. Ever since they got their lease, children are going to school. Almost every child in the village is getting an education.

They're free to do what they want to do. People work as much as they want to work. Economically, they are better off because they are earning more. That is the big difference.

CALLAHAN: When they [Sankalp] come in and tell people, "You have certain basic rights," what rights do they tell them? What do they say: "You have this, you have this, you have this . . . "?

SEEYAWATI: We essentially talk about three rights. The right to life, to be safe, and to make progress. For example, the right to life, we talk about medical benefits. The government has given us certain medical benefits that don't reach the villagers. Vaccinations, polio drugs, vaccinations against tetanus, malaria, issues like that. It's also very important for ladies who are pregnant to be vaccinated for themselves and also for the child. Nurses are supposed to come in remote areas, but they don't. The villagers, especially the females, decided to go to the village and talk to the nurse themselves and ensure that she comes to the village for the medical safety of themselves and the children. These are the rights.

CALLAHAN: This work is very difficult, moving from village to village. It's frightening sometimes. What keeps her going? What motivates her?

SEEYAWATI: I just hate being home. I hate it. Even if it's one day that I will sit inside my house, I can't describe it, but something eats me up from inside. There's this constant feeling: "What am I doing here? I should be in this village or that village. I should be out, I should be doing something." I can't describe it in words, but that's just the feeling.

CALLAHAN: You sounded a little frustrated with the women today during the meeting. You were tough.

SEEYAWATI: Well, I wouldn't say I'm frustrated, but when I hear about these issues, there is simmering anger that is built up inside me. This anger is with authority. The government has made certain schemes and given us social security benefits which never ever reach the poor people. The middlemen in between, just the corrupt officials, eat up all the benefits for their own sake.

Take, for example, the nurses. They've been given a job to do. They don't do it.

Take, for example, the school. Three masters have been allocated to come and teach. Today I got to know [that] only one comes.

What is the point? They get a salary. They should do their job. And how do I compel them to do their job?

There's no point running an institution like this where there is no education. You might as well switch it off, shut it down, and I'll see the children a better job. When I hear about these instances, anger built up inside me.

CALLAHAN: But I was saying she was tough on the women. I mean, she was like, "Come on, get with the program. Do something about it!"

SEEYAWATI: Well, I won't say I was tough, but you see what happens is . . . even earlier on, take me, for example. When I would leave my house and started working in the field, I would be shy, I would be coy, I would hesitate to speak in front of people. But now I don't. Four people, ten people, makes no difference.

Similarly, I want them to speak up, to voice their fears, and I want to instigate them to get them going. That no matter who comes, which local authority, if you keep silent, nothing is going to change. I compel them and let them shed their inhibitions. And that's why I behave the way I do.

CALLAHAN: Was she a bonded laborer ever or a slave?

SEEYAWATI: No, I wasn't. I wasn't either bonded or a slave.

CALLAHAN: Why does she think the Sankalp's way of doing this works, when so many other people, so many other organizations aren't very successful?

SEEYAWATI: I would say a big reason for the success has been persistence. A lot of other organizations would come, come once, visit the village, and not appear ever again. Sankalp that way ensured that they made repeated visits to a number of villages, spread out in a large area, to see that there was compliance with what they said the last meeting, whether children had been freed from bonded labor or not, whether the child labor was getting abolished. Our persistence, continuous persistence, is what our success factor would probably be.

CALLAHAN: When they start a self-help group, what do they have to come back and help with? I mean, I've heard things like they help keep records. They help, if they [the villagers] are saving money together, they help keep records for that. What kind of things did they do to facilitate self-help groups?

SEEYAWATI: During our meetings itself, because the villagers are predominantly illiterate, you would help them in maintaining registers and records about the savings, about how the money was being spent, how much they had saved up to that point of time. So our meetings were also incorporating all these documentation elements.

CALLAHAN: She's been working at Sankalp for the last how many years now with the self-help groups? And as the self-help groups start working with each other, does she see any overall changes in the villages?

SEEYAWATI: There is a huge difference. Earlier on, they were not aware of their rights. As long as they got two square meals, they were happy, irrespective of if they were exploited, their children went to school or not—they didn't really care.

Now the awareness level has gone up. They themselves come up to us and demand—demand amenities, demand their rights, demand the school functions properly. Whether it be the land, the lease, education, sanitation, health care, they demand them because they know this is what they deserve. Not only do they demand, but they also make progress and steps toward attaining the demands themselves. We're going to the local district authority. We're going all the way to Allahabad. They are willing to do it all by themselves. That is a difference.

CALLAHAN: What do you dream for the people you work with?

SEEYAWATI: My dream for these people is education for the children. Also education is very important, that similar education be imparted to all. Right now the situation is that in nursery [school], English is the medium of instruction, whereas in primary [school], Hindi is [the] medium of instruction. Therefore, when the common exam comes, the children who have English education manage to scrape through, whereas children who have primary education usually fail.

If this continues, the vicious circle will come right back. Because the children, once they fail the exam, will have to resort to labor to survive. Something should be done to check this.

CALLAHAN: Is there anything else she would like to add?

SEEYAWATI: My last dream is that every child anywhere here associates himself with some means of education, remains free, and gets all the rights and benefits that he or she is entitled to. My last dream.

CALLAHAN: Why should we care about these people? I'm living in another country, I'm doing fine. Why should I care about people who slave somewhere else?

SEEYAWATI: Why not? Why not? It's all the same family. Look at me. I don't belong here. I'm not a bonded laborer. Why should I care?

But that's not the right thought. The thought that comes from inside, a thought that says, "Look, I've reached a level of progress. And I'm here; they're not." The only thought that should be is "How is it possible for me from that position to get the people from here to join me?" And that thought should be the running thought in every individual whose moved beyond this.

If you don't care, how would things ever change?

SUNIT SINGH, NONGOVERNMENTAL
ORGANIZATION CONSULTANT

Mr. Singh's interview has been abbreviated because it was too long to include in its entirety. Unlike the other interviews in this section, this interview was conducted entirely in English.

CALLAHAN: Can you please introduce yourself? Tell us your name, spell your name. And tell us about you and where you work.

SINGH: I am Sunit Singh, and I am working with the G. B. Pant Social Science Institute. And I'm also engaged in consultancy to grassroots-level nongovernmental organizations [NGOs] working with the disadvantaged sections. Primarily, I'm engaged in research particularly related to rural areas, particularly related to rural poor, and in that sense I'm also involved in social intervention programs along with NGOs like Sankalp.

CALLAHAN: They [Sankalp] seem to be successful in ways that other groups have difficulty finding the same success . . .

SINGH: Sankalp is also a grassroots-level NGO and is working with the bonded laborers employed in stone quarries in the areas, in the remote areas of Uttar Pradesh.

Sankalp was busy in finding sustainable solutions to make the bonded laborers free, to help the bonded laborers free, to find solutions. In fact, Sankalp initiated its work to get the child laborers removed from the quarries and send them to school. But it was . . . they find it difficult to bring children to school if the parents are in the bondage. And then Sankalp started thinking to find new

ways, alternative ways, firstly to get the parents free from bondage. These laborers were migrant laborers, but still they were staying in this area for the last forty
years. Two or three generations have grown up in this area, but they didn't have
any house sites of their own. They were staying on the contractor's land. They
were getting wages barely to survive. They didn't have any agricultural land to
produce food grains for their survival. And in that situation, whenever they
were caught in the conditions of distress, they're forced to take advances from
their employers or contractors.

So these laborers, they're forced to go from one bondage to second bondage, to third bondage, fourth . . . [for a] number of reasons. With that, at some
times, they seek advances for food grains. On other occasions, if there are . . .
[if] any member of their family is ill, they seek advances for the treatment. If
there is anything they want to start as a microenterprise—for example, they
want to purchase some goats—again they will ask for advances. In a way, they're
always trapped in it—debt-like conditions.

So Sankalp thought that they must find solutions on which these laborers
can—what you will say—on which they can, you say it like this . . . Sankalp
thought, "If we want to get these laborers free from the bondage, we will have to
find some occupation which will start giving earnings to these laborers without
any time lag and on which they can work without any newer skills required."

So we thought that since they are working on quarries, they have skills to
break stones. So it is better to get a quarry for these laborers on which they can
start breaking stones as soon as they leave the sites of the contractors.

CALLAHAN: Can I interrupt you for one second? Because you're great at talking.
Is it, in your view, is bonded labor another form of slavery, and are contractors
another form of slave owner? If that is true for you, when you speak, can you
use those terms, or can you say "bonded labors or slave owners"?

SINGH: In fact, when we say "slavery" or "slave owners," most people think of the
days of seventeenth or sixteenth century. And they didn't feel comfortable to
accept the term *slavery*.

But we must understand that slavery has also been transformed. There is a
new form taking up and in which the slave owner doesn't prefer to hold the
slave with him. So you may find that workers are staying outside freely; [the]
contractor is not putting his pressure on them; they are free to move around
their locality. But they are not free to move away from the sites of work because
they have taken advances, so they are in a bondage. They cannot raise voice to
get the statutory minimum wages, and if not the statutory minimum wages, at

least the prevailing market wages. They're not free to ask the contractors because they have taken loans. They are not free to ask: for certain periods, we are
not ready to work on the sites.

So the relationship between employer and employed is such that they are
under bondage. The laborers are under bondage. The arrangement is not free.
The relationship is not free. Although they're not enslaved in the manner as
the slaves were enslaved in the period of the seventeenth century. You may find
indentured laborers, the history of indentured laborers. The first, it was called,
slaves of Negro origin. That was one stage. In the second stage, we find indentured laborers in which Indian laborers were—what do you say—immigrated
to certain colonies to work on plantation farms. And this is a third stage. This
is the third stage in our world history when laborers [are] being bonded in a
different form.

Don't you agree? Eh?

CALLAHAN: So it's okay when we are referring . . . to you, it's absolutely permissible,
when we're describing this, to describe it as slavery. It's a new form of slavery,
but it is absolutely slavery. And the contractor . . . see, in the United States contractors are some guy you hire to build your house. You don't think of contractors as slave owners or, like we've heard yesterday at the village, where contractors came in and did horrible things to people. It just has a different term at
home. So we're just trying to make sure we can communicate at home and here.

SINGH: Here in India we don't call it slavery. Most people prefer to call it "bonded
laborers," "bondedness."

CALLAHAN: Is that because they are uncomfortable with the word *slavery*, or they
just don't think it's slavery?

SINGH: They're uncomfortable with the word *slavery*. It's because they're
uncomfortable.

For example, even people are not ready to accept *bondedness* even. They'll
not say that bondedness is slavery. In fact, we will have to appreciate that when
we are negotiating with the world, which is engaged in the business activities,
engaged in academics, engaged in politics, or the world which is controlling the
resources, they are not ready to accept the term *slave* because that hurts their
mental makeup since they are controlling the society. They claim that they have
achieved democracy. They claim that here is the country in which everyone is
free to participate in elections. Here is a country in which government is taking
care of all the people. So they are not ready to accept that there is any slave in
this country, that there is any bondedness in this country.

But if we confront ourselves with the reality which is prevailing at the grass-roots level, we will find that there are people who are living without shelter. There are people who are working, who do not earn wages which can provide two square meals to them. There are people who do not have access to public health facilities in the period of their illness. There are people whose children die due to malnutrition. There are people whose children don't go to school; they themselves are illiterate, and their children are also illiterate. They don't have any piece of land to produce food grains for their family. They don't have passes to move out from their houses. They're under threat at the local level.

So if these situations are prevailing, we should not hesitate to call them as slavelike conditions. People feel shy to call it [a] slave-like situation. They will say it is a "situation of extreme poverty." They will say "chronic poverty." But I would say that if it is a chronic poverty, it is a condition of slavery. We should not hesitate. Because unless we accept the reality in real terms, we'll not be able to find solutions which are workable, which will help these people come out from the situation which we are calling slavery.

CALLAHAN: Can you talk to us about the strategies, as you described in the correspondence that I read of yours, that are usually employed to bring people out of slavery and how Sankalp is developing a fourth strategy, as you described it? Can you talk to us about the average three, the first three that people usually use, and then the fourth, that Sankalp is using?

SINGH: Sankalp's strategy, in fact . . . we were dealing with the people who are under slavery conditions, yet they have some freedom also. Because in the new form of slavery, slave owners do not keep these slaves under strict control. They have temporary control over these slaves. So they have freedom during certain periods.

So Sankalp decided to organize these slaves or bonded laborers. And their strategy was different in the form that Sankalp asked these laborers to find solutions for themselves, to understand the complex dynamics of indebtedness, to make them aware about the arrangement of advances through which they are being enslaved. And then ask them to find out solutions.

The laborers, obviously, since they had the skill only to break stones, they felt that if they are able to get mining leases, they can break stones for their own self, and their returns will be high, and their incomes will raise by three times or four times. And then they will be able to purchase land for their own shelter, clothes for their family members, and they will start sending their children to schools.

It was convincing enough. So Sankalp decided to take up this idea with the district administration and the state government. Fortunately, the district administration got sensitized, and they accepted the idea and granted a mining lease to one group in the year 1999.

The results were amazing. The income rose three times. The workers constructed their own houses. They started sending their children to schools. They purchased some goats as an additional income-generating activity. With the outcome of that quarry—on the one hand, administration was convinced that this, this experiment, can provide greater revenue because these laborers gave substantial amounts of revenue during the period of one month. And on the other hand, the laborers located in that particular region also started seeing this experiment as an emancipatory experiment. A good number of laborers approached us [saying] that "we are also ready to organize ourselves in self-help groups. And please help us to get mining leases from the administration."

Again we said, "It's not our job. You have to organize yourselves. You get yourselves organized. We will just be a facilitator to get the mining leases from the district administration."

Finally we were able to get around twelve to fourteen mining leases from the administration, on which something around thirty or thirty-two self-help groups or members of those groups are working. And they are living happily.

In the meantime, we found that economic empowerment must be supported with a social involvement also. That also formed a part of our strategy, because if empowerment has to be sustained, it has to be supported by the social empowerment. The children must go to schools. They must increase the access to public health facilities for better health. They must participate in the improvement of biodiversity. They must participate in the family-planning program. And we encourage these self-help groups to come forward.

[A break here for a video camera adjustment.]

CALLAHAN: Can you tell us about the three typical strategies that people use to free slaves and how Sankalp has developed a fourth strategy?

SINGH: In fact, in our country the most prevalent strategy is the rehabilitation strategy. It's a legal approach, in which people say that bondedness is illegal, unlawful, and if a person is employing a bonded labor he will be punished under law. But the problem is that you will never find any person on legal grounds employing a laborer under bondedness so you will never be able to prosecute him in the court of law.

Second is a relief and rehabilitation approach, in which if you find a person under bondedness, you'll ask the district administration to get him free and then provide him a rehabilitation allowance, which is around 10,000 rupees [about U.S.$200] to start a new life, a free life. But this is also not workable because the corruption level is so high that firstly you will not be able to find evidences to ascertain that a person is under bondedness. If you were able to ascertain that he is under bondedness, and he requires rehabilitation allowance, the government department which is responsible to distribute that allowance will take out some money from that amount. And finally the laborer will be able to get only 50, 60 percent of that amount, and that amount is so meager that he will not be able to survive in the conditions beyond bondedness. And again he will be forced to ask for a debt or loan from the same contractor or any other contractor. So again he's in the situation of bondedness.

Then there is a third approach in which the district administration, since India is a democratic country, the district administration is asked to pursue certain welfare policies. So they are asked to provide certain facilities to the people living in the conditions of poverty and in that course of action they support these laborers to some extent. That is also a very ad hoc way of dealing this complex situation.

Sankalp has a different strategy, which we call a fourth approach. In this we prefer to involve district administration, even the courts, governments, and organized laborers in the form of grassroots labor organizations. So grassroots community organizations, district administration, courts, government representatives, social activists all join hands to remove the situations of bondedness. They all come together. It is a partnership approach. And while organizing these laborers in the form of grassroots community organizations, Sankalp trained them, educate them to earn a self-respect and self-confidence, to earn the capabilities to run their microenterprises independently, to earn the capabilities to forge partnership with NGOs and other higher-level organizations, and [to] work for the social empowerment or social transformation of the region also.

This is the fourth strategy. And this provided ... and in that course, Sankalp also tried to find out solutions in which these laborers could move, without any time lag, to earn their livelihood after leaving the quarries of their erstwhile contractors.

CALLAHAN: Now, there are slaves all over the world. Some fish, some do only agriculture, all kinds ... and there are people all over the world that want those people to be free. What can we learn from Sankalp that could apply universally? What do you think they have to teach us?

SINGH: First thing: the laborers must be organized in grassroots community organizations, whether in the form of self-help groups, whether in the form of mutual aid groups, or whatever. But they must be organized in grassroots organizations.

Second, they must learn to forge partnerships with higher-level organizations, local-level NGO, regional-level NGO, national-level NGO, and also international level NGOs. They must learn to find out the solutions which are workable. They should have the capacity to understand and analyze the situation prevailing around them.

And lastly, which is the most important, that they must earn a self-confidence and self-respect and the feeling that they could achieve freedom and they could sustain their freedom, that they could work for a better tomorrow.

CALLAHAN: It seems like what Sankalp does is so fabulous because it combines what's very practical—you need to make a living today so that you can feed your kids—and also somewhat spiritual—in that to make real external changes you need to make some internal changes. Would you agree with that? It might be too simple, but . . .

SINGH: No, it is true. It is true that external forces are of course responsible for the conditions of slavery, the structure, the system, the legal system, the political system, the economic system, the relationship between employee and employer. All are responsible. But then [at] the same time, if you are moving ahead to achieve freedom, you will have to earn that inner strength, which makes you able to think that, "Okay, we can change these situations, we can change these structures and can create new structures." This internal strength is also essential for moving forward.

CALLAHAN: When you see the work that's being done, and you're such a pivotal part of it . . . it must feel really pretty good inside. What's going on for you when you look at the great strides that have been made?

SINGH: Pardon me. Please repeat your question.

CALLAHAN: How does it make you feel? What happens to your heart when you see the strides that are being made? When you get to tell stories of villages that have just done amazing things. What does that do for you?

SINGH: I'm not getting the point again.

CALLAHAN: Okay, I'm sorry. I'm not asking it very well. Does it make you feel good inside when you see slaves freeing themselves?

SINGH: [Long pause.] It does, it does a very . . . if I'm . . . there are many different approaches. If I am working as a researcher, and I am going to field, and I am pursuing my research, that is a different approach. I look for results. It would be an experiment for me.

But I'm . . . I'm not . . . I feel that research cannot be isolated with the action. Research and action must go side by side. I mean, in that sense I am equally involved in this project because I feel that it is not a question of simply freeing the laborers. It's the question of liberating ourselves also, the research community, the academic community. We must also understand what the reality is and how to participate in the process of transformation, which is part of our society, part of our economy in which we are living.

If we are committed to build a free society, if we are committed to make our democracy strong, we must participate in such transformation processes sincerely and honestly. And when I see that laborers are organizing themselves, they are participating in the activities which are affecting their life, they are participating peacefully, they are raising their voices nonviolently, they are exerting pressure without any violent move, it certainly gives me a great satisfaction because I find myself a part of this movement.

CALLAHAN: Why should people like me—I live in southern California, I have a great life—why should I even care that there are slaves anywhere in the world?

SINGH: Yes, a very pertinent question. It's not a question of [just] yourself. Many people in India also ask me, "Why should we participate in such movements?

If a person is employed in a university, he's a professor, if a person is employed in a court as a judge or is a good businessman, why should he participate in this movement?

My point is if there are hungry people, if there are unfree people around you, you cannot live peacefully, not only because it is hard on your sentiments, but also it is the dynamic of the society that if a large number of people are starving, one day or another they will take up arms in their hands and become violent, and it will demolish all of the achievements which you have achieved so far. That is one point.

Secondly, if you have to grow, if the economy has to grow, you will have to unfreeze all these productive forces. I'm taking a view of global economy; you will have to unfreeze all these productive forces. Then only you will be able to utilize the potential of human kind for the welfare of human kind. That's why I think whether you are staying in California or anywhere in the world, you must participate in the movements of freedom in any part of the world.

MUNNI DEVI

Origin: India   *Trafficked in/to*: Sonbarsa, Uttar Pradesh

Form of enslavement: Bonded labor   *Current status*: Enslaved

Source: Interview conducted by Ginny Baumann for the Free the Slaves' film *The Silent Revolution*; translated transcript reproduced with permission.

MUNNI DEVI: My name is Munni Devi. I'm about thirty-five to forty years old.

BAUMANN: Does she have family?

MUNNI DEVI: My extended family does not live with me. I essentially live just with my immediate family.

TRANSLATOR: How many children do you have?

MUNNI DEVI: I have four children: two boys and two girls.

BAUMANN: Is she working in the stone quarries?

MUNNI DEVI: Yes, I work there.

BAUMANN: How long has she been working here?

MUNNI DEVI: I've been working in the quarry for a long, long time. Many days. Maybe twenty years, maybe more. I'm not sure. My husband died while working there, and now I have to work there myself.

Life is very tough. I've taken a loan, because of which I'm bonded, or I'm a slave to the person from whom I've taken the loan. And now the situation is getting even worse. I'm in debt. I can't work that much, and he's threatening to throw me out of my house.

My poor son is just running from pillar to post to organize things. I don't know what's going to happen.

BAUMANN: She's been here for twenty years?

MUNNI DEVI: Yes.

BAUMANN: With this one contractor?

MUNNI DEVI: I've been working under the same contractor. I had taken one loan, and now it seems to have doubled to become two loans.

BAUMANN: What was the loan for, and how much was it?

MUNNI DEVI: I've taken a loan, but because of the fact that I'm not really earning too much; my amount is increasing. I'm not sure how much the loan was for.

BAUMANN: What was it originally to pay for?

MUNNI DEVI: My original loan was for 9,000 rupees [about U.S.$185], and I've been trying to repay it for a long, long time. It just seems to be increasing.

BAUMANN: What was it to pay for? A funeral? A marriage?

MUNNI DEVI: I took it for the marriage of my daughter.

BAUMANN: How much does she think she's paid back over that time?

[The translator is not able to understand or translate. Lots of side talk among people gathered there.]

BAUMANN: How much does she get paid?

MUNNI DEVI: I'm not paid any money or salary per month, excepting once in a while, when the lorry comes to be loaded, I'm paid about 400 or 500 [rupees, about U.S.$8 or $10], depending on his mood.

BAUMANN: That's about every fifteen days, is it?

MUNNI DEVI: The lorry only comes when all of us are able to break down the hard rocks into tiny pebbles. As and when the tiny pebbles are ready, the lorry turns up. I would say the process of [turning] hard rocks into tiny pebbles takes about fifteen-odd days, approximately.

BAUMANN: Does she feel like she's forced to work? How do they make her work? If she is sick, for example, or isn't able to work, what happens?

MUNNI DEVI: I am forced to work.

TRANSLATOR: What happens if you are sick or have something important to do at home?

MUNNI DEVI: I am forced to work. Even if I'm sick, I'm made to work. If I'm so sick that I can't go to work, it's very simple: I don't get paid; they don't look after my expenses, my food. There's no nourishment coming from that side whatsoever. Because of this, when I'm not working and since I pay back my loan because of my earnings, my labor, my loan amount keeps escalating when I'm sick.

BAUMANN: Has there ever been any physical threats given to make her work?

MUNNI DEVI: I have been threatened—verbally, that is. The threat has been that he's going to throw me out of my house. He keeps coming over once in a while and saying he'll throw me out, put a lock on my door so I can't use my own house. We're trying to do something about it. Once when he did come earlier, we all got together, abused him, and made sure he went out of the village. But I'm not sure how long that tactic will work.

BAUMANN: Does she feel frightened of him?

MUNNI DEVI: I am scared. I am scared because at least in the daytime I have my children around me, and it's possible they will protect me. But then that's the daytime. But in the night when my children are not around me, I'm more vulnerable, and somebody could just come and do anything.

BAUMANN: What does she think he might do in the night?

MUNNI DEVI: Beat me up, thrash me, what else?

BAUMANN: Given how much she's worked and how little she's been paid, does she still feel she owes him that money?

MUNNI DEVI: I've taken a loan, and I have been working to repay for a while. But I'm not sure how much I've paid. I think I must have paid about half by now, and half might still be due. But then again, that's not taking into account the fact that he may be duping me or cheating me. If that's the case, I'm not sure how much of my loan has been repaid. He forces me to go to work, and I don't know about the accounts.

BAUMANN: When people take out a loan in this way, and they're forced to work under threat . . . does she think that India's laws allow that to happen?

MUNNI DEVI: No, what he's doing is not right. I don't know what the law is, but, no, I don't think it's right.

BAUMANN: How does she feel about that? The wrong that's being done to her?

MUNNI DEVI: I know it's wrong, but I have no choices. Where will I go? What will I do? Even if they beat me and they abuse me, this is my house. This is my home. And this is the only way I can survive because I have no money, so that is all I can do.

BAUMANN: So does she feel like she can't run away? What would happen if she tried to run away?

MUNNI DEVI: How will I run? Where will I run? What will I run toward? I'm here. I spend my whole day here. My family is here. My brother is here. His children are here. My children are here. Why should I run?

BAUMANN: Given that what's happening to her is so wrong, why don't the police do something?

MUNNI DEVI: The police don't listen to us. They only listen to us if you bribe them. We have no money, so we can't bribe them. If we can't bribe them, they can't listen to us. So there's no point in complaining.

BAUMANN: Do her children have to work with her?

MUNNI DEVI: My daughters, they are young. They are about that high respectively [gestures to height]. So they do work with me. But my husband's brother's son, he's about twenty, so he works with me for sure.

BAUMANN: So the younger children do work with her? What do they do? [The translator asks Munni Devi several different questions, trying to ascertain whether the children work.]

MUNNI DEVI: My two daughters are both working in the quarry. My daughter was studying in school until she lost interest and they asked her to work, so she started working in the quarry as well. My son was studying, however, 'Til the contractor or the slave owner came in and asked him to work. That was something he was not keen on doing, so he has run away.

BAUMANN: Does she know where he is?

MUNNI DEVI: He hasn't told me. He's just about run away, so I don't know where he is.

BAUMANN: Is she worried about him?

MUNNI DEVI: I'm worried because I don't know where he is. I have no information about his whereabouts.

BAUMANN: She said her husband's died. How did that happen?

MUNNI DEVI: About eight years ago, he was sick and not keeping well, and therefore he expired.

BAUMANN: Has she heard about other groups that have managed to get their own lease and then work for themselves? Is that something she could ever imagine doing?

MUNNI DEVI: I'm not aware of any other groups such like.

BAUMANN: Does she think her situation ever will change?

[Translator asks several questions before coming to an answer.]

MUNNI DEVI: Sometimes I do think I don't want to work under the contractor anymore. But then I also realize I've taken a loan, and I vowed to repay it. To such time that I can repay my loan, I will have to work under him. And then who knows?

[Munni Devi begins to move away from the camera to a seat with the other women gathered there. The interview stops at this point.]

VIVIANA: When I talk about this now, I am scared. But now my life is better . . . I will come home now. With the help of my last boss. He has a heart, and he wants to organize my papers. . . . I dream so much to go home, I hope that it happens. Deep in my heart . . . I was so weak when I came here.

P

Origin: Albania	*Trafficked in/to*: Belgium
Form of enslavement: Forced sex work	*Current status*: Free

Source: Narrative collected and translated by the Association of Albanian Girls and Women, 2005; reproduced with permission.

Context: See O's narrative in chapter 1 for more context on the narratives gathered by the association.

When I was a senior in high school here in Tirana, I met a boy who did not go to my school. He was kind, attractive, and treated me well. After a time, we fell in love with each other—or so I thought at the time. He was my "first love," and I hadn't had much experience with boys romantically prior to that.

After dating for a time, he convinced me to go to Belgium with him. He said that he could get a good job there and told me about what a wonderful place it was: how clean, how beautiful, and how many opportunities there would be there for us. He proposed to me, and our plan was to leave Albania illegally (since we would not qualify for visas) and get married once he found work there. I was in love, and I believed him.

Once we got to Belgium, however, he totally changed. He became abusive of me and violated me many times. He threatened my life and the lives of my family members. I did not speak the language there and was totally dependent on him; I had nowhere else to go and was afraid. He trafficked me for six months. I don't want to talk anymore about that time. It was the worst period in my life. It is now in my past, and I have closed that door behind me.

I was able to find a shelter there with people to help me return to Albania. I wanted to return to my family here, but my father would not accept me and was abusive of me and my mother. My mother decided to leave my father to help me, even though this is something unheard of in Albania, for a woman to leave her husband. Women here can't really find work to support themselves and have to rely on their fathers or husbands for their livelihood. My mother gave up everything for me, and for this I am grateful.

After living in the shelter for as long as we were allowed, my mother and I are now living together and trying to support ourselves.

JAMES KOFI ANNAN

Origin: Ghana   *Trafficked in/to*: Ghana

Form of enslavement: Forced child labor

Current status: Free, founder of the nonprofit organization Challenging Heights

Source: James Kofi Annan's written personal narrative, "Child Trafficking: The Experience of James Kofi Annan"; reproduced with permission.

Context: James Kofi Annan volunteered to write the story of his life specifically for inclusion in this volume. He is currently in the process of writing a book-length narrative of his experience. His work has been celebrated by organizations and universities around the world.

I'm giving you a very small detail of what it means to be a victim of child trafficking in fishing in Ghana. My aim in sharing this experience in this book is to assist you to make that decision—to resolve to assist in the repair of shattered lives.

One of my greatest challenges is getting people to gain insight into what it means, practically, to be a victim of trafficking. No matter how crafty and skillful a writer or an artist may be, nothing on paper can parallel the experience for its length, intensity, and emotions.

I no longer call myself a victim. I'm a survivor because I have overcome the shackles of impunity, of bondage, and of slavery. I'm now a free person independently living my life. But because of my great insights into what it means to be working under oppression, I am unable to rest—my soul is constantly agitated and troubled to do something, and that explains why after years of lucrative employment I still cannot boast of any personal material benefit I can truly call my own. I continue to trouble my personal sustainability and sometimes look practically ridiculous before people when it comes to light that after five years of such a lucrative employment, rising to become a manager in no less a bank than Barclays Bank, I'm unable to afford to change my 1994 Nissan Primera [for a newer car]!

Well, the truth is that I can afford it, but it gives me no pleasure when I know that that [a] little nine-year-old girl, Esi, is currently being raped in that sunny afternoon in that rugged stone hot savanna bush, and this rapist glees with satisfaction that his continuous desecration of this little girl is what will give him strength for his work! And this heartless man leaves this little girl grimacing in the bush, staggering in pain, and yet her parents are oblivious to what their children go through.

Having this little knowledge, of what patience should I have to try and rescue Esi? So all I have I continuously sink into the repair of lives, assisting victims to regain hope for life, and engaging in [a] rescue effort to prevent other children from becoming victims.

This explains my passion and unrestrained quest to fight child slavery in Ghana. In fact, as I assist other children out of slavery, it becomes a personal healing for myself, too, because all that I saw happen to others and all that happened to me are both reasons to be personally traumatized. I believe I can repair my life if I continue to assist in the repair of other children's lives—a healing balm for myself!

I was initially trafficked from Winneba (my hometown) to Yeji at the age of six. According to sources, I was initially sold for two years for $10. This earned me the ordeal of working in about twenty fishing communities along the Volta Lake, between Yeji and Buipe, which are about eight hours' drive apart. Children trafficked to these areas are aged between four and fifteen years. These children are engaged in fishing day and night in the longest river in Ghana and the largest man-made lake in the world, Lake Volta.

Shelter was usually made of mud, sticks, stones, and thatch, usually located close to the river and the bush. This made our shelters fertile grounds for the breeding of mosquitoes, snakes, scorpions, frogs, worms, and other wild animals. There had been a number of occasions when poisonous snakes and scorpions had lived and lurked in places where I slept. Snake bites and malaria were common, and because of the absence of medical care, a lot of children died as a result.

The river served a multipurpose of being my destination for fishing, my source of drinking water, bathing (directly in it), defecating, all in competition with such animals as cattle and pigs. The river breeds a special kind of worm which lays special kinds of eggs which infect children with bilharzia (schistosomiasis). This disease can be more painful than gonorrhea. Especially when the disease intensity nears a quarter of one's urine coming out as blood, then the blood urine will start clotting, and the affected child will need a louder shout, a harder hit on [the] abdomen, and a tighter squeeze on the genitals before you can pass a small amount of urine. Bilharzia affects nearly every male and about 50 percent of all female fishing-trafficking victims. I do not remember when exactly I contracted that disease, but what

I know is that I never lived without that disease until somewhere in 2003. I was still carrying this disease even while I was in the university, and I got healed of it only about six years ago, sixteen years after my escape!

I worked at several villages along the river, applying different methods of fishing, which demanded high degrees of physical strength and precision. My typical working day started at 3:00 A.M. and ended at 8:00 P.M. from Sunday to Sunday (seven days in the week), with hardly any days off. Children regularly worked without closing for days. In this case, we rested in the canoes on the river, and food would be brought to us via neighboring canoes, and in this case there will be no shelter, and we will be at the mercy of the changing weather (hot and cold) day and night.

My typical day's duties included carting the outboard motors, paddling the canoe, casting the nets, dragging and pulling the net, diving to remove trapped nets (typically about fifteen to twenty yards deep, depending on the location of the day), mending nets, shadowing fishes, removing fishes from nets, fetching firewood from the bush, etc.

Diving is one such dangerous activity undertaken by child slaves. No one taught new entrants how to swim or dive. It is one of the activities which comes as a result of our quest for survival. The older people will throw us into the lake at unexpected times and locations, and you are expected to survive. You will be allowed to gulp water, choke, lose breath before they realize that you are finally drowning; then they will rescue you. This exercise is meant to signal to you that you would need to know how to swim and dive if you wish to survive. If you don't, the next time you are abruptly thrown into the lake, no one will care about the quantities of water you gulp. These simple exercises ended the lives of many children.

Diving is a common activity for all male children. Due to the [tree] stumps left in the wake of the flooding of the lake, cast nets are often trapped. But because the net is more expensive than we the children, instead of pulling the net, which could result in damages to it, we were required to dive into the lake to disentangle them—ages did not really matter. Often due to some technical reasons, children are trapped under the lake by the nets, and some of them die. I saw children die under trapped nets. On several occasions, children died without their remains being recovered from the river after having been trapped by nets. I remember my personal trauma of having been trapped under the river and miraculously finding myself on shore with blood oozing out of my nose, mouth, anus, ears, and skin pores.

Suffering physical and sexual abuse was an accepted part of children's daily work. Whether in the high rivers or at home, older people could hit children with anything in sight: sticks, paddles, clubs, thorny fishes, rope, slaps, blows, etc.

The girls are useful for three typical reasons: as fishmongers, as cooks, and as sex materials. I saw children as young as eight years old being sexually abused, sometimes even in the course of work! It was normal, for instance, for a girl to be raped and get impregnated by older men. [There were] no protection and no law enforcement because of the remoteness and inaccessible nature of the locations.

Typically, children here are either under debt or contracted bondage. They will have to serve a number of years. At the expiration of their bonded periods, their masters will go back to their parents to renegotiate for an extension of the bond. If you are lucky, your master would go with you when he is going to renew the contract on you. This makes the children lack the ability to speak about anything that concerns them. They are given scanty food, no medical care, no school, no freedom and have insufficient rest. Their slavery conditions are worsened by the fact that their working locations are not easily accessible to provide opportunities for escape.

As children, we had no rights, no dignity, and no protection. We had only one, but very "important" aspiration: to grow into adulthood so that we could also abuse other children! The cumulative effects of all these were psychological nightmares, flashes, aggression, and intermittent panics that I went through after my escape.

Due to the diminishing in the stock of fish in the river, there emerged a concept of multiple trafficking, where children were initially trafficked by a particular person, then retrafficked to another person unknown to the original source. This sometimes can go on for a number of times and a number of years, thereby making the tracing of some children quite difficult.

After twenty-one years of uninterrupted freedom, and with all my education, I still shy away psychologically from remembering some of the traumatic experiences of child slavery and child labor—the abuse, the pain, and the impoverishment. This explains my passion toward helping other children out of slavery. I have been there before, and after a good education I know that something urgent needs to be done to help these children recover their lives and hope for a better future. There are still many children in the same situation, suffering similar abuses and enduring the same conditions, and I stand privileged to do something for them.

In my case, no one rescued me. I rescued myself! It had been back and forth, with a lot of battles between my parents, but after several attempts I finally succeeded in escaping from the pain of modern slavery, leaving behind several other children—boys and girls—anguishingly working for the economic gains of older persons.

Briefly, how did I perform so creditably in school, to the extent that I set an unbroken academic record? After I escaped, I enrolled myself into two schools: classroom education and poverty! I faced the challenge of combining looking for food to eat and looking for knowledge for my future. I am grateful that in the end I could do both: I fished and farmed to pay my way into school from basic to the university.

Enrolling in school in class six at age thirteen without even knowing the alphabet was another trying moment. I had to humble myself to learn the alphabet and the numerals and how to spell my own name, from kindergarten and class one, in order to build on. Overall, I came last in our first-term test out of nine children. In the second term, I came seventh out of fifteen children. In the third term, I came sixth in the class of twenty students. This qualified me for a promotion to Junior Secondary School One.

In Junior Secondary School One, I came in seventh out of twenty-five students for the first and second terms, and in the third term I came in first! I topped the class, simple! Since then I came in first in all areas until I sat for my final examinations. When the results were released for the final basic schools certificate, I did not only top the school but set a performance record which is still unbroken (1991–2009). You see the talent that was to have been wasted? You and I can never tell how many more of such talents are being wasted under the greedy economic eyes of traffickers, ably assisted by lack of law enforcement!

I then entered Winneba Secondary School and became one of very few students to qualify for the university. I gained admission to the University of Ghana in 1996 and graduated in 2000. I gained employment with the Barclays Bank of Ghana.

Life kept changing with each passing day after my escape, but it took determination, endurance, hard work, dedication, and humility of heart to get me this far. Though it was CHALLENGING, I am getting to my HEIGHTS steadily. This is the origin of CHALLENGING HEIGHTS:

way to make money quickly. Within two years, I would have a lot of money, so I could come back and build a new home and give a better life to my child.

TODD: Let's talk about Sri Lanka. Why you would have to leave to make this better life? Tell us about the conditions and what life is like.

FERNANDO: Well, at the moment during that time I was so unaware of so many things. I was brought up in this overbearing community that you had to live up to their expectations. So in my family, my father was a hypnotist and a homeopathic doctor. So, because of his title, we got the respect and the standard and the class in our society. So therefore I could not go and be a housemaid or go work in the farm like a laborer—a third-class job.

TODD: Because that would bring shame to your family?

FERNANDO: That would bring more shame to the family. So the only way for me, because I didn't have the college degree at the time, in my rush to grow up I got married without finishing my education. So the only way out was to leave the country. So when I met this agent, when he promised me I could get paid largely and that I would live a good, luxurious life, I thought, "Wow, this is like winning a lottery."

TODD: Boy, you were in for a big surprise, though, when your passport was taken. You were actually even warned by a fellow Sri Lankan not to do this.

FERNANDO: Yes, on the plane to Lebanon. The gentlemen who was sitting next to me—we happened to talk to each other, and then he asked me where I was going. Hesitantly, when I told him, he said, "Why are you going there? Don't you know what's happening to the women who goes there? They were raped; they were killed; they were abused." So he kind of told me, "Go back, turn around, I'll pay for you; when I come back, I will find you a job if that is the reason you are going." But I was already on the plane, and how could I trust a stranger—let alone a man?

TODD: Right, right. Now once you got to Lebanon, you had no more contact with your family. That was cut off. As I mentioned, they took your passport. At that moment, that in itself had to be a terrifying experience.

FERNANDO: Yes, the first sign was when the agent, who was a total stranger, at the airport, when he asked me for the passport, I was hesitant because I was a naive young woman, but I knew I am in a foreign land and this is the only identity I have. I have no friends, no family, and this is the only connection. But you know, the way we grow up, we don't question our elders. So because of that value, I held my tongue. I doubted to question him; I was afraid to question him. So I just, even knowingly, gave the passport, knowing it wasn't right.

TODD: Now, the woman that you worked for kept you prisoner in her apartment. You survived by eating the children's leftovers. She beat you with a brush when she saw you crying. As you read through this book . . . it's just, I mean . . . I can't even imagine the frustration and desperation that you had to be feeling.

FERNANDO: That is correct. I can write a hundred books about what happened and how it happened, but I cannot really explain how it feels when you hit the rock bottom. You are so helpless, you are so desperate. You know there's no going forward, there's no going back. That is when people turn around, and they give in, give up, and become suicidal, or you sell your soul. But somehow it was my luck, I guess, when I hit rock bottom, I somehow managed to find whatever the strength left in me because I had two reasons to live for. One was my son; I knew I cannot give up, I cannot give in, or I cannot be suicidal. The other thing was I believed in God. I believed somehow, if I hold on to that faith, that will come through for me.

TODD: Tell us what a typical day was like. Did this woman treat you this way in front of her children?

FERNANDO: No, no, the children were never home most of the time. She would take them in the morning, and she will return sometime during the day. Those are the times she would beat me, when the children are not home. Sometimes at night, late at night when they had all gone to bed, and that's the time she would come to my room, and she would just say that I had not cleaned something or that the plant is dying or something. She would just find an excuse. She would just touch the wall and say it's dirty, it's not washed. And she would just grab me by the hair or push me to the wall and bang my head on the wall or kick me to the floor or stomp on me or . . . she would hit me with anything she could get her hands on. Anything.

TODD: Now, you carried a note in your pocket that read, "Please help me. I'm in danger," and you never got the opportunity to pass that on. But you were always looking for them. We should mention for people who say, "Why didn't you just leave when she wasn't home?" that she locked you in. You couldn't leave.

FERNANDO: I was locked in, yes. I was on the fourth floor. The whole fourth floor was her home, and there was only one door out. The other out was off the balcony. So when I tried to open the door, the doors were locked. The telephones were locked, so I could not communicate with anybody. So I had the note. Even though it was my desperation that I wrote the note, but I know when you really think about it, in the whole housing complex there is a yard and a few yards away the ground, and then off the ground there is the eight- [or] six-foot wall that surrounds it, and the road is beyond that. So even if I saw somebody down the road, I don't think that piece of paper would reach the road. But I was desperate. I was ready to try anything.

TODD: And so, showing your desperation—you truly were desperate—you decided you were going to jump off of that fourth floor balcony.

FERNANDO: [Pause.] Yes, it was not to kill myself. It was not an act of suicide. That was the only way out of that house because I had tried all of the other possibilities to escape this home. And when I knew, when I finally really realized, that I was going to die, that she was going to kill me in this house, I thought, "Why wait for her to kill me?" So that's when I found the strength and courage, and I realized that we are born with this human spirit that is so strong that can go beyond your human confines. And I held onto that, and I thought, "I will sacrifice my life. I will take that risk, with the hope of living, not to die."

TODD: And you did not die, but you were paralyzed with a broken back and hospitalized for fourteen weeks. And all this time, while you're going through all of the pain and trauma of that, in the back of your mind you don't know if, when you are well, they're going to send you back to this woman.

FERNANDO: Yes, that was the fear. When I came to, when I had a glimpse of this little girl, walking back and forth, and all of a sudden I thought, "Oh my goodness, I am okay, nothing has happened to me, and they have come to take me back." And that's when my body went into a shock, and I was unconscious again because of the fear. Unconsciously, I had screams, saying, "She's going to kill me, she's going to kill me!" And that's how the physical therapist found out that there was something off.

TODD: And you write in the book [about] the whole ordeal of getting through that and getting back to your family, which you did eventually get to do. And so, you've really, obviously . . . you're a survivor, and you've made your way to the United States, and now you're trying to help others. But maybe you can give us an idea of how widespread this problem is in Sri Lanka and around the world. How big of a problem is this?

FERNANDO: This is large. This is the second-largest crime, the trade [criminal trade], in the world. In Sri Lanka, when I went to Sri Lanka last June after twelve years, to visit my family, and I had high hopes; I thought things will be different. But I was so ashamed; I felt so bad because it was during, again, the Beirut war, and it was the month of June. There were seven thousand housemaids returned to Sri Lanka due to the war that was going on. And I had the opportunity to go and meet with some of the victims, and they are ready to go back. In two or three months back [in Sri Lanka], they say they're going to go back [to Lebanon]. And we asked the question why, and I understand why they go back: because when they first went, they borrowed money to pay to the agency, just like I did. So once they were there, their passports were taken away, they were not placed in the right homes, they were abused, some were raped, some were killed. And when they come back empty-handed, with all that trauma inside, and they come back to Sri Lanka—even though the communities now have accepted people going abroad, but when they come back abused, still the stigma continues. They cannot share their stories; they cannot find help or support. At the same time, they are still in debt. So their problem is not solved; no one is there to support them. So what else they can do? They have to turn around and go back. The other main thing is their mentality has not changed. They believe, just like I did for so many years: this is my fault, this is my fate. So if I go through another agency, to another home, things will be different—I'll get lucky.

TODD: And that rarely happens, as you know.

FERNANDO: No, next time she will not come back.

TODD: Now, describe some of the—there is a lot of poverty. And that is why you made the decision to leave your son; it was because you needed to make some money.

FERNANDO: That is the reason, yes.

TODD: And are these mostly women who do this? Or are there men as well?

FERNANDO: Yes, there's men, women, and children—because of the poverty.

TODD: So with this poverty, the promise of work is obviously very hard to resist.

FERNANDO: It is.

TODD: And now these agencies that are, in a sense, scamming because they're giving this loan of money, and I imagine [at] a high interest rate, and you're never ever really going to be able to pay that debt, to catch up with that debt.

FERNANDO: Sometimes they do, but in Sri Lanka, if you want the numbers, we have 18.5 million total population. From that, one million are already living outside of Sri Lanka. Out of that, 80 percent are human-trafficking victims. And at least two hundred bodies return to Sri Lanka every year, according to the reports.

So the thing is the government also encourages these women to take up the jobs. Like when I went to Lebanon, this was done secretly. The women are very shy, and they don't want to tell anyone that they are going abroad to work as maids. But now it has become like a competition. It is not only the poverty that is feeding into this slavery; it is the competition. The next-door [neighbors], they have gone abroad, they came back, they build a home. That's what they see; they don't see the abuse that is hidden inside that house. So they want to compete. So they say okay, I have a chance, I'm going to go, the government is supporting me. So they're going to go. So it's not only the poverty anymore.

TODD: Now, it's hard to imagine this, but as you mention, some of these women come home, and they're not greeted with open arms, as you might expect. They're often punished further by the stigma. Maybe you can explain a little bit about that.

FERNANDO: Yes, like if you see a woman down the street, a little modernly dressed with lipstick on, wearing modern [clothes], and the boys passing by her would make comments on them. "Oh, that's Dubai goods"; that's what they call them—"Dubai goods" or "Middle East goods." So they look down on them. And if they were raped, the husband will not accept the woman. Or if they came home with the children, they have no homes to go to. So they go hidden. Even when I went to speak to these women, they would not tell me the real story. They said, "Everything is fine; I didn't get paid, but they treated me okay." So they never tell you.

TODD: So when you work with the Nivasa Foundation, what you are trying to do is to reach out to these women, especially, and say, "Don't leave your children behind." So what options would they have if they were to stay?

FERNANDO: Well, with my own experience I realized most of these women leave Sri Lanka to support for their children, to give them a better life. This is every mother's dream. So if I give them a solution to that problem, take away that burden, and give them a chance to stay back, give that security to the children, give a safe environment to them because I will take up the responsibility of providing for the children, to educate them. With education you can break the poverty, when you break the poverty . . . also, by not sending the women back to the Middle East or wherever, I am breaking the cycle of slavery. Because the cycle continues—mother goes, come back, and three months later she goes again. Or sends her daughter. So I am putting a stop to that because they have to stay home because I am giving them funds to educate the children. The funds I support the children with . . . the funds will take care of the child's education, medical needs, clothing, and food. And so the time is for the parents to get job skill training, start their own business, and we are also thinking about providing microcredit, so they can start up their own business and make a living.

TODD: Now tell me about starting up this organization, which all sounds great, but I'm thinking this sounds like a lot of money. This sounds like you're going to need a lot of money. You're talking about the population, and this is just one country we're talking about, and there are many countries in which this is an issue.

FERNANDO: Yes, so I thought since I am from Sri Lanka, I have to start slowly, and I thought first my goal was to find one child, support one child. I thought that would mean that I am just replacing my guilt for my child, for one child—that should not work. So I went looking, and there were so many families that need help, that would rather stay home if they can find support, but they would leave if they don't find support. So I thought I would start with ten children. With ten children I will support the funds. I will go around speaking, and I will raise funds, have fund-raising, and somehow raise the money to support ten children. Once I get enough funds, once I have enough sponsors, then I will take another ten and another ten, and it will grow from there.

TODD: So how many are you helping at this point?

FERNANDO: Ten children.

TODD: Ten children right now. You mentioned that you have gone to visit. And you are planning another visit to Sri Lanka this summer. And what is it like when you go back? Tell me what you are feeling when you go back and visit. I know you mentioned you were disappointed.

FERNANDO: Yes, in a sense of . . . when I went back in June, I was very happy to see my parents. But then I felt like I was disconnected; I felt like an alien in my own country because I don't feel any connection to my family, my friends, my nieces—they're all grown and married. That's when I realized the damage I've done to my son because he's a young man now, but when I brought him to Sri Lanka, he has no connection, he has no roots there. He felt so alone, and I felt so hurt. On the other side, also, this rising of slavery, the human trafficking—how people are so ignorant. They don't want to speak about it; they don't want to think about it. All they want to do is compete and just don't listen to you. So that's continuing, and the government is not really doing enough. They say they are doing [something], but it is not enough. One thing I saw different this time was the children are not around. Because in my time I saw children on the streets, working in the streets, working with the families on the farms, going fishing. I did not see any of that. So the law is at least working to do that.

TODD: That was going to be my question. A few years ago you testified before Congress about slavery. Tell me about that testimony and then what actions you feel government leaders need to be taking.

FERNANDO: Well, I testified to the Congress in support of legislation to provide security and protect the victims here because in this country, and anywhere, a victim is hesitant to come forward because of the fear. They would think, "Oh, if I come out, they will deport me." They come here with a dream, just like I went there with a dream. My idea was I thought if you can kind of get the agencies to pay for this, make them accountable when an employee returns home abused or raped or whatever abuse. That's what I told the Congressman Smith that we should look into—that to somehow make these agencies accountable. And he said that that was the first time anybody even thought about it, and he was going to look into that. So far nothing has come out of that, but the legislation was signed last year. And it is in effect. Now the victims here in this country can come out. They will not be deported. They were issued a visa that they can stay, and they have a choice to go back or stay here. They will provide them with support, counseling, and education. Whatever support they need.

TODD: Let me ask you about your talking about victims being reluctant to tell their stories and thinking back to your own story. Surely it's against the law to keep someone prisoner and beat them and starve them as this woman did to you. Was she ever prosecuted for anything?

FERNANDO: No, no. It was back then when my father really told the media, my story went on the papers, and that's what brought more disgrace to the family and to myself. But he did this in order to get the government's support to prosecute this woman. But when my mother went to one of the ministers in Sri Lanka, he shut the door on her. So they [the officials] didn't believe it; it was just my word against hers. From my point of view, I was so scared of this woman. I thought she can find me anywhere, and if I say anything against her, she is going to find me. So I really did not tell the truth. I let the gossips make the news. So the people just believed what they want to believe, and they created many other stories, and I was hesitant to tell the truth. It was after coming here, after so many long hiding years, I decided to come out and tell my story.

TODD: And you told your story, as we mentioned, in your book *In Contempt of Fate*. Let me ask you about that. When you were putting the book together, you had to relive all of that. What was that experience like? It's like going through it all again.

FERNANDO: Yes. It is a past that I tried to hide from. It is a past that I didn't want to think about *or* speak about. I'm surprised that this is exactly what I'm doing now. But when I came here, I somehow found the peace and the freedom, and that gave me a pair of glasses and hearing aids. I, all of a sudden, gained this awareness. I realized it's the way you look at things. Things are different. Also,

I have to say, this country—the compassion, the want, and the freedom in this country gave me the courage. I knew I need to heal my wounds. I realized that I cannot hide from my past. It never works . . . because the pain on my back kept reminding me what I had overcome. And so I thought, as a child I have turned my suffering pain into stories and poems, and when I came here, I was so lonely, it came to a point where that I needed to find peace, I needed to heal my wounds, so I thought I will write them down. So writing the book was just for myself, when it started. But when I started to relive it, I remembered so many things that I tried to forget, and even I have forgotten, and that's where the transformation began. I started to wake up. I realized all the lessons I have learned, the courage I had, and the spirit a human could have.

At the time, I was not aware I was the victim; even then while writing the book, I was not aware of human trafficking or modern-day slavery. I did not think that I was the victim, but looking back, reliving my story, even though it was so painful, I realized that I have something that I can give to other women just like myself. Because there are women being abused all over the world, and I know there are women who are feeling helpless, thinking they have no way out, there's no hope, they have hit rock bottom, they are suicidal, they kill themselves. I thought I can reach out to them, show them they have the power they have in them. That's how it all started. But now it's a different ballgame; I mean that spirit is not enough. You and I have to get together and help them out. Because it is the freedom you are born into, and they deserve that freedom—every human.

TODD: You know I have to say that you talk about the spirit and courage, and I got that sense in reading the book that you had this incredible sense of courage and spirit, and even in the worse conditions, something that just seems to be inside of you—and I know other people have it—but you never let go of that. Even in the most desperate times, where people might normally give up, we never get that sense. We feel the helplessness, but you never give up.

FERNANDO: I think I am a fighter. I think the way I was brought up—the culture, the values that I grew up in—I think have toned me and helped me to survive any battles. Also, I should not forget my dear father, that I didn't mention enough of him. He's the hidden strength in me. He's the only person in my whole life that told me that I can do anything. When the world was against me, he said, "Don't worry about what they say. You do what you think is right. Hold on to your strength and believe in yourself." It took me long years to understand it, but I think that's what kept me strong.

TODD: As far as individuals who want to help, what can the average person do? We talked a little bit about what governments can do. What can the average person do?

FERNANDO: All they can do is awareness; tell each other. If someone hears this today, share this news with another person because you can read books and listen to the news, and you do not believe it. But when you hear from a victim, a survivor, you have to believe it. This is the truth.

8

Becoming an Activist

THE INSPIRING ACTIVISTS WHOSE SPEECHES, interviews, and narratives are collected in this chapter could have been included in any of the previous chapters. Like the other survivors in this collection, they suffered through the degradation of enslavement, through the extraordinary and enduring fear of their slaveholders, through the enormous difficulty of escape, and through the complicated return to freedom. Like the authors in chapter 7, they all found their voices, despite the enormous burden of creating meaning out of such meaningless suffering. They all found a way to articulate their experiences, not simply to heal their own wounds, but to help others who find themselves exploited, degraded, enslaved.

All the contributors to this chapter are survivor activists—people who have come out of their experience, as James Kofi Annan did—to find the power to speak out against the twenty-first century's most embarrassing and appalling crime: modern-day slavery. All of the authors represented here have made a life out of protecting, liberating, and rehabilitating people who have been enslaved and of defending countless others from the prospect of enslavement. They have made it their life work to use their voices to speak for those who remain silenced in our world. They have dedicated their strength, energy, determination, and even their anger to the cause of freeing the world's enslaved people. They have decided that, for them, being a survivor had to mean more than simply survival. Because they are among the lucky few survivors of modern-day slavery who live to tell a tale of freedom, they have dedicated themselves to ensuring that others can do the same.

stories and reclaim their own voices in order to speak out against human trafficking and sex slavery. In October 2009, she received the Fredrick Douglass Award given out by Free the Slaves.

ANYWAR RICKY RICHARD

Origin: Northern Uganda   *Trafficked in/to*: Northern Uganda

Form of enslavement: Conscripted child soldier

Current status: Free, founder of Friends of Orphans, Uganda

Source: Interview conducted for the Free the Slaves' documentary film *Friends of Orphans*, dir. Peggy Callahan (2008); transcription reproduced with permission.

Context: This interview was conducted by Free the Slaves for a video to celebrate the awarding of the 2008 Harriet Tubman Award to Friends of Orphans, Richard's organization. As a result of the awards ceremony video's needs, Richard is asked to repeat himself succinctly several times. The original interview consisted of several hours of footage, so only selections have been included here. Three asterisks indicates where sections have been removed. Peggy Callahan of Free the Slaves is the interviewer. Richard narrates his own story in English, his second language, without a translator.

RICHARD: I'm Anywar Ricky Richard, the founder of Friends of Orphans, based in northern Uganda in Pader District. We work with former child soldiers. I know a lot about former child soldiers because I was one time I was child soldier. I was abducted when I was at the age of fourteen years and forced to fight adults' wars. We work to rehabilitate former child soldiers, reintegrate them, and empower them so that they gain their life back. Our experience with them and my personal experience as a former child soldier is that a child soldier doesn't destroy only the family or the person, but they destroy the whole community.

CALLAHAN: That was fabulous. You did a great job. Tell us how child soldiers destroy an entire community.

RICHARD: A former child soldier, as I said, doesn't only destroy the life of the child, but they destroy the life of the family and the life of the community in that to regain back their normal life, to be useful people, useful citizen, is very difficult. Because they go through a lot of trauma in the bush and the child soldiers, they are made to fight adults' wars. They are made to do things not of their own will. These destroy first of all their emotional feelings about human being. They feel so bad about human being; they feel human being destroyed their life because they did not gain the normal childhood life any other children can experience.

CALLAHAN: Can we back up and you walk us through what happened to you? What happened to you is unimaginable, and I know that you know it happens to many children. It's just most of them don't come out of it the way you did.

RICHARD: Yes, when I was abducted, I was abducted with my elder brother and other three children from this same village where we lived. Then we moved in the bush, and we were tied up with our hands behind us, and one rope was connected to another person, so we were in chain and tied up with our hands behind. We moved for about three days with no food, no water, until the fourth day; that's when they gave us some food and some water we took.

From there we kept moving, and I saw horrible things in the bush. First, I'd never seen this kind of beating which these people could do. Whenever they get you, they'd beat you, they'd kill. I'd never seen that before, so it was horrible for me to see people being killed, people being beaten, especially the women and children. It was really so, so bad for me. I didn't like it, and I saw it as something I never wanted to do, and I never wanted to be in there, but unfortunately we were guarded twenty-four hours by the commanders. We could not escape. There was no way we could escape. So we remained in there. I always tried my best, but if I could get any chance, I would escape. But you couldn't get any chance to escape.

In the night, we undressed and [were] tied up together so that you have no chance of escaping because they believe that in the night maybe somehow, somewhere you could get a way of escaping. They could send us scaring messages every day that if you escape they would kill you in the most horrible way. And they used to do that. We used to see that some of our friends would try, some of the children try to escape, and they're brought back when they're caught, and they kill them.

At one point, I remember they brought some man who had escaped. He escaped like today, then the following day we got him, and he was brought. I saw about fifty people beating him in all parts. And . . . I don't remember what happened next, but somehow, somewhere, someone told them, one of the commanders said, "Please stop, stop," because he was lying [there]. Then he woke up. He got up. And when he got up, the jaw was broken. One of the finger was also broken and was looking weak. They [the commanders] call us together, then they told us, "Uh huh, today you've seen"—that's after only, I think, two days of—yeah, two days when I was abducted, then that happened. And they brought up this man. They didn't tie him; they made him to sit down. Then they call out us around, and they told us, "Okay, you people, you want to escape. I know some of you are planning to escape, and today we are going to show you if you escape what will happen to you."

They brought some boy called Patrick with the *panga* [a large knife] to cut him up. So one of the commander went in front when he [the man] was seated down like this, then pointed a gun at him, [and said] that "look at my eyes straight, and if you dare to run, I will be the one to shoot you. I'm going to kill you." He mentioned his name, then he hollered at Patrick to cut off his neck. So Patrick was fearing, but there was no way. He didn't show, though, that he was fearing, but from the action I saw that he was fearing because when he cut off once, the *panga* went off.

Then there's another person now, one of the commander came and cut him off, then they told us that, "uh huh, have you seen what happened? If you escape, we are going to kill you in that way." What pained me most is that the boy didn't cry. I never heard him crying till he died. And the most horrible thing about it is that the sister was there seeing, and it was so bad; it was so painful.

To me, what I saw is when—because when they cut off the neck from behind, he fell down on his back, then they started cutting the neck, the face, and everywhere. So I was close to my brother. Now they told us, all of us, to cut him, so people started cutting, the recruits. You cut him until they see that you now, you are not fearing to kill, then they tell you that, okay, leave, pass the *panga* to the next person; he cuts like this.

So I was behind my brother, my brother came and cut him, and he was completely chopped up. So one of the commanders said, "Stop. The rest, go." Then unfortunately the next person who followed me behind, they told him, "No, no, no. Now what you do, you move, you walk on him." So people walked on him so that they would get the courage of killing, the courage of doing atrocities. And when we all passed, then they stop us again.

They said, "Uh huh, do you know what happened? We didn't kill this man; it's you people who have killed him. So the spirit of this man will keep coming around whenever you escape, will keep guiding you back until you come back to us because you killed him. That's you. He escaped . . . so now you have also escaped, so you have done the mistake, and you should be killed as well." So that's what they told us about him. We went and slept.

*   *   *

CALLAHAN: I know I'm getting ready to ask you difficult questions, so I apologize in advance. So when you were abducted—well, first we're sitting—you're sitting on the porch of your family's house.

RICHARD: Yeah.

CALLAHAN: And you were abducted right around here, true?

RICHARD: Yes, please.

CALLAHAN: Can you tell us a little bit about that and what happened to your parents?

RICHARD: Yes, what happened is that it was on Friday, the 3rd [of] May, around 3:00 P.M. We heard a gunshot. We were staying at home, in a nearby market, which is about one and a half kilometers away from here. There was some rebel groups who had come to raid the market. I think there were two groups who didn't know themselves that they were around our village.

So one group came first and went and shot in the market; they raided the market. So when we heard that, we were curious, we wanted to find out what happened. Did they kill people? What did they do? So we moved from home with my elder brother and sat just about fifty meters away from home along the road side. Then some friends of ours from the village, other children, also came and joined us.

We were waiting for any possibility of someone had escaped and could come and tell us the story. Then I think it frustrated another group when they heard a gunshot in the market, so they decided to raid our village, and a man came riding a bicycle. He was putting on civilian clothing, and he had a gun boot for the army. So we were contemplating who is this, and he came and stopped and started conversing with us. He was very friendly.

He was just trying to buy time so that other people with guns could come in in a bigger group. So the next thing I saw was a man who was dreaded [gestures to indicate dreadlocked hair], bare chest, and putting on army uniform with gun boots. He came—we were sitting down. He came and started kicking us, and I got scared, and I knew that, oh, today we are being abducted.

So another person came in as well, and they started coming in and all that. So our parents were fifty meters [away] at home. I could see them peeping, looking at what was taking place, what they were doing at us. So as we were abducted, they did not run. I think to them they said, "No, since Ricky and the brother has been abducted, there's no way now. We cannot run."

So they stayed at home here. They were behind, right at this house. So this one [who] was dreaded came in and had was beating people hard and doing all these kind of things. Then at one point they call us in, we came, and what I saw is they were putting them, all of them, my mom, my dad, my sisters, my brothers, and some three people from around the village; they got them from the eastern side. They came with them.

shot cannot get you—you'll not be shot by the bullet. So these are some of the stories they could tell us.

Then on the action side, that is the theory of it. The action side is that when they bring people, when they want to punish people, it's the children to do that. When they're beating people, they want to beat someone, they order you, the children, to beat them up. And when they're killing, it's the children to do that. The commander doesn't kill—it's the children to kill. And when you kill, that's when they tell you, "Uh huh, you've killed, you see, so you have nowhere to go."

And especially when they are abducting you, they make you to kill your brothers or your parents, whatever they see you with, or the relative or the family of village members. So they said, "Oh, Ricky, you see, you are not going to escape because you've killed your own family members, you've killed your village members, and now you have nowhere to go. They will hate you. So you have to remain with us here." So that's what how they indoctrinate the children in their system.

And I think that's why the trauma comes most to the children. Because if the children were to do it, the commanders don't do it, so it's the children. And they get the trauma a lot because of killing, beating, doing their . . . fighting. They're the one taken to the battlefield, and in many cases they are used as [a] seal for the bullet not to touch them [the commanders] because they are far away, and they leave the children to fight.

CALLAHAN: You've said that when you met [Joseph] Kony, that he actually didn't seem like a crazy person. He seemed pretty nice. Can you describe that?

RICHARD: Yeah, Kony himself, when you meet him, you can't believe that is the one doing all this what he's doing. He looks polite. He likes telling stories a lot. He tells you how he lives, where he lived, and he lived in—he told us he lived in Lira Palwo [Uganda], and all this kind of stories. He liked children around him all the time.

But there comes a time when he's possessed with the spirits. He could tell the commanders that, "Okay, well, now civilians are doing this to us, and we are not going to spare them. So go and kill any civilian you have seen." So after thirty minutes he could say, "No, no, no, no, I don't want any killing. Nobody should get killed." But when the commanders had already left, and we had no communication system, so you keep killing until you go back to him. So there was that gap of communication which created a lot of problems and atrocities.

CALLAHAN: Could you tell us where we are and which—not specifically what area, but you know in this part of northern Uganda, in the such and such year war with Kony and the rebels, we think, we guesstimate this many people have been killed, this many people have been displaced, and this many children have been abducted. Can you give us a big picture like that?

RICHARD: We are right now in northern Uganda, where the war has been going on for the last twenty-two years. Two million people have been forced to leave their homes and live in refugees camp. An estimated number of five hundred thousand people have been killed, and twenty-five thousand children have been abducted and to go and work as child soldiers doing a lot of atrocities in the same community they have been home. [Repeats this three times to articulate the numbers clearly.]

CALLAHAN: Tell us basically when child soldiers—children are abducted to be child soldiers—tell us basically what boys do and basically what girls do.

RICHARD: When a child is abducted from his village to go into the bush, basically the boys are used as fighters, and the girls are turn out to be wives to the commander[s]. But at one point all of them are used as carriers for the loads, for the sick, for the wounded, and as cook for the commanders.

That's what they use. And at one point depend, when the longer you stay, the more you are faced with the war directly where they take you to fight on regular basis. But at first when you have just been abducted, you are used to carry loads, carry sick people, carry the wounded people, and cook food, prepare food for the commanders. As they train you, you keep going on through training and all doing all the atrocities and the indoctrination until just a time when they know that you have the courage now; that's when you go directly to fighting.

And there was one thing I wanted to mention now is that the war in northern Uganda, which has taken twenty-two years, is the most unique war around the world. This war has never been fought in any part of the world. Why am I saying this? When we look around the world like what happened in Rwanda, it's different community fighting different communities. What happened in Liberia, it's different communities fighting different communities.

But in northern Uganda it's the same community fighting themselves. That makes the war so unique. How do they fight themselves is hard to explain. When assuming they abduct a child from this family, if the child was made to kill the parents, kill the brothers, kill the sisters. So if any of them is killed, assuming you killing your sister, then the rest of the family members will turn against you now. At war, this is our enemy: "he killed my daughter," "he killed my sister," "he killed my brother." So it's the same community. You will have problems at personal, family, and community level. So it has made a lot of conflicts among the community.

CALLAHAN: Can you go back again and tell me—can you tell us briefly what boys and girls are forced to do when they're abducted?

RICHARD: When the boys and girls are abducted, the girls are used as sex slaves by the commanders and the boys are used to commit atrocities in the community.

CALLAHAN: Thank you for such a short answer. That's amazing. You said yesterday that you could tell that when kids in the bush, when they started enjoying killing, when they had reached that point of no return, that, in fact, they were going to die soon. Can you talk to us about that?

RICHARD: Yeah, what I realized, I noticed from the bush, is that when someone begin [to] have the urge of killing all the time—"Oh I need to kill, I need to kill"—he talks about killing all the times, and he's involved, you see, on a daily basis, is killing, is doing a lot of atrocities in the community . . . I noticed that that person will not last long. Either he's going to die in the next two, three days or one week. It has happened to a lot of kids and a lot of commanders I saw in the bush.

CALLAHAN: Help us understand what happens, and if this is too difficult for you to talk about, just tell me that. But for people who are listening to this for the first time and trying to understand and maybe even parents who don't understand what happened with their child, help us understand what goes through your head and heart when someone is over you saying, "I will kill you if you don't cut this person" or "If you don't shoot this person, I will kill you." What happens inside that allows people to be able to do that?

RICHARD: When you are forced to kill someone, when someone tells you, "Oh, if you don't kill him, I will kill you," what happened first of all you look around and look at your security; that's what happened. Then you decide—they all happen so quick. You decide, Should I do this or I don't? Is there a way I can escape it? Can I escape doing this? Then you look around, if you see when you don't have any way to escape, then you have to do it, because if not you will die. And you also value your life. Do I want to die now, or I don't want to die now? So that's what's happening to your head. That's what you think about.

CALLAHAN: Did you ever have to kill someone close to you?

RICHARD: What I did when I was in the bush is that I made sure that I couldn't kill any person [that] I could see directly that I'm killing someone. I could not do that; I could dodge it. When we were told—when they give us someone to kill, like, "Hey, kill this person," then I could move as if I'm doing it, but I make the children—I could be like at the back of it, I never wanted to do that myself.

And that's what helped me. It's a theory, I think, or a thinking I developed when I was in the bush. When I realized that those who could have the heart of killing all the time, they die soon, then I thought to myself, I prayed to God, I said, "God, I think you shouldn't make me kill anybody when I'm seeing. And with that I will remain, I will leave, I will escape, I will go back home, and I will do all this."

So I made sure that I didn't kill anybody. I didn't participate on the beating, which is to death, to killing. I participated in beating people as a punishment, which they give me to beat and do that kind of things. But for the killing, no. I made sure that I didn't rape any girl, and I made sure that I didn't raid anything off anybody. That way I thought it would help me out, and that's why I managed to come out without any gunshot, not even a scratch, and I fought a lot of battles. I don't know how I managed to come out of this if I can imagine now. I went through sprayed bullets and through gun ship, which could send dense smoke so it could be seen for many miles away bombing us, and I managed to escape these. I feel it's a miracle, I can believe that.

CALLAHAN: Did you make a deal with God? "If I get out of here, I'm going to do something else, I'll be good, I'll . . . "—so did you make—I'm just wondering. I know that I start making deals, even if I don't believe in God; I'll start making deals with God, "Oh God, please . . . "

RICHARD: What happened is I come from a Christian background, and I was going to a Christian school, so when I went to the bush, before, I was like any other child. I didn't have that heart of helping the people. It has never crossed my mind. I was just a child, and that's all. But my experience in the bush started cultivating any thought for children in my life. I started seeing things different, and whenever I could see people suffering, I could say, "Oh God, I think I wish I could help." And those I help and those who I could, I think I helped them. I thought, "No, these people are not doing the right thing." That's how it started. I felt that, no, we need to do something about this. I need to do something about it. And . . . oh, I got lost a bit about . . .

CALLAHAN: Why do you think you . . . well, first off you said, "I never did this, I never did this. . . . It was a miracle." Can you tell us that?

RICHARD: What I was saying is that what happened to me in the bush, like carrying a gun, I can't do it now. And what I went through in the bush is difficult. Life there is like carrying an egg. You know when you carry an egg in your thumb [gestures to hand], anytime you just stand like this, and it's off and you lose it and you never gain it. That's how life is in the bush.

I went through a lot of fighting. I fought many battles, a thousand battles, I think, in the bush. And I went through sprayed bullets. I went through a lot of fighting. I went through gun ship where it could pass through dense smoke which can be seen from far away. We were shot at with gun ship and all that kind of things.

CALLAHAN: But you didn't get hit?

RICHARD: I didn't get hurt. My belief is if I don't do anything on any human being, then nobody could do anything on me as well. That's why I came out without any bullet wound, without a scratch.

I used to believe in that a lot. I couldn't think of raping, killing, and whatever they do. I could see as if they're not doing the right thing, and I could caution even other failed children.

Like one time I sat a child down, and I told him, "Please, you know what? These people have been killing, you see." I gave them example, this one was doing this and this, was doing a lot of killing and is no more, and this and that kind of things. So some . . . the boy was kind of understanding, but I think at times [shakes his head no].

Then we had some conversation with other children, like when I ask him that as I wanted to escape. I knew that at one point I need to leave if I get the chance, so I could not put on their hat. You know when you keep on putting on a hat for a long time, it makes a mark here [gestures around top of head]. So when you come back home, they will know that, "oh, this is a soldier." So I never wanted to do that, to make any mark. Then carrying a gun here [gestures over shoulder], if you carry for a long time will make a mark here. I avoided that.

Then putting on gun boots. When you keep on putting it every day, it makes a mark around the leg [gestures to leg], so I never used to do that because I knew when I escape, and someone sees that will know that, oh, this has been a soldier, and it would bring problems to me. And that's what I could tell, even these other children, that, "please, avoid doing that because you know, at one point, we know we will get a chance of escaping."

And some could tell me, "Oh, Ricky, no, for me I don't want to escape. That's why I've started putting on the things, you know, because I killed my parents, and I'm not going anywhere, I don't have where to go. Oh, they made me to kill one of the village members, so I'm not escaping. I'm staying here now. This is my home."

That's what they could tell me. Some would tell me, "Yes, Ricky, I think I understand, and at one point I know we will do it if God willing."

Then when I was departing with my good friend, he was transferred to the next group. We shook each other's hand. Then he told me that . . . [speaks to himself in Luo] . . . I don't know how to frame this, but you know this baby— you know the baby soul? Do you know the baby soul? Baby soul . . . is this one they carry with the babies.

CALLAHAN: Okay. Yeah?

RICHARD: So he told me in parables that whoever will go back to the baby soul first, go and greet them. Which he meant that if you go home first, go and greet them. Or if I go first, I will tell them you are still alive. So that's the kind of experience they know.

CALLAHAN: What happened to your brother?

RICHARD: My brother came back first from the bush. Then when he escaped, I think he was too traumatized. First, he couldn't cope up with the experience he got. In that one time, he was made to carry a wounded soldier on his back when he was still fresh bleeding, and he died on his back. Then I think seeing our parents being burned down alive and the kind of atrocities he went through—he was forced to kill a lot of people. Then I think he couldn't stay with that, and he committed suicide when he came back. That's the report I got from the village. I didn't see him, though; I saw him last when we were still in the bush.

CALLAHAN: Is he part of your motivating factor to work so much? I mean, you are so dedicated to working with children.

RICHARD: Yeah, I dedicate my work to my parents who died because of me. They had all the opportunities to run away and leave me with the rebels, then they said no. I think in their mind I was so special to them [puts his head down and covers his face with his hands to hide tears]. I think let's leave it for a moment. . . . I need to walk around.

*   *   *

CALLAHAN: Why do you think, you were around so many children, you watched so many children have such a horrible time, what is it about you that allowed you to hold onto your head and your heart in a way that I . . . you clearly didn't come out unscathed. No one could come out unscathed, but you were able to, in the face of atrocity, say, "That's not who I am. That's not what I do." When other people just couldn't hold onto their own humanity, that it was just too horrible for them, what is it about you? Why do you think you somehow were able to do that?

RICHARD: Yes, I think what happened is that I started realizing myself and my role when I was abducted, when I saw a lot of atrocities being done. At one point,

I never accepted it, that that's the right thing to do. And at one point, I never accepted it—[that] this is where I'm supposed to be, this is where I belong, and this is the right thing to do. I knew it clearly that all of what they were doing was wrong, but I didn't have the power by then to stop them.

But at one point, as I got integrated into the system, I got a lot of problems with my thinking, my different thinking about what they're doing. They felt I was disrespectful, and all the time I was in jail, they removed my shirt, they don't give me the gun. I sleep under the cold without any blanket, without anything to cover me. At one point, my friend tipped me that they wanted to kill me, so when I got a chance of getting a gun, I did not release that gun at all.

I saved many people from the bush because I could move in front while I was in abduction, and whenever I see you, I could tip you, "Hey, please come here, run away. I have this group, big group, coming. When they see you, they will kill you."

Then my brother also at one point brought a wrong report, and he was supposed to be killed. So they brought him. There were a few—we were a few group with one of the commander, who was insisting that he [my brother] was supposed to be killed. So I crossed a line [gestures as if to draw a line in the sand]; I said, "My brother, come this way," [and then to commander,] "If you want to kill him, cross here." I opened the ship. And I think they saw from my expression that I was annoyed, and I was ready to kill. Then they left him.

Then I told you a story of how I saved this boy whom I was supposed to beat or kill because he threw away the bag. And all that. And what I could see [I] could create a new faculty for children in my life. I keep thinking about these children; I keep thinking about the suffering, how best if I could help.

So when I came back, I got the chance that I went out of the war zone completed; I was in Central [Uganda]. And I got the chance of going back to school. When I finished, I got a job, but I wasn't satisfied. In my mind, something was telling me, "No, go and help these children. They need your help." So I have to move from the Central and came and live in the IDP [internally displaced persons] camp and started helping the children.

CALLAHAN: So I'm going to ask you . . . I'm going to ask you just to rephrase that for me to make it easier for people. So you went to college, you got a really good job in the government, but still you kept feeling called to do something else. So you came back to where all this horrible stuff had happened to you. You came back to your home to work with refugees and other kids who had been—okay, can you say it kind of like that? If it's true for you, say it like that?

RICHARD: Sorry?

CALLAHAN: If that's true for you, say it like that.

RICHARD: Yeah, that's true; that's what happened in my life. Okay, I begin? Yeah, what happened is that when I finished my college school, I was lucky. I got a job, a good job, with the government of Uganda with [the] minister of education and sports in Kampala in Central Uganda, where it is very peaceful. And I would get good money, but I left the job. I felt I wasn't satisfied with the job. I felt I need to go back and help my people. And I came back to live in the refugees camp, helping children, former abductees who could come back from the bush, and give them support so that they become rehabilitated; they become another child altogether.

Like any other person, most children or most people when they finish school and they get good job, before even getting good job, most people want to move to the city, where they feel their soft life. They want to lead that kind of luxurious life.

But to me, I'm not satisfied with that. My satisfaction is not about the best—about to be known of the best car I'm driving or about the riches or physical riches, how many land titles are in my name, no. I feel more satisfied when I serve people. As the saying goes, if someone see a child dying along the road and kneel down to help that child, he stands more taller than someone who stands and watch that child dying. So I go by that principle.

What drives me most is seeing former child soldiers getting rehabilitated. I feel very happy; I feel very satisfied. And many times when I see the hopeless children who have come back from the bush, they were about to die, and the abduction—they came back, I rehabilitated them. They are very happy people now. I feel more happy about that. And whenever I see them succeed in life, I feel very, very much satisfied. I feel so happy.

CALLAHAN: Yesterday you said to me after, I think, we met your adopted mom, you said to me that after everything that's happened, you still really believe in people. Can . . .

RICHARD: Yeah, you know, as I always put it, that as a child born out of trouble, the trouble came as a result of a human being doing a lot of atrocities in me when I was young. They abducted me; they forced me to do a lot of things I never wanted to do. They made me pass through sprayed bullets, through bombs from the gun ship, which could produce dense smoke which could be seen from many miles away. They made me to sleep under the cold. They made me to stand guard them while they're raping young girls. They made me to see people being killed, which I never wanted to do that.

But that—that does not put me off because it's the same human being that helped me when I came out from abduction. Though I was living in this village as a slave as well, I could dig in return for food. If I don't dig, nobody give me food. But still that inspire me because if they didn't give me food, I would have died anyway, you see. If my second mom didn't help me . . . they're all human beings. I wouldn't be there. So I felt that, yeah, I think human beings are good people, and I need to help them; I need to be with them. So it gives me more love for human being when I think positively, you see. And I always keep thinking positively about human beings.

CALLAHAN: Despite everything you saw?

RICHARD: Despite everything I saw. I said maybe those are the wrong elements, but human being needs to be helped, you see. And that's what I believe in.

CALLAHAN: Could you say that for me again, "despite everything I saw, I still believe in human beings. That's what I believe in."

RICHARD: Yes, despite of everything I saw, I still believe in human being. They're very important to me. I love them and I feel . . . it's . . . that's what I believe in— I'll keep helping human beings.

CALLAHAN: For those of us who don't understand anything about this war here, can you just give us a short answer, if there is one, about why people think that Joseph Kony has been fighting this war for twenty-two years?

RICHARD: Sorry? Say that again.

CALLAHAN: Can you explain what this war that's been going on for twenty-two years, what this war's about?

RICHARD: Yeah, the war in northern Uganda has been going on for the last twenty-two years, and the war is being fought by two parties: the government first and the Lord's Resistance Army. The Lord's Resistance Army want to overtake the government of Uganda. They have mistrust in the government. The government also doesn't want to leave, so they went into war. And it kept on and on until twenty-two years from now it has been going on.

The government of Uganda . . . the Lord's Resistance Army started reinforcing its troop by abducting children from the villages to go and fight the war. And the government, on its part, decided to put people in the IDP camps so that they're protected from abduction. That made the rebel to do a lot of atrocities at home in the villages, like they burned them down, and they set land mines in all the strategic places they think people could come back and . . . like a path, water places, under the trees, the fruits, in the churches, schools, and all that. If people come back, they would get blown up by these land mines. You see?

CALLAHAN: So basically the Lord's Resistance Army starts fighting the government. The government . . . the Lord's Resistance Army needs people to fight the war for them, so they abduct children.

RICHARD: Yeah.

CALLAHAN: The government fights back, but really what happens is the civilians are in the middle and getting hurt by both sides?

RICHARD: Yeah, as the two parties fight, the government and the Lord's Resistance Army, it's the civilian who are caught up in the crossfire, you see, between the two warring parties. So as the saying goes, that if two elephant fights, it is the grass who would suffer the most. So I think it's the civilian who has suffered the most in this war.

CALLAHAN: Anything else you would like to add here about your personal story because later on we'll interview [you] at the vocational center about Friends of Orphans.

RICHARD: Yeah, I think my background has inspired me a lot to do what I'm doing. And I dedicate all the work I'm doing to my family, who are not there now and cannot see what I'm doing physically.

But I believe that somewhere, wherever they are, they are seeing what I'm doing, and they're happy about what I'm doing. That's what I presume. And I believe that this is the only way I can pay them back. I know I owe them a lot. They died because of me, and if I became a wasted human being, in a sense that I couldn't help anybody, then I think there was no meaning for them to die because of me.

They died. They thought I was so important to them. And maybe in their mind they thought that I would be very important to the community. That's how I feel that my background has really motivated me and has inspired me to do what I'm doing right now. And I feel happy about what I'm doing. I get a lot of satisfaction in what I'm doing.

The sad part is that they miss it physically. They will never see it again. But still I believe that wherever they are, they would recommend that I'm doing the right job, and they wouldn't be ashamed of me. I think they would walk with their head up, very happy for what I'm doing. I think that's what . . .

CALLAHAN: So out of something so horrible, something beautiful has come.

RICHARD: Sorry?

CALLAHAN: So out of something so horrible, something beautiful has come.

RICHARD: Yeah. Out of the horrible things which I've gone through, I've created a very beautiful thing for the community. And I will live with that. Many times

I tell people that when I die, I shouldn't be recognized as a hero, but I should be recognized as a servant who has dedicated himself for them. [Wipes tears from eyes.]

I know in the process of serving my community I went through a lot of things as well, as I told you. At one point I headed into an ambush, and I was shot at in the waist, but that has not derailed me from what I'm doing.

I never thought in my mind that, "oh, Ricky, your life is at risk because you're working refugees camp, you're in the battlefield, and maybe one time you will die." I never thought of that, though. Instead, I feel that my personal life is not important in the cause.

But what is important is seeing that people, especially the child soldiers, come out of what they have gone through, their help. Because human beings have to die anyway, but the cause have to continue, and that's what I believe in. And that's what drives me.

SOMALY MAM

Origin: Cambodia   *Trafficked in/to*: Cambodia
Form of enslavement: Forced sex work
Current status: Free, founder of the Somaly Mam Foundation, Cambodia
Source: Christopher Shay, "From Brothel to Boardroom: Interview with Somaly Mam," *Phnom Penh Post*, November 3, 2008; reproduced with permission.
Context: This interview was conducted by Christopher Shay, an American reporter, for the *Phnom Penh Post*. His stories for the *Post* tended to revolve around the pressing social issues that affect the most impoverished people of Cambodia. Mam does not typically like to talk about her experience as a slave, so this interview focuses on the important strides her organization has made in creating an antitrafficking coalition in the region. Mam responded to the questions in English.

SHAY: How do you feel about your newfound fame?
MAM: I'm not famous. We're still AFESIP as normal. I feel normal. I just hope we can change the country, and we can get more people to pay attention to trafficking. People tend to keep talking and don't do enough acting. I'm fed up. I don't think I'm famous, but I'm here letting people know about what's going on in trafficking. People outside the country have to know, too. AFESIP does our work, and we are still small. We try to find solutions. We are a local organization; we cannot find all the solutions. We have to have the political commitment to change.

SHAY: Where does AFESIP get its funding?

MAM: A lot of funds come from the Spanish [government], but also from the [United] States. We have funds from Queen Latifah and Barbara Walters. I was also lucky to meet Susan Sarandon, who helped me a lot.

SHAY: What is your opinion about Cambodia's new anti–sex trafficking law?

MAM: It's complicated. We should have law. The problem is the people who implement the law. When we passed the law, no one understood it. They didn't talk about it to the people. Afterwards, there were people playing with the law—the police—who always manage to find a way to take money. I think we should have the law, but we have to work very strongly on the law enforcement.

SHAY: A few months ago sex workers came together to protest the new antitrafficking law—

MAM: I know that the law is not easy to understand. I know the law is not perfect for protecting the victims. I know that some articles are not clear. What I don't like is people who take the victims—I don't want to call them prostitutes, they're victims—who use them to fight against law. I just want to say to them, "Stop using these girls." They have to make their own decisions. When I saw associations using victims for politics, I wanted to know, "Why do you have to use them to fight?"

SHAY: What's the state of the sex industry in Cambodia right now?

MAM: If you go to the streets, everything is closed down, but they're just closed in front. Underground, we have the problem again. We cannot say that right now is better. In my opinion, it's getting worse and worse. We cannot see them [prostitutes]. We cannot access them to give them condoms or bring them to hospitals. They are afraid of the law.

SHAY: Could you explain how you work together with the government?

MAM: We cannot work without them. It's not easy. Some of them are bad. There is corruption, but some of them are good. Right now, we've identified the people who are working hard, like the Ministry of Women's Affairs and the police. We still have a problem with justice. The problem is the court. We also have some problems with the police in the countryside. They don't understand law enforcement involving victims. In Phnom Penh, it's better now.

SHAY: When police take sex workers into custody, do they bring them to your clinic?

MAM: We work with the antitrafficking police. Yes, they bring them to us. We also work directly with the [Ministry of] Social Affairs. They have a shelter. When they save the girl, they'll call us. We go there and try to talk to the girl and tell them about AFESIP. If they agree to come [with us to the clinic], we bring them.

SHAY: If a sex worker decides to come in the clinic, what happens then?

MAM: If they want, they can come. Some of them, we just say, "You should come visit us." It's not our staff always going to talk to them. The victims themselves come. Sometimes they agree to stay one week, and then they make the decision to go home or stay longer. If they ask us to bring them home, we bring them home.

SHAY: Do all the girls make the decision to stay at AFESIP?

MAM: Not all of them. Some of the victims are young. They are under age. We cannot let them go back into a brothel because they are seven or twelve. They stay because they are children. What I like to see is them becoming children again. They take off their makeup. It's my dream to see them playing and laughing again.

SHAY: How does your organization, AFESIP, do its brothel rescues?

MAM: We are not rescuing. We are cooperating. When we know something, our investigations team tells the trafficking police. They are the best. They can work with us. We cannot go into the street. We work with them. When they have our complaint, they go into the brothel to make sure there is a problem. Then, if someone signs an agreement saying we can go into a brothel to save the girl, then we go in. We are not saving them. We are going with the police.

SHAY: How does your organization determine which women are sex workers and which are sex slaves?

MAM: A lot of them have been raped before they become part of the sex industry. A lot of them, when I go to see them, and I ask, "Why are you in the brothel? Why don't you want to get out?" A lot of them have psychological problems. They agree to sell themselves. They are sex slaves because they have to survive. A lot of them say they are free, but, for me, they are not free. They are the victims of the situation.

SHAY: Are all women in brothels victims?

MAM: Yes. It's really hard when someone comes to me and tells me, "I had more than ten clients who raped me with a plastic bag." I tell them we have AFESIP, but they tell me, "I cannot now." I am surprised at all the girls who do come to AFESIP. Many of the girls, they are destroyed. They have problems because they feel guilty themselves. Give the victims time and try to work with them and prove to them that you really want to help them. You have to have patience.

SHAY: How has your background as a former sex slave affected the way you run AFESIP today?

MAM: I work by my emotions. What I was denied, I want to give to others. I want to give them love and trust. I'm not a manager. I have my team who manages for me. I work by emotions. I just want to take care of the girls. We need both. We have to have heart and patience. I can find money for AFESIP. Normally when you're president, you have to stay in the office, but I hate staying in the office.

SINA VANN

Origin: Vietnam	*Trafficked in/to*: Cambodia
Form of enslavement: Forced sex work	*Current status*: Free

Source: Documentary video interview by Free the Slaves for the Frederick Douglass Award ceremony, 2009; transcription reproduced with permission.

Context: This interview was conducted by Peggy Callahan for Free the Slaves when Sina Vann won the organization's 2009 Fredrick Douglass Award. Vann works for the Somaly Mam Foundation and is the leader of the Voices for Change program there. Vann's work involves training young women to speak out about their experience of enslavement. A translator simultaneously translated her testimony, so many of the questions are directed toward the translator. Some off-camera directions to the translator have been edited out of the transcript. As with the other award videos, Callahan sometimes asks Vann to repeat herself for the sake of the video.

VANN: My name is Vann Sina. This is my Cambodian name, but my original name is Vien Ti Bet. So that was V-a-n-n S-i-n-a was spelled in English, and I don't know how to spell my Vietnamese name.

CALLAHAN: Can you tell us how old she was and what does she do for work?

VANN: I'm twenty-five years old, and I work in the Somaly Mam Foundation. And I'm in the Voice for the Victims. Before coming to work here in Somaly Mam, I worked in AFESIP for six years.

CALLAHAN: What did she do with AFESIP?

VANN: And I work in an outreach project, and I went to brothels. I went to the brothels, and I educated the sex workers about HIV, AIDS, and STDs. And also [as] part of my outreach project, I investigated new girls who came into the brothels. So when we received the information that there are new girls in the brothels, we report it to the investigation specialist, and they come to rescue the girls. I'm very happy with my work here in Somaly Mam. So what I do here at So-maly Mam is I collect all the voices of the victims, and I want to tell the outside world that they—that the sex workers—do not want to do that work. We don't

And the brothel owner threatened me: if I don't go up into the room, I will be killed. I was forced into the room, and I had to sleep on the floor, not even on a bed.

[Crying] I felt very lonely then. I really missed my grandmother, and I really missed everybody there. I realized that I would die there. I don't know what I'm doing there. I was sleeping like a kitten near a table. I got up, and I was very thirsty, and I saw a coconut nearby, and I drank it. After then, I don't know what was going on. And I woke up; I realized that I was in bed. I opened my eyes, and I realized that my life is completely ruined. I opened my eyes; I saw the mattress over me. With blood. All over. I didn't know where the blood came from.

I was hurt. I could not get out of bed easily. I had to crawl out of bed.

I went into the bathroom; I was sitting on the toilet; I was spraying water over me, wondering, what am I doing, what am I doing? What happened to me? Why is there blood all over me? And it was very saddened. I don't know where to go. I don't know what that place is. Surely it's just—I don't have anything to say.

A little bit after that, a customer came in. He slept with me, and he kicked me out of bed.

I knew that this was not my dreamt [of] life, but this is me, my real life. And I was hurt. And I was very hurt then. That's why I understand what it is like for the victims. Because it's really hard, and it's really unbearable.

I was sleeping with a customer; I was kicked out of bed. And the next day I was taken back. The café owner gave me two medicines. After taking the two medicines, I didn't know what happened next.

I woke up again. I was in a police station. My new life started then, and I started to have hope. I was asked by the police, "Where do you want to go?" I told the police, "I want to go to Vietnam." But my hope was destroyed again. . . .

CALLAHAN: How long was she enslaved at the first brothel before the police raid?

VANN: I don't know how long I was there in the first brothel. I know how long I worked in the second brothel. In the first brothel, it was raided by the police; I was rescued. I thought I could go back to my country because the police help people. Instead, the police took me back to the brothel. That made me really feel hopeless. I went back to the brothel, and I worked as a sex worker there.

In a long while after that, I was transferred to another brothel. It's called Thor Kup area. I was doing sex work there for more than a year. The time period of a year is just like my lifetime. My life there was like a life of a dog. I was beaten to eat chilies, and until now I eat a lot of chilies. I was electrocuted. I was detained under a bed, naked. I used to be detained in a dungeon underground. That's my life. This is my life. I was taught how to do that in my childhood.

All the pain really gives me strength to help other victims. In the brothel, I worked nonstop to earn money. Though I was sick and shaking, I had to service customers. If I didn't service customers, I would be detained in the dungeon with my hands tied at the back. It was really hard, really difficult. On my body there is scars.

CALLAHAN: Sina, when you are speaking, can you . . . if it's true, can you say "sex slave" versus "sex worker"? Because "sex worker" sounds like you made a choice. "Sex slave" sounds like you didn't have a choice. And you didn't have a choice. . . . And that's only if it's true for her.

VANN: So the brothel owners are very smart nowadays. They allow the girls to go to hotels and anywhere. And they drug the girls, and after a while they will come back to the brothel owners to get more drugs. After being drugged, they cannot make their own decisions; wherever they go, they need to come back. They have to work to get money to buy drugs, so the brothel owners just give enough to make them get high, and they have to work for money to get drugs. That really puts their lives at risk. They don't care about their health. They do whatever they can to get money to buy drugs. They go with the customers. Some customers even take them to sleep in the bush. They even go with a gang.

If you want more information, tomorrow I can ask the girls—then you will know what is going on in their life.

CALLAHAN: Was she given drugs, and if so, what kinds of drugs did they give?

VANN: I was given drugs in the first brothel. After taking the drugs, I never thought, never cared about my family. The girls that I worked with, they used *yama* [a methamphetamine] and crystal ice, a new kind of drug. And the price range is different, too.

CALLAHAN: Can she describe what is it like in the brothel on a typical day?

VANN: In the first brothel, I could communicate because there were Vietnamese there, and I could eat the food there. In the second brothel, it was like it's us and them. And me kind of separate from them. In the last brothel, I experienced a lot of beatings, a lot of detention, and I was forced to eat chilies. I was not forced to take drugs—it's me myself, I took drugs. I remember every step of it.

There was a demand for me to service twenty to thirty customers if it's on the weekend. If I don't do that up to the standard, I would be forced to eat chilies, and I would be beaten. So every day I would call the customers in, and I would do anything to get the customers. I was scared that I would be beaten. To put it plainly, I'm just like a little bird in their hands. I was very scared of them. I didn't know what to say to them [to get them] to stop beating me. In a day, I could eat only two meals. I would work until dawn and would sleep after that. I was doing that [when I was] thirteen years [old].

[Translator's conversation with Callahan about her timeline interrupts Vann.]

So when I work in AFESIP, I was asked when I was born, and then they did the calculation to see how old I was. Then I knew that I was fifteen, then, when I worked in AFESIP.

CALLAHAN: Now it's complicated. Now we talk about numbers. I thought she came here when she was thirteen. I thought she was free when she was sixteen or seventeen. And I thought she worked for AFESIP and Somaly for seven years. So can you check those things for us?

VANN: So I came to Cambodia when I was thirteen. I worked in AFESIP for six years. And I came into AFESIP when I was fifteen.

CALLAHAN: She went into the [AFESIP] center when she was fifteen, or she started working for them when she was fifteen?

VANN: When I first came into AFESIP, I learned there for about a year . . . about a year or two. And then I started to work in a garment factory. So I worked hard, and I know that I have a love for children. And so Somaly took me back to work in AFESIP.

CALLAHAN: Can you tell us how you came to be free?

VANN: I worked in a brothel for over two years, and my feet never touched the ground. I never imagined that I can stand here. Because every day I would receive punishment. I would service men. I would miss my family. If I wanted to get the sun, I would poke my head out of a little window to get some sun.

In the brothel, I wanted to escape, but I didn't know how to. So the house, the brothel house, was above water, and even in the water they planted sharp spikes. It's not just me that tried to escape; even the [other] girls there tried to escape, too. I had a friend of mine there; we never talked with one another. When it was time to go to bed, we just went to bed. We were not allowed to talk; otherwise we would be beaten. I didn't know that that friend of mine sawed the wooden floor, and she jumped down, and she was caught in the spikes. She was not taken out of the spikes immediately; she was left there for about ten minutes. After, she got taken out of the spikes. They threatened us; they told us, "Look: if not, your life is just like that, too." They took her out.

They didn't take her to the hospital. They locked her in the room. Then every one of us was very scared.

So no one cared about others; we just cared about ourselves. When we heard our name called, we shook. When I was beaten, I was also tied. I was tied in the dark room. Very dark. Could not see anything. And I thought that I was dead back then. My body ached, my hands were tied to the back, and the mosquitoes were swarming around me. I was naked. What I was only thinking about was that I could do anything as long as the brothel owner didn't beat me.

At that time, I would think that "now it's over; it's good now." When I opened my eyes, I think that now my fate comes again. Every day I would tap my pillow so that I would dream about my parents, my grandmother. I really missed them.

Then AFESIP, along with [the Ministry of] Social Affairs, went to rescue us. When they were doing the raid, the brothel owner asked me to jump into the water, but I didn't do that. Because there is a place that we could jump into the water safely, which is in the kitchen. So why would I jump? Why would I go with them, with the police? They would take me back. If I went with them, I would die. If I went with the police, I would die.

So I was rescued, and I was taken to AFESIP. I was asked, "Do you want to go to an organization? Do you want to go to a center?" And I didn't know what an organization or a center is. I answered them, "Wherever you take me, I know that I will end up in the same place."

In fact, I was taken to AFESIP. When I got to AFESIP, I felt scared because I saw a lot of women there. When I got there, there was a Vietnamese staff member there. She took care of me, and she explained to me what they do there. I didn't believe her easily; even the police took me [back] to the brothel, let alone her. And I asked her, "When will you sell me?" And she explained to me that, "no, we're not selling you." She would sleep with me, and she would show me the picture of her children.

Somaly [Mam, the founder of AFESIP,] would explain to me that "we would help you." She would take me to her house. Then I understood that the organization is trying to help us. She showed me the pictures of the Vietnamese girls: where they are from, what province, and things like that. Then I felt like my life was hopeful again

But I still have the bad dreams in my life. Nowadays I have freedom to do whatever I want, to go wherever I want. But my spirit is dead.

My dream was to be a teacher. My dream to be a teacher in childhood ended. And now I have another dream, and I achieve. I realize the dream as a teacher now. And it's a new life.

Though I have freedom to do whatever I want, to go wherever I want, I cannot look at myself in the mirror alone. Even in my room I don't have a full-length mirror because looking at the mirror, I would think about my past life.

Sometimes during the day, when I was sleeping, and I would think that I'm still in the brothel, and waking up, I felt very scared. The first couple of nights, I could not sleep, so the dream was still in me. So I tried to not think about that, but I felt like the dream and me are just together.

All this—this experience in my childhood—is the strength for me. It makes me want to help all the girls out of slavery because I understand what it is like.

CALLAHAN: Can she tell us . . . one of the things I'm most amazed at is that I heard that she wanted to jump in front of a car . . . to do something to commit suicide to get out of that life. But she didn't. She remained so strong. Can she talk about that?

VANN: Because I was hurt very badly, I didn't know what to do. To put it plainly, I didn't know what to do right. I wanted to kill myself, but I know it hurts to kill myself. I wanted to hold my breath to die, but I couldn't. Actually, I wanted to kill myself many times, but the ways to do that are really hurtful. I could not find anywhere to even strangle myself. The plate and the spoon I ate with are plastic. Only the cooking pot is made from iron. Even the kitchen, when everything's finished, the kitchen is locked, and after eating we sleep.

When I was really in difficult times, only cigarettes could help me. [Pointing to her wrist] This is the mark from the cigarette that I burned myself with because I was having a very difficult time, and I didn't know what to do. There is a scar on my head when I was hit with a flashlight. And now even, if I stay in the sun for a long time, I start to have a headache. I don't know what happened to my head. Because I was hit on the head. I was beaten. They didn't get me treatment, but still they detained me. I feel like my head has developed tetanus.

That's why I said that my life has now ended. And I said to myself, this is not Sina from childhood, but a different Sina. This is different Sina, that people have helped me to become who I am, and I will pay them back. And the people who have hurt me, I wanted to destroy them. I wanted them to stop what they're doing now, and according to the religious teaching, it's sin. Doing that is just like killing. Just like I said, the old Sina was dead. And this is a new Sina, and I will help those whom the brothel owner is trying to kill.

CALLAHAN: Has she ever seen any of the people who hurt her? Because she does a lot of work in the same community, has she ever seen any of those people?

VANN: No, and I want to see them. When I see them, I will give them a good gift. Because they gave me a good gift, and I want to return the good gift to them. I tried to look for them, but I don't know if I have a chance to see them. And I want to say thanks to them for helping me to be who I am now. And I want to help those people who they are trying to kill.

CALLAHAN: One of the things she says is [that] even in freedom she wants to remember every single thing from the day she was enslaved. Why is it important to remember every single thing from her enslavement?

VANN: It doesn't mean that I try to remember. I try to forget, but it never goes away from me.

Though there are good things happening to me now, but they don't equal to the things that happened to me in the past. I really try hard to forget. I met with a lot of people to get help from them, but that could not help me. Whenever I tried to forget, I still remember.

CALLAHAN: How do most girls in brothels who are sex slaves in Cambodia—how do most of them get trapped or become sex slaves? . . . She told us how she came from Vietnam, but she has worked in this field a long time. So how do most girls get fooled or trapped into sex slavery?

VANN: When I was in the brothel, I saw the girls coming to the brothel, and I didn't know where they came from because I never got to talk to them. Looks like a lot of them like their work in Cambodia. So in Cambodia the tradition is really embedded strongly in the people. They will do whatever they can to help their parents. Because of poverty, because of divorce, because of domestic violence, the girls have no choice but to enter into sex work.

Even some girls are forced to work in garment factories by their parents, and the first salary they get is only $45. They have to work another year to get $50. And that does not include the rent and daily expense. They have to work to send money to their parents. If they cannot do that, they do whatever they can. They will get a boyfriend. They will work extra hours to get money. So they do whatever they can to get money to their parents because they love their parents. That can cause them to fall into sex work without knowing. Some fall into the trick to work in brothels. Just like some are trafficked from Vietnam, are tricked to work in sex work. So there is a lot of human trafficking happening in Cambodia, and a lot are forced to work in sex work.

CALLAHAN: Is it sex work or sex slavery? There's a difference. I just have to be clear for what I am reporting.

VANN: So the sex work . . . it's twofold. One is sex slavery—they are forced; they are tricked into it. And sex work is what they do when they have problems in their life. And their life is ruined, and they have no other options. If, even when they think of going to work in garment factories, they have to bribe [someone] in order to get the job.

[Conversation between translator and Callahan on the difference between the two. The tape cuts off.]

CALLAHAN: [Continuing.] You said that you were electrocuted. What do you mean by that?

VANN: So it means that I would be soaked with water; they would splash water all over me. They would put the electricity on a very long stick, and they would electrocute me. They would tie my hands and tie my feet, and they would splash water over me, and they would shock me. [Pointing to her forearm] So this is the scar from the shock. Because I was trying to protect myself, and I was shocked by the electricity, and it burned. So when I was shocked, and I felt like my spirit just left me and didn't know what happened.

The life in the brothel is like the life of a dog in a house. In this life, I experience enough of it now. Actually more than enough.

CALLAHAN: The women who were freed when you were freed—what has happened to them?

VANN: Some of them went back to their hometown, and some have died. They have died of AIDS.

CALLAHAN: Your friend who you came here with—Giang—have you ever seen her again?

VANN: I tried to look for her in different provinces, but I didn't see her. I would try to look for her again. I met with her mother, and I asked her if she sees Giang. She said no, she hasn't seen Giang. I don't know if she has arrived home or not this year because her family has moved from their original place, but I will try to look for her again.

CALLAHAN: Have you ever seen your grandma? I know you used to think about your grandma when you were in this horrible place. Have you ever seen her again?

VANN: I met with her after I left the brothel. Up until now, she has been dead for three years.

CALLAHAN: The customers at the brothels where she was enslaved, who were the customers?

VANN: There are two brothels. In the first brothel, there were a lot of foreign men. There were no Cambodian men. The second brothel there was a mix of customers. I don't know what nationalities they were, but there were a lot of good men going there.

CALLAHAN: What was the very worst thing about being a slave in the brothels, and what is the very best thing about her life now?

VANN: So talking about the worst. It's really, really bad for the life in the brothel. And usually for Asian women, we are shy. But for sex workers, they are not shy—they can sleep with whoever they want to, as long as they get money. So it's really bad for the life in a brothel, and it cannot be forgotten. So coming to the [AFESIP] center is the start of my new life. I am able to stand to speak in the society. As you can see now I can stand, I can speak up, I can advocate for other girls. What I am very happy about is that I can stand up for other girls. I can tell others that they don't want to do that, to do that kind of work, but there are many things that force them to do that. I want to speak to the customers that go to the brothels: "Don't look at their smile, but look into their eyes. Though there is a smile on their face, but look at their eyes."

CALLAHAN: Does she ever talk to the customers? Or brothel owners?

VANN: I talk with the Vietnamese customers, but not very much because the wall [at the brothel] is not very thick. I asked my customers to help me to escape, but when I was finished and I came out, I was beaten because they [the pimps] eavesdropped. Because there is a lot of abuse and violence in the brothel, they would eavesdrop on us, and if they hear anything, they would beat us. I told the customers that I was sold to the place, but they didn't believe me. They even told me, "How can it be? Look at you, you look happy." They didn't believe me. They looked at me, saw my smile; they thought that I decided to do that.

And I could not ask for a day off when I feel sick. Even an hour, when I ask the brothel owner that I was not feeling well, and I remember that it was only the first time I asked for an hour off. And when I asked—I didn't get to rest at all. I didn't get any rest. I got the beatings instead. That made me not want to ask them again. The only time that I could rest was when I was beaten and put in a dungeon. And the time that I got to rest was when I finished my work from 5:00 p.m. to 5:00 a.m. And that was my rest time.

CALLAHAN: You used to ask the pillow fairy to see your grandmother. What do you ask the pillow fairy for now?

VANN: If I miss my grandmother, I would tap the pillow, and I would turn it over, and I hoped that I could dream of my grandmother. My grandmother used to tell me that when I want to have good dreams, I would tap the pillow, and then I would have good dreams. Or if I want to see somebody I missed in the dream, I would tap and think about that person. I miss my grandmother the most.

CALLAHAN: What is the most important thing she does for survivors now? The women she helps and works with.

VANN: So I help to rescue the girls from the provinces. Looking at my life in the brothel, if I would have been rescued earlier, I would have helped more. My work nowadays is very good and very important. I help a lot of people . . . AIDS patients. And if I see the victims, I would report to the police. My work nowadays is I can help worldwide because it is not [only] Cambodia that has fallen victim.

But I want to say that victims have hurt, too. No matter where they are, no matter what country they're in, they all have pain. What I want to say to them is for them to move on, to go forward. I'm very happy with our work. I know the voice for the victims is getting stronger.

People will understand more about victims.

CALLAHAN: You once said that no matter how hard it gets, that you won't hesitate. Why is that?

VANN: Just like I said earlier, the previous Sina has died. This is a different Sina; the brothel owner has shaped me. My childhood dream has been destroyed. There is only hurt and revenge.

My hurt has become [the] strength for me to help others to not fall victims like me. Up until now I cannot forget my past. No matter how far I go, it cannot be separated from me. So that is something that I can get advantage of to help others. When I help a victim, I feel very happy.

I'm very happy that they are free. I'm very happy that I have destroyed the work of those people.

CALLAHAN: What does winning this [Frederick Douglass] Award mean to her?

VANN: I never thought that I would get the award. I'm very happy that the world was supportive of the victims. And the award for me is not my money, but it is their money. It is the money that comes from their hurt. I won't get the money myself. I will use the money to help them. I have plans to do that. Just like I mentioned earlier, some of the victims have started a new life. They go back to their home town, they do business, but they might have some problems in their families. So I have plans, and one of them is to help strengthen families. Because the girls work alone to support their family. They will fail. So I need to help them. We need to help their families so that they can stand stronger in the society.

So the second plan is for the victim group. So I want to help them to learn Khmer, English, and computer, and especially for the speaking. And they also need to learn about the law very clearly to help them when they speak. So one of my plans is also to help victims who don't have a goal in their life. So in our center, some of the victims don't have a goal in their life, don't have a family, and they don't know where to go. They finish their studies; they don't know where to go. And some of the victims in the victim group know how to cook. They can cook very well, but they don't know who to cook for.

Another idea is to open a fruit shop and to help the victims who don't have a plan in their life. And the income will be used to help them. The plan is to help the victims who don't have a goal, who don't know where to go.

Another plan is for me and for other victims. Why do I say this? Because when I go into the brothels, I see AIDS people. When they get the disease, they cannot earn money, [and] they get kicked out. I take them to the centers that take care of AIDS patients. In our center, we don't have money to help the AIDS patients. I always spend my own money for them. Since I have the money now, I will save some to help them because I know that the AIDS patients are very hungry. They didn't get to eat enough when they were in the brothels. When they got the disease, they got kicked out. They didn't get to eat enough. They got beaten. They got the disease. They got kicked out of the brothel. Looks like their life is just for torture and punishment. As a former sex worker, I would like to help them with the money until their last breath. Now we cannot do anything else to help but to get them food and to sleep well.

These are my plans. I don't know if I have enough money for that; if it's not enough, we'll ask for more from Somaly. [Smiles.] I would not keep even a hundred real for myself. Because I experienced poverty in my family and even now, it doesn't mean that I have more than enough. But I understand that the victims really are in need. I know that I'm okay right now, and I know that it's really, really hard for them.

CALLAHAN: You said that you love children. Do you think that you will ever meet someone and have a family?

VANN: No. I never thought about that. I know that there are a lot of good men, and there are some bad men. But through my work going to the brothels, that doesn't make me think about getting married. Only after I came to work at AF-ESIP, I started to talk with men, but when I was in the brothel, when I saw them, I would stare at them, I would not talk with them.

CALLAHAN: What does she hope and dream and pray for now?

VANN: My dream is that I hope that there will be no more victims. I hope that the world will understand more about victims. My dream is to see that there will be no victim in Cambodia and other countries. This is my biggest dream.

CALLAHAN: Anything else she'd like to say? God knows I didn't cover . . .

VANN: I would like to thank the people who have helped me so far, even to the point of getting the award, and I would not disappoint you. And I will take what you give me, your love and your mercy, and give it to others. I will tell them that there are a lot of people who are supporting them. I will tell them that "this is the money I get from the people who love me, who show me mercy, and I will use the money to help you." Thank you very much.

[Interview continued several days later.]

CALLAHAN: Sina, one thing you said to us was that your heart had four compartments. Can you talk to us about how you share those compartments of your heart. Can you tell us that again?

VANN: Everyone has four compartments in their heart. And two we can open up and share to others, and another one we can share with our families. And the other compartment is a secret place that I myself don't know how to get into that and to share out of that compartment.

CALLAHAN: So what she said the other night was that in one of those, the private compartment, there were no words to describe that. So can you . . . so she was describing the other day that there are some places in her heart that she cannot even find the words . . .

VANN: So I tried as much as I can, but I don't know how to get people to understand that in that one private compartment . . . because it's really hard to get into that compartment and to really make people understand. Just like I said, we all get hurt, and we all have different hurts and different depths of hurt. So some people, they get hurt in their heart, and they can get healed, but another type of hurt cannot get healed.

If we get hurt over the loss of our family or relatives, then we can get over it in a few years, but then the hurt's inside of us; there are scars in there and cannot get healed.

Just like the girl we met earlier; she was sharing with us—though on the outside she looked happy, but on the inside there is much more going on that she cannot find words to describe what's inside of her. I understood that she was feeling very hurt when she was sharing, and that's why I asked her to stop.

CALLAHAN: One of the things she said to us the other day was in the brothels, the brothel owners get the money, and the girls get debt. Can she say that to us again because we weren't rolling tape?

VANN: So the girls get trafficked into the brothels, and they get to use drugs, and every time they get drugs, they have to pay for the drugs. And everything is recorded in her debt: accommodation, food, electricity, and water. And for a set of clothes, it's double [the] price. And finally what they have left is the disease and nothing else.

That's why the brothel owners get all the money, and then the sex workers get all the debt. And no matter how long they work, they cannot pay off the debt.

CALLAHAN: One of the things she talked at length about the other day was vengeance. And anger. That it fuels her. Vengeance and anger keep her going. What happens if that vengeance and anger ever go away?

VANN: I think that is impossible. That anger and vengeance cannot go away until I [have] died and get reborn because the scars are inside of me and the hurt in me, so it can never go away. I'm not Sina as before. I'm a different Sina now. One Sina: Vietnamese and Cambodian.

I'm the product of the people's anger and punishment. My childhood experience, all the beatings and the torture and the punishment, and I believe they will never go away from me.

If I can just get rid of it, it will be ridden from me, but I cannot. So there will never be a day that it will go away from me.

CALLAHAN: What are you angriest about?

VANN: What I am angriest about is why the world is full of a lot of evil people. Why good people die early and why a lot of evil people live longer. So I don't know if there are angels in this world, good spirits, or not. Because evil people, wicked people, get richer, and the good people they try their best to earn money, and they never get better.

CALLAHAN: Talk to us about Voices of Change. Why Voices of Change is important.

VANN: We understand that some sex workers don't have their voice. They cannot express their voice. So the Voices for Change can be the voice for the victims that can be expressed throughout the world. And we want to do that to tell the world about us, about what we experienced and about other victims.

And we share our experience, the experience of trafficking, so that people are aware and know what's going on. For me, personally, I think the Voices for

Change is very important. It can be a voice to the government so that they can do something to help the victims in time.

Also, internationally, they hear the voice, and they come to help. Only the victims know what their real needs are, and the first step is to show them compassion, and they do need warmth and love because they lack love and warmth in their life.

CALLAHAN: What do you hope and dream and pray for all the women you're helping?

VANN: So my hope for them is to see them stand on their own and to help to have a family themselves and also to help other victims.

So what we want to see is that the victims can stand on their own, that they can survive, that they can stand in the society. And my hope is that the voices of the victims are heard worldwide. My hope is that the world will support them. They will support the victims, not just in Cambodia, but everywhere in the world. So we are *former* victims. So please help us, and without you there's nobody to help us.

CALLAHAN: I have a feeling that as long as she's living and breathing, everybody in the world is gonna hear about this.

VANN: [In English] Yeah! Thank you.

CALLAHAN: Anything else you'd like to say? And then we can look at the tape from the other night so she can talk us through it.

VANN: [In English] Yeah. I have. [Translation begins again.] I really thank you for the award, for me and for other victims. I never expected that. So my work is out of my desire, my satisfaction, out of my heart. I never expected an award or a medal, but I do my work out of my heart. But I am very happy to receive the award and also to help the victims. So we want to say that we won't disappoint you, and we will carry on. And I want to share my experience and also to get support and to tell others that people are helping us.

Thank you very much. I'm very happy. When I go to the provinces, I will tell them that our people love you and don't worry. I have a lot of love in me, and I will share that with you. Thank you.

9

Case Study

COALITION AGAINST SLAVERY AND TRAFFICKING,
SURVIVOR ADVISORY CAUCUS

WHEN THE CALL FOR CONTRIBUTORS went out to inquire whether survivors of human trafficking might be interested in including their stories in this collection, people responded with narratives they had written for their visa applications or with testimonies they had given to Congress or to nonprofit groups. Others wrote their stories for the first time in order to be able to have their life experiences included in this volume. Several nonprofit organizations and journalists contributed the narratives and interviews they had collected with the permission of the survivors they had interviewed. The Coalition Against Slavery and Trafficking Los Angeles (CAST LA) suggested that its Survivor Advisory Caucus might be interested in participating.

CAST LA was founded in 1998 in the wake of the infamous El Monte, California, sweatshop case in which seventy-two Thai garment workers were held in debt bondage and forced to work up to fifteen hours a day for almost eight years. Since then, CAST LA has been fighting modern-day slavery through a threefold approach: advocacy, outreach, and client services. It builds coalitions among organizations and service providers advocating against slavery, creates training programs for law enforcement officers and other service providers who come into contact with victims of human trafficking, and provides rehabilitation services for survivors of modern-day slavery.

CAST LA is a model for understanding the rehabilitative strategies that are necessary in abolitionist work. The people who turn to CAST LA for help after they have escaped enslavement are provided with the shelter they need, psychological and physical health care, job and life skills training, and a support network of other survivors. These services are integral to helping survivors of modern-day slavery avoid the vicious cycle of enslavement that often results from being part of an extraordinarily vulnerable pool of immigrant laborers in the United States. CAST LA's program is a model service provider whose philosophy is built around a unique survivor-centered approach, through which the survivors who utilize their services also are eventually involved in directing the organization in its mission, goals, and programming.

Despite their enormous successes, it was clear to the staff at CAST LA that even though survivors had liberated themselves from slavery, learned to negotiate life in America as free adults, managed to find legitimate work and a visa or green card, and even addressed members of Congress to fight for their rights, many of them, even those who worked with CAST, continued to be vulnerable to rights abuses and had to seek a way to make meaning out of their experiences of being enslaved. In response, CAST LA instituted its Survivor Advisory Caucus in 2003. The caucus is a survivor-led group that is a "one of a kind leadership program" in which "members of the Caucus organize to speak publicly on behalf of all survivors of trafficking."[1] The caucus was conceived as a leadership development and empowerment program for survivors of all forms of modern slavery who had successfully completed their rehabilitation with CAST and had graduated from their social services program. The diverse caucus members are asked to help set strategic goals for the larger organization. With their help, CAST is able to know, for instance, precisely what legislation is most needed by survivors and what kinds of awareness programs might most readily reach people who are enslaved. Caucus members aid new clients who have turned to CAST for help and act as informal mentors for those who are working through the rehabilitation programs. They hold workshops regarding workers' rights, self-defense, and healthy relationships. Caucus members also advise CAST in how to provide effective rehabilitation services. Through working directly with the survivors, CAST learns what programs are most effective in aiding survivors in the transition to their life as American citizens.

The Survivor Advisory Caucus has had enormous success since its inception. In 2008, its members went to Sacramento on Immigrant Day to advocate for better policies for trafficking survivors. That same year they met with

California's First Lady, Maria Shriver, and participated in the annual Border Governors conference, where they discussed the issue of human trafficking and recommended policies to the governors. They organized a petition and letter-writing campaign to influence the passage of the Trafficking Victim Protection Reauthorization Act of 2008 and the publication of green card regulations. Green card regulations are a critical issue for the caucus because survivors of human trafficking are left in an ambiguous situation in terms of their status in the United States when their visas expire, and, as a result, they can be denied employment and are unable to visit their families in other countries. The work that caucus members have done to insist upon transparent regulations and expedited services will likely help thousands of survivors like themselves. In 2011, the caucus initiated the National Survivor Network, which hosts and leads conference calls and retreats that "bring together a community of survivors of human trafficking, by creating a platform for survivor-led advocacy, peer-to-peer mentorship, and empowerment that embraces all survivors, regardless of gender, age, nationality, or type of trafficking experience."[2] The caucus uses these collaborative events to create working documents that provide recommendations for service providers as well as for media, government, and law enforcement personnel who interact with survivors. Its program is constantly expanding to meet the new needs and interests of the survivors in its network.

The caucus has also participated in the Los Angeles Marathon for the past several years. The marathon reminds these survivors of the power and freedom they personally possess and provides them an opportunity to raise awareness about their cause and money for their programming. Running or walking in the marathon symbolizes for them the strength they have gained since liberation and the power they have to make change in the world.

Caucus members have become increasingly interested in advocating for abolitionism by telling their own stories, thereby turning their experiences of slavery into a powerfully liberatory weapon against slavery. Thus, in the past couple of years, they have made it one of their top priorities to work on their public-speaking, advocacy, and media skills. They decided to have a retreat dedicated to storytelling in the summer of 2009, which would help prepare them for media interviews and other public appearances. This book provided them the opportunity to practice telling their stories and to have a venue through which to have their stories accessible to people who want to know more about modern-day slavery.

The members of the caucus were asked to contribute their stories to this collection, but no direction was given to them about precisely what they should produce. They decided that they did not want to produce individual written testimonies. Instead, they decided to interview one another in order to demonstrate their leadership skills and to show that through support and training the victims of trafficking can transform themselves into powerful agents of change. The interviews are a collective effort—sometimes up to four people are speaking in the same interview. These collective narratives reveal how much the survivors have helped one another in the process of learning how to recover from the suffering inflicted upon them in slavery. They are clear evidence of how crucial a social support system is to freedom.

All of the women who tell their stories in this chapter were enslaved because they thought the United States would provide them with the opportunity for legitimate paid work that would help them support their vulnerable families back home. They all were deceived into situations of forced labor but were lucky and brave enough to escape their enslavement. Like so many of the other activists included in this book, the women in CAST LA's Survivor Advisory Caucus find it difficult to tell their stories. As Kanthi says, "It wasn't easy to talk about our stories over and over. Even if we don't talk about it, it is still there, but when we talk, it is very emotional. But still, we need to do it. It was worth it." It is worth it because, as she says, "I fought for my freedom. So now I want to fight for other people's freedom, too."

The women who speak in this chapter are willing to tell their stories because they know how relieved they were to meet people who had suffered as they had but who were also working to ensure that others might not suffer in the future. They know how crucial it is to a survivor to know that what she is claiming has happened to her is not going to be ignored or misunderstood and to know of people like herself who survived, who are free, who are on their way to citizenship in the United States, and who have managed to speak out and make real change in the world.

CAST members feel empowered to decide their own futures, to speak, to lobby legislatures, to protect each other, and to reach out to others who are enslaved. They consistently speak of their own power to change the situation for immigrant workers coming to the United States—a situation that they felt held them captive just a few years earlier. Through their interviews, we learn that these survivors are ambitious and recognize the importance of the work they are doing. They suggested in their interviews that they wanted to meet the president—and in 2012 Ima was held up as an example of a survivor of slavery in President Barack Obama's speech at the Clinton Global Initiative meetings in New York City, where she was able to meet him in person. The Survivor Advisory Caucus also decided during the interviews that they want to go on *Oprah*. These are not the naive goals of star-struck fans. They are the ambitions of savvy survivors who understand the importance of public awareness and recognize the most successful avenues for raising awareness in this country. We hope that Oprah will respond as Obama has.

WATI

Origin: Indonesia	*Trafficked in/to*: Singapore and Los Angeles
Form of enslavement: Forced domestic labor	*Current status*: Free

Source: CAST survivor-to-survivor interview in English, 2009; reproduced with permission.

WATI: My name is Wati, and I am from Indonesia.

KANTHI: And how did you come to the United States?

WATI: My boss brought me come to the United States from Singapore. First, I work for my boss in Indonesia, then they bring me to Singapore, then they bring me to U.S.

KANTHI: How much did you get paid?

WATI: They promise me at first 2,500 rupiah . . . Indonesia money.

KANTHI: How much U.S. dollar is that?

WATI: I think it like $10, something like that.

KANTHI: And how often did they pay you?

WATI: They never paid me one penny . . .

KANTHI: And how long you was with them?

WATI: They locked me up for seventeen years. From 1983 until December 2000, when I escaped.

KANTHI: And you were never paid in seventeen years?

WATI: Never.

KANTHI: Did you go out?

WATI: No, I didn't; they never let me out. In Singapore, yes, I could go out with the driver. The driver took me to the doctor.

me, and the lady point at me. Then the policeman on the motorcycle came and talked to me. He asked, "What is your name? What happened? Where are you from?" All I could say is, "I hungry." I didn't have any food to eat. He asked me "Where you live?" I point to the house said over there . . . behind the wall. "You jump from there?" he ask me. "Yes."

And then he ask me if I wanted to go back inside, and I said, "No, no, no!" Then three more police came, with a car and ambulance. I'm not scared, but I was cold. Then two police came and ask me if I was hungry. And I said, "Yes!" And they went to the car, and they both gave me their lunch. That is so nice. Gave me fruit and drink, and they say, "Okay, you eat first, then we talk." I just sat there eating, and then afterward they say, "Tell me." I said my boss lock me inside the house for many weeks and left me alone. The boss's son came by once, but he say that he did not have time to bring food for me. They ask me where my boss was, but I didn't want to tell them the truth because I did not want them to make me go back to them because I would be dead. Usually I have the phone number and address of all of their houses in San Marino, San Gabriel, La Canada, but I did not want to give them to the police, so I said I did not know. They asked me what I needed, and I said, "Please take me to immigration Indonesia." They asked, "Do you have money? I will call a taxi for you." I said "No, I don't have any money. They not pay me." "Okay," they said, "you stay here and let us talk." So the three people just talking, talking and talking. I thought, "Why they no do anything?" [Laughs.]

So they took me to the payphone, and they talked to somebody on the phone. They took me to the police station and told me to stay there to wait for someone will coming from my country, and they will speak my language. They gave me some towels and showed me to the bathroom, but I didn't have a chance to go to the bathroom because the people from the Indonesian consulate came. I was so skinny—I'm like a grandma, so skinny. I have a little hair, but long . . .

KANTHI: I remember you then . . .

WATI: Yes, because you were there when I first came over . . . I met you the first day.

KANTHI: With a CAST social worker, me and some others went to see her. Then we meet her, and we talk to her; she was really skinny, and I remember that she didn't know how to wear the shoes! [Laughs.]

WATI: Because in my life I have never worn shoes! The CAST social worker gave me boots and want me to use, but I've never used shoes. They were like high-heeled boots, and I couldn't walk in them!

KANTHI: For me, it was good to see Wati because I didn't know that something like that could happen to other people. Everything was new to me. And I hadn't spoken to anyone outside of the family that I worked for, so for me it was a good support to have other people who went through what I went through, but that were now okay . . . that even though I have a difficult time, that I will be okay.

WATI: We have been helping each other from the beginning.

KANTHI: We learned everything together: how to take a bus, how to go to the store. We didn't know anything: how to make a phone call, how to use the payphone. The first time I took a bus, a lady from the shelter asked if I wanted her to teach me to take the bus, and I asked my CAST case manger if it was okay. For two years, everything I did, I would call her to ask for permission. Because before, I was a little girl with my parents, then when I was with my employer—they forced me to do what they wanted me to do, not what I wanted. So I was thinking that I would have to tell everything to my case manager. She would tell me, "U.K., you can make your own decisions! You have to learn to do it!"

WATI: "Where do I put the money?" [Laughs. Then, she asks Kanthi,] Did you speak English before you came to the U.S.?

KANTHI: No, I didn't. I didn't know any English.

WATI: So you learned from here?

KANTHI: Yes. I learned from here, from ESL [English as a Second Language classes] when I go to school.

WATI: CAST helped me a lot to go to school. CAST bought a bus pass [for me] to go to school when I was at the shelter. They helped find a shelter for me and helped me with papers, like work permit, green card, everything.

KANTHI: What are you working on with the caucus?

WATI: We learn about human trafficking and how to tell our stories. I want to tell my story from beginning to end, and maybe it can help somebody, and maybe we can go to the Indonesian newspaper, something like that. I like that we are talking about how to help people and how to find new trafficking.

KANTHI: And what do you want to tell other people who are still in trafficking?

WATI: I want to tell them not to believe people when they tell you that they will bring them back to their country . . . because it is not true.

KANTHI: Have you visited your family?

WATI: No, I haven't—I haven't seen my family for, like, twenty-nine years.

KANTHI: Do you have a green card?

WATI: Yes, I do. I already got my green card a few months ago. I was so happy. I no worrying anymore. Because I already get the green card, and I can now go home and visit my family. Now I need to get my passport.

KANTHI

Origin: Sri Lanka   *Trafficked in/to*: Los Angeles
Form of enslavement: Forced domestic labor   *Current status*: Free
Source: CAST survivor-to-survivor interview in English, 2009; reproduced with permission.

KANTHI: My name is Kanthi, and I am from Sri Lanka.

WATI: When you coming to the U.S.?

KANTHI: I came in 1998. I used to work for the family in Singapore. I work for them for two years there, and then I came to the U.S. They were an old lady and her husband. They needed help because they could not go alone on such a far trip, so they asked me to come with them.

WATI: How long you stay with this family?

KANTHI: After I came here, the old couple left to Canada. They say that they going to come back to get me. They left me with their daughter, but after about two years they did not come back. The whole time I didn't get a chance to talk to my family. I didn't get paid. I had to work with their daughter, taking care of the kids, cleaning the house, doing the gardening, washing the car, folding clothes, and cleaning the kitchen . . . everything.

WATI: Did you enjoy your job?

KANTHI: No, I didn't! Not at all! [Laughs.] That was the hardest part in my life. It was altogether four years, but I felt like it was four hundred years. Because I couldn't go out, I couldn't talk to my family, sometimes I would cry for two or three days straight . . . because I didn't have anyone to talk to, I didn't have break. I had to work, even though my feet hurt, my hands hurt, or if I had a headache or I didn't sleep for two days . . . I still had to do what they asked me to do.

WATI: How long have you not seen your family?

KANTHI: I didn't visit my family for eleven years. And I didn't talk to my family for four years and two months. I always asked my employer to go back to Sri Lanka. I said I did not come here to stay and that I needed money because my family is very poor, and they need to buy food, and my mom need medication. And so I would cry and ask her, and she would get very upset and angry, and she said I can never go back because if I do, she don't have anyone to clean her house and take care the kids, so I just cry and keep asking her every six month or so. Then somehow the neighbor heard me crying, and they heard my employer say that I could not go back, that even though I ask many time, it's not going to happen. So the neighbor called INS [U.S. Immigration and Naturalization Service], and they came to get me out from the house.

WATI: How did you get out of the house?

KANTHI: INS came to the house a few times. The first time my employer said she didn't have anybody, but the second and third time they told her that they know somebody is in the house. She didn't let them see me first. She kept me in the garage when they came. She brought me her dress and made me wear it, and she told me to tell the INS that I was her niece and that I was just staying with her. But they didn't believe it. So they took me outside. I went with them, but I told them what she told me to say because even though they say "immigration," I didn't really know who they were . . . I had no idea what that was. At that time, I didn't speak English. And I had no idea. Even though I didn't tell the truth, they took me out of the house, and I stayed in a shelter, where I met [someone from] CAST. And then, you know, they didn't force me to say anything. But then, two weeks later, I told the person from CAST that I really wanted to talk to her. And then she came right away, and I told her my whole story and what happened, and, you know, I feel better.

WATI: Who brought you to CAST?

KANTHI: INS brought me there. CAST helped me to find a lawyer, and then they help me to find a place to stay, and they help me to find a school, and I learn English. And they help me even until today!

WATI: You already get your green card, right?

KANTHI: Yes, I do.

WATI: Do you have plan to go back to your country?

KANTHI: Yes, I do. And I can't wait to go see my family. I am very happy because now I don't have any worry. Before I got my green card, I always worry that if something bad happen to my family, if somebody have a bad sickness or some-body pass away or something, I always thinking, how am I to go? And right now I don't have that feelings, and I feel good, and I know if anything happen I can just go home.

WATI: I feel that way, too.

KANTHI: Same with my family. I talk to them, and they say that they don't have that bad feeling anymore. When I talk to my sister, she say that before I got my green card, she always felt like she have no idea when I was going to come. And is like at least six years since I applied for green card, so she don't know if going to take six more years or six months or sixteen years . . . so right now, she feel good. She knows if anything happen, I will be there.

WATI: What you do with the caucus?

KANTHI: Well, the caucus is the group who was trafficked, and after they graduate [from CAST services training], they start this group to educate people about human trafficking and how to stop it. Because it is hard to end, so we get together every month to plan what we are going to do.

WATI: How you fight for your green card?

KANTHI: We went to meet with the legislators, and then we talk about our story, and we told them why it was important for us to get the green card. We went to meet with many people, and we wrote letters. One time we had to get a signature from many people, like a petition. We gave it to everyone we know! I told them, "Take it to the work, take to school, and get as many signatures as you can."

WATI: Yes, I took it to the people I work with, and they say, "Oh I already signed for Kanthi." But I said, "This is for me! It's the same thing!" But they didn't sign for me because they couldn't sign it twice!

KANTHI: It was hard to do because we had to take the day off of work, and sometimes we lose the money for not working that day. It wasn't easy to talk about our stories over and over. Even if we don't talk about it, it is still there, but when we talk, it is very emotional. But still, we need to do it. It was worth it.

WATI: What are you most proud of? I am proud of working with CAST, to get my green card. And an education. I learn English, I have my own apartment, and I found a job.

KANTHI: It is hard to pick one thing I am most proud of, but maybe getting the green card because we fought hard for it. And we never give up until we get it; we kept fighting for it. The other thing that I am proud of is that I am over with my case. Because it was hard, especially when I had to see my employer there, and I had to talk about it. And it was very difficult, without my family, but CAST support me at the trial; that felt good. And now I am working, and I try to go to school. I am also proud of running the LA Marathon . . . four times! With the marathon, I prove that I am strong. I also know this because I was working for four years nonstop without a day off. I never got eight hours of sleep. I fought for my freedom. So now I want to fight for other people's freedom, too. Wati, are you going to run this year?

WATI: Oh, I don't know . . .

KANTHI: You can walk it!

WATI: Oh, but a few days ago I was walking, and it was long! I was so thirsty! I never walk! . . . What do you want people to know after reading this book?

KANTHI: After the people read the book, I want people to put more attention . . . like if they know somebody who work in the house or restaurant or anywhere, that if they are quiet and don't talk much and don't go out much, I want them to find out if they are trafficked or not. We were both helped by someone on the street or a neighbor. So that is a lot. And if they know somebody, they have to help—don't be afraid to help.

WATI: Because there is a reason some people do not want to get help; they are afraid, and they don't trust people.

KANTHI: Because you know it's not easy to be there, to be working for someone and not get paid, especially in a different country. And you know, in my country, my family need money because they don't have money. That is why we come here. And so there is not only one person is suffering; their families are also suffering. Because I have been there, I know how hard and how difficult, and I don't want anyone else to feel that way.

WATI: I would like to go on *Oprah*! I would like to meet her. She could help us end slavery, to make people promise to be good to their housekeepers and pay them, and they have to make a policy for this. My boss kept me like a bird locked in a cage, but now I am free like a bird. But sometimes that is crazy, too! Life can be really difficult, but not as difficult as it was!

I am proud that I met CAST. Because if I didn't, I don't know what will happen. They were my guardian angels. If I didn't meet CAST, I would have been sent back to Indonesia and back to my employer. But CAST help me find a good lawyer. Now I send money home for my sister and brother every year, but I can't send much because I don't make much money

KANTHI: I send money every month. It is hard, but it makes me feel better. Even for me, if I need money, I know that I can take it from the credit card, and when I get paid, I can pay it little by little. But my family, they don't have that. I am the only one that is going to help them. I am the only one.

WATI: Me, too, it makes me feel better. If I couldn't send the money, I couldn't sleep. My brother and sister, they have a better house now. It is wood with hard mud floor and tiled roof. When it rains, the water comes through the house and mixes with the dirt, and it looks like coffee! [Laughs.] Oh my goodness, I am sorry for them!

I had to work long hours. At 4:00 or 5:00 A.M., I started sewing only with a little needle with no lights until 8:00 A.M. The other workers came at 8:00 A.M. and turned on the lights, and I had to act like everything was normal.

A truck was parked in front of the door. There was no room to escape. I sewed, then ironed, then sewed. When the workers left, I had to sweep the huge shop and then take out the garbage. Then sew again until 1:00 A.M. She said I wasn't allowed to go to bed until she finished working. I tried to convince her to let me leave with a coworker. She said no. I was desperate. I felt like I was living a nightmare. My back hurt so much.

I ate only when she told me I could eat. I only had ten minutes. I was losing hope. My mother had always told me don't forget to pray. Even when I was so exhausted, I prayed. Mom told me not to forget to pray.

I remember one day I asked her to allow me to go to church. I said I really wanted to go, but instead she gave me more sewing. I said, "I don't care if I have to sew day and night, but I want to go to church." I was so stubborn that I couldn't give up. She told me that I was stubborn. Finally, she said I could go, but only after I had finished sewing. I was so happy. My tiredness went away. I worked all night.

She said so and so church was on so and so street. I had no idea where it was. I had never been out. She asked if I knew where I was. I said of course, but I had no idea.

That day I woke up early, finished working. I was nervous and excited. It was the first time I had been outside in forty days.

The sewing teacher, who was also a victim, had tried to leave, but she had been punished. So I was scared. That day I finished working, and I walked out. I didn't know where to go. I was scared and kept thinking, "What would happen if the trafficker showed up?" A coworker came by, and she asked if I was alone. I didn't answer. I gestured to a person [my sewing teacher] hiding in the grass. She [the coworker] gave me paper with a phone number on it and left. I found a payphone and picked it up, but the operator was in English. I didn't know English. I didn't even know how to put in a coin!

It was a Sunday. There was no one on the street. No cars passed by. I wasn't planning to escape; I just wanted to go to mass and come back. Finally, I saw a Spanish-speaking person. He helped me with the pay phone and then asked, "Have you just arrived?"

"No." I said.

"How long have you been here?" he asked me.

"Forty days." I replied.

He didn't know what I had been doing. He dialed the number. My coworker answered the phone and asked, "Where are you?" She said she could come and get me.

I was so scared to upset my trafficker. The coworker picked us up and took us to a restaurant, and the food was so good. But I was so nervous. When we got to the restaurant, it was the first time I'd ever talked to the coworker. I'd been so silent. She said she knew something was wrong because I would never speak.

I told her I didn't speak because the trafficker was threatening my family. We spent the night at her house. Then she went to work. The trafficker was so mad. She hit my coworker. While we were at her house, we cleaned the whole home and didn't go anywhere. Finally, my coworker came home and told us we had to look for a place because the trafficker threatened her. She called a friend in San Diego to pick us up. We stayed there until Valentine's Day.

At the house in San Diego, we were with a young pregnant girl. The trafficker found the phone number and kept calling and asking for us. Finally, the husband came home, and the trafficker asked to speak with him. She asked if he had seen me and my sewing teacher. Then a crew of people came to the house. One of them was a coworker. I was scared. How had they found us?

They took the husband outside and put handcuffs on him. His wife was scared. I was scared she'd be so stressed she'd lose her baby. I'm like, "Oh my God, she might lose the baby to protect us." I felt so helpless. I said, "Call the police," but the police just passed by. In Mexico, people who have money have justice. It seemed the same. I was scared they would kill me. I felt desperate. I thought to escape through the backdoor. But then I thought maybe they have guns, and they'll just shoot me. So I just waited, and I thought this is my way to die. I was crying and crying. I felt like it was the last minute of my life. I saw another coworker, who knew everything. She saw me crying and asked why. I said I thought this was the last day of my life.

She told me not to worry about the trafficker. Someone had called CHIRLA [the Coalition for Humane Immigrant Rights of Los Angeles], and CHIRLA had called INS, and they were already investigating the case. But I escaped a few days after they came to rescue me. They said all the coworkers were in jail, but the boss was free. She said I was the only one who could set the coworkers free. The coworker that had helped me had been blamed by the trafficker as the instigator.

But another coworker had started for one day, and she was an FBI agent. She had a camera in her lunch bag and had taped everything. So when the trafficker denied everything, they brought in the FBI agent.

They said if I can cooperate, I can help, but I have to go with them. They said I could stay legally, and they would protect me. I wanted to free my coworkers, so I said okay. They took me to INS. It was top security. CHIRLA had told INS, but they wanted the rights of workers to be respected. They took my fingerprints and interrogated me. I thought whatever is happening here, it's just as bad as with my trafficker. But I wanted to free my coworkers.

We couldn't communicate, but he was really nice. Then I went to the CHIRLA office, and I stayed with Angelica, the director. I stayed there until July, when I came to [the] Alexandria House [shelter]. CHIRLA then brought me to CAST.

The trafficker only got six months of house arrest. She never stopped chasing me. She went to visit my mother and tried to pay my mother $20 for information about me.

But from CAST I learned how to change the situation.

IMA: What do you want people who are reading this book to know?

FLOR: This is a monster without a face or hair. It has so many different faces. Faces like forced labor. It is slavery; we're not free. Sex trafficking is another face. We need to be working hard to fight all faces of human trafficking. We need to work hard and educate people and our politicians. We need to bring opportunities to origin countries so women and children wouldn't have to migrate. We can implement better trade so they can have life with dignity.

IMA: That's why people come here.

FLOR: They work really hard, but it's not enough to help children. After witnessing your child passing away, it changes your life forever. Right now it's a huge darkness. Let's spread the light. Living in trafficking, they take the light out of you—they not only take away your freedom, but your right to dream.

IMA: And your hopes.

FLOR: They did it to us, and now we are doing everything possible to stop them. We have the power to take back that power and spread the light. We can do it. We are just starting, but we cannot do it alone. As I said and I always say, just do something. If you yourself cannot help, then call the police. You don't need a coin to dial 911. Sometimes I feel like crying because this should not happen to anyone else. No one should go through what I went through.

IMA: Sometimes I can't believe what happened to us. We were slaves, and now we're free.

FLOR: I am proud of the caucus. We are growing and are learning.

IMA: There were only three people in 2005 when it started.

FLOR: I didn't understand it when it started. I thought I was the only one. Now I'm a leader. I am proud to take be a caucus member. To be a leader. I am a stakeholder in the caucus. Ima, you make me feel like that. You make me feel special. I don't have sisters, but in the caucus group I can laugh, cry; I can tell how I feel. I'm not judged when we are a group. At the caucus, you can speak freely. I can't do that outside the group. I have friends, but for safety reasons I can't tell them what happened to me. I keep my shades down all the time.

IMA: I didn't necessarily want her [my trafficker] to go to jail. I just wanted her to leave me alone.

FLOR: The FBI asked if I wanted her to pay for my work. I said, "No. I just want to be free." I'm proud of the caucus. We went to Sacramento to see how we can make a change.

IMA: I can't believe people like us can talk to lawmakers. We can ask them to change the law. In Indonesia, we can't change the law. . . . What do you want in the future?

FLOR: I want my children to be proud of Mom and to be part of the movement. They were not with me because of my trafficker. I want them to join this movement because people have heard enough from me. But people should also hear my children's experience growing up without a mother. Also, if I have the opportunity, I want to be a police officer. I want to inform the police and help others.

IMA: This is the reason I want to get my GED! To get a better job.

FLOR: Ima, don't be discouraged like me. I get discouraged with school.

IMA: What would you say to a person still in their trafficking situation?

FLOR: First, I would tell them not to lose hope. Second, that there's a lot of people who are working hard to end this issue. Say something to someone. You can tell a police officer, and they know about trafficking now. See how far we have come? Monsters use the silence. That's why we have to raise our voices and say something. This is not fair to someone—a child, a stranger, etc. We all have a feeling . . . if you suspect something, ask questions. We can start questioning. Without the caucus, I would feel lost, like there is no one who cares. No motivation. Because we enrich each other and empower each other each time we see each other. We encourage ourselves to help each other. And we have food at our meetings! We eat together first, and then we discuss issues and check in.

IMA: Without the caucus, I don't think we can fight for our rights to be legal. No green card campaign. No people to lobby Sacramento. And our dream is to go to D.C.! We want to meet the president and tell him about us so he can help!

FLOR: Now that I'm with CAST, I feel like I'm allowed to dream.

IMA: I'm dreaming, too!

FLOR: That's what was taken away, and now I'm dreaming. Dreams can come true.

IMA: I agree. I can't believe it myself that I've been here for ten years, and now I have three children.

PASI

Origin: Indonesia   *Trafficked in/to*: Los Angeles

Form of enslavement: Forced domestic labor   *Current status*: Free

Source: CAST survivor-to-survivor interview in English, 2009; reproduced with permission.

PASI: I'm Pasi, and I'm from Indonesia. I coming here with my niece. Someone brought me here to work in America.

FLOR: How were you trafficked into the U.S.?

PASI: Well, a family bring me here, and I work for them always long hours. And then said they pay me $150 a month, but I never received the money. My niece same thing. I stayed here two and a half years. So I became a trafficking victim.

FLOR: So how did you escape?

PASI: First thing was I wrote a letter to a neighbor, but the neighbor never responded. I can't take it anymore, so I wrote letter to police. So police take me away from that place, and they take my niece away from the other place. The first time I didn't know any English, so the first time I wrote the letter, I just wrote a few words because I didn't know how. After, I started looking through children's books and dictionary and see how to use the words. From those, I wrote the letter. I kept looking and looking for three nights. Then the police take me away and go to the police offices. I stayed there like a whole day, then the police tried to match my handwriting to that letter. They asked me if I wrote this letter; I said no because I'm scared. I didn't know what to say. My heart was beating.

Then one police asked me to write ABC, so then they know I wrote the letter because they matched the handwriting. Then they asked if I wrote the letter. I said yes. I understand I'm making them crazy, but I'm scared.

They took me to the jail. They said, "You're not going to jail, but you'll have to stay here." There was no other place for me. They tried to make me not scared, but that whole night I'm thinking that the whole world is falling. [Laughs.]

FLOR: Now it's like a joke, but now we see how far we have come. They didn't know that you're not supposed to go to jail. Now we have shelters. Now we can laugh, but we know how you were feeling.

PASI: Now I was scared . . . we're not sleeping a whole night. Now they're taking me to the fingerprints and then taking picture. I didn't understand property, you know: hold my bag, my things, my clothes. I didn't understand. Police say, "Take your property." I didn't understand. They say, "Take your things with you." I said okay. I had to wear the jail clothes and everything. I stayed there the whole night.

Then finally we stay all day in there; then tomorrow night they take me to central jail, then to another jail in Santa Ana and another jail. I don't remember how many days. Maybe twenty?

YUNI: Oh my God, I'm so sorry. I'm so lucky.

PASI: At that time, CAST had no shelter, no Indonesia translators. From the jail, one day we supposed to go to Indonesia. CAST case manager come in. I didn't know them. I didn't trust them. The case manager gave me the card with the office phone number. I was about to go back to Indonesia, but I have no money, no clothes. I think people won't understand and won't believe me. Then one day I go to sign the ticket back to Indonesia. I start crying. The police were ten of them are all around. I say, "No, I'm not going home. I cry. I asked them to call CAST. The agent called the case manager to pick me up. Finally, she come around 9:00 P.M. and took me to Good Shepherd shelter. I stayed there six months. I was only supposed to stay there three months. Then I move to Alexandria House for one year. Now I have my own apartment and work permit and my ID.

FLOR: What do you enjoy most about being a member of the caucus?

PASI: I enjoy working with the caucus because they help us, and we are supporting one and another, and we're working to make the world better. A caucus meeting is really good for me because I learn a lot from one another.

FLOR: What do you want to do in the future?

PASI: I want to learn more. I want to learn because from the beginning my whole life I never learn anything, especially in school. The case manager pushes me to go to school, and thank goodness. I had to walk so far to go to school, but I went.

FLOR: How did you feel when you get your green card?

PASI: I don't have one yet, but I have T-visa on extension. I think they're waiting on me to get a green card. I'm exciting. I'm happy for everyone who already get it.

FLOR: What would you say to someone who is still in trafficking situation?

PASI: Well, I can tell someone that when the boss not home, whenever you doing what you're doing, watch the TV so you know how to use money or where to go for help. To feel independent or try as much as you can to be free. I didn't understand anything. Zero. No English. So you must learn. From then, you can get your help.

FLOR: What do you want people who are reading this book to understand about trafficking?

PASI: If you see someone in the situation, when you watch TV or when you have a magazine or whatever, then try to change their life. People get more blessings when you're helping one another.

FLOR: What would you think it would take to end slavery and trafficking?

PASI: That is really hard to end because it is really big, especially people who want to come to America to make a better life. It's very hard to make that stop, but I hope that other people can learn, and the lawmaker can make a changing, and we can make that happen to stop them.

FLOR: What changes do you think are needed to help survivors of trafficking after they are free?

PASI: I want people to support us. This is changing my life and my needs. I hope that people understand and can help us.

FLOR: What do you want people to do to help to end slavery?

PASI: If people read the book, then they must understand what the situation is. Number one, they must open their mind and be understanding. Please help and try to help those people. Maybe your neighbor or your apartment neighbor—if you know that these things are happening, you need to make a help.

FLOR: What are you most proud of in your life?

PASI: Myself. First thing, I am very proud of myself because I learn so many things. How to speak English. From CAST, they support me and make me proud and understanding and a better life. So thank you—I cannot forget for one second or one minute about CAST, and they make me so proud. Especially when I am happy. Sometimes I am happy, but I start cry. The whole thing combined make me happy and proud and mad.

IMA: That's what I'm thinking. I don't want to move far away from here, from CAST and the people who understand me.

YUNI: Even though I live far away, I make time to come here.

FLOR: How would your life be different without the caucus?

YUNI: We wouldn't be like who we are now.

PASI: Without CAST, I'd be gone in Indonesia.

FLOR: We're like family.

PASI: When we see each other, everybody really cares.

YUNI

Origin: Indonesia	*Trafficked in/to*: United States
Form of enslavement: Forced domestic labor	*Current status*: Free

Source: CAST survivor-to-survivor interview in English, 2009; reproduced with permission.

IMA: How were you trafficked into U.S.A.?

YUNI: Someone offered me a job to come to this country to take care of a baby. So they promised me that they pay me $100 a month. That's why I came—because I wanted a job and to have a good opportunity.

IMA: How long were you trafficked?

YUNI: I was here three years. I was scared because my boss went to Indonesia, and I stayed here with her husband. While she was there, she was always screaming and yelling.

When I escaped, I had heard of an agency from my trafficker. At that time, I had no money. Not even a dollar. I had my own jewelry from Indonesia. I found a taxi and asked them to take me to Chinatown to sell the jewelry. I had to pay the agency $100 to get a job. I worked in a restaurant. A year later I got contact from Ima, and she asked me to come to Los Angeles to get help from CAST. I was scared to go with Ima. The trafficker threatened my family, saying if she finds me, she'll kill me. Then CAST take me to the FBI, and they explain that she can't hurt me. And I went to CAST, and now I'm comfortable.

IMA: What do you enjoy most about being a member of the caucus?

YUNI: I feel like a part of a family when we get together. I get to do a new thing and learn new things about life.

IMA: Why is being a part of the caucus important to you?

YUNI: It's important, but I've never done it like Flor. . . . I haven't gone to speak in public. But I like being a member of the caucus. People speak in public.

FLOR: We get together and support each other, and in those meetings we find ways to advocate.

YUNI: CAST did so much for us, helping us to be independent and improve our lives and be educated. I keep coming to learn more things and be a support to the group. I just want to say thank you to CAST because they have already done so much.

IMA: What are you most proud of your life?

YUNI: I feel very proud because I have a beautiful baby, and I'm very happy. I have a nice family, and I am very proud of myself. I can start from the bottom and be a better person, and every day I can learn new things. I'm very proud because now I can help my family.

IMA: What do you want to do in the future?

YUNI: I want to make my dreams come true. I want to have my own business. Any kind of business, but to work for myself. Me and my husband are thinking in the future we can open a restaurant. My husband loves Italian food, and he knows how to cook. We will have to work hard, and hopefully some day . . .

IMA: How did you feel when you get your green card?

YUNI: Oh my God, I feel very happy. God was blessing me, and it's hard to get a green card, and I was so happy. I cry, and I say, "Thank you so much, God."

IMA: What would you say to someone who was in the situation like you were?

YUNI: I can say we have to do something. We're trying to help. Hopefully we can guide the person to get help and escape the situation. Maybe I can tell this person I want to try to help you to get out of the situation. Maybe it's not easy, but I would give them a phone number of CAST, so she can get help or someone can help her. I can leave her the number in case she changes her mind.

IMA: What do you want people who are reading this book to understand?

FLOR: I realized that slavery still exists. I realized I had no freedom to go out or see family. We can say it still exists because it happened to me and to other people also. Still there is a lot of victims. And I know it's hard to believe, but it's true and it's happening. I'm a proof. I experienced it. I was a victim of slavery.

IMA: What do you think we have to do to end human trafficking?

YUNI: I think we have to educate people. That way the people knows that this thing should not happen again. If they see in the newspaper that we have this kind of problem, the people will know not to use the traffickers. I would tell people to stop human trafficking. It's going to be hard to stop it because it's coming from everywhere. But it's not impossible to stop it.

IMA: What do you want people who are reading this book to do to end slavery?

YUNI: To educate more the public and to give advice so that we can stop trafficking so that it doesn't happen again. We want them to do something about it. To tell the other people. I would tell people to go to an agency and report that they saw slavery happening in this house. They can give a phone number to call and report problems.

IMA: How would your life be different without the caucus?

FLOR: I would feel lonely and lost and like nobody cares about us.

IMA: I feel like if there's no caucus we can't make a change about slavery. We would be lost without each other.

IMA: We wouldn't understand anything, and we wouldn't be able to help others.

FLOR: Now we can talk to the lawmakers and have them change things. We wouldn't have that much power to say anything without the caucus.

FLOR: And we decide.

IMA: Yeah, we can decide what we can do.

FLOR: After Sacramento, we saw that we have a voice and that we can change things.

Twenty-first-Century Abolitionists—What *You* Can Do to End Slavery

WHEN WE LEARN ABOUT THE history of slavery in the United States, we often think to ourselves that we would have joined forces with Harriet Tubman or the Quakers who were so instrumental in forming what we call the Underground Railroad. Knowing that slavery exists today, how can we turn away from the reality that abolitionists are needed even in the twenty-first century? How can we let slavery last yet another century? How can we allow our children to live in a world in which slavery still exists? How can we hear the voices of these survivors and not join forces with them today?

Ending slavery is not all about kicking down doors and carrying victims to safety. Ending slavery is most certainly not about buying people's freedom, which only supports the market for slaves. As we can see from the powerful stories collected in this book, working to eradicate slavery today involves raising awareness, raising money, and raising a storm of action. Many of us feel helpless when confronted with the enormity of the problem: 27 million people enslaved. We should not feel daunted, however, because mathematically this number is the smallest percentage of the world's population to be enslaved in all of human history. What we have to do is make sure that people speak out about their intolerance of slavery and that governments enforce their laws. There are so many ways you can help to stop slavery at both the global and local level, and just a few of them are listed here.

Become an abolitionist.

AWARENESS

1. Encourage your reading group or your classmates or your friends and family to read this book and discuss ways you might get involved in the cause. Give out copies of it for holidays and birthdays. All author proceeds from the book go to antislavery organizations!

2. Remember the facts. Tell others. Memorize statistics about slavery so that you can make people see how urgent and important this issue is. And remember the stories shared by survivors here. Tell friends and family and strangers about the very real people who are being affected by slavery every day.

3. Make your commitment public. Post links and information about modern-day slavery and your activism for this cause on Facebook, Twitter, Tumblr, or your website or blog. Put a sign in your window or on your door reminding people that slavery still exists. Encourage friends to find out more and get involved.

4. Invite a speaker to your school, community group, or religious service. Many of the people who contributed to this book are brilliant public speakers and are eager to tell your community more about modern-day slavery. Their contact information is included at the end of this book. You can also learn about survivor activists who are speakers at the Survivors of Slavery website, www.survivorsofslavery.org.

5. Have a house party or host a screening of one of the documentaries listed in the "Suggested Reading and Viewing" section of this book (appendix C). Many people turn these parties into fund-raising opportunities as well.

6. Write an op-ed column for your local paper to alert people to the problem of modern-day slavery.

7. Make help available in public places: distribute posters, brochures, and other materials about trafficking in places where many people gather, such as cafeterias, cafes, classrooms, public libraries, community bulletin boards. Make coffee holders and coasters to give to restaurants and bars. Download materials from the U.S. Department of Health and Human Services "about trafficking" web page, www.acf.hhs.gov/trafficking/about/form.htm.

8. Keep a blog about recent human-trafficking cases and the development of laws to eradicate slavery around the world. Ask your local paper to run your pieces on its website.

9. Prepare caretakers and encourage health care providers and law enforcement officials to be aware of the signs of human trafficking. Give repairmen

this information because they are often the people who witness what goes on in a home. If you work in one of these environments, download resource guides from the U.S. Department of Health and Human Services "Rescue and Restore Campaign Tool Kits" web page, www.acf.hhs.gov/trafficking/campaign_kits/index.html.

10. Keep yourself updated on laws, trafficking prosecutions, and breakthroughs in the movement to remain a reliable source of information for the people you are educating.

11. Watch for cases of human trafficking and call the National Human Trafficking Resource Center hotline at 888-373-7888 if you know someone in need. A list of signs that someone has been trafficked or is enslaved is given in appendix B.

12. Tell your children. We can hope that by the time they are adults, slavery will finally be history. This is not a problem we want to pass on to the next generation.

ACTIVISM AND CAMPAIGNING

1. Volunteer or intern for organizations such as Free the Slaves, the Coalition Against Slavery and Trafficking, or the Coalition of Immokalee Workers. The many worthwhile organizations fighting slavery listed in appendix A would be happy to put you to work.

2. Utilize the skills you already have. If you are a web designer, artist, printer, researcher, writer, publisher, journalist, photographer, teacher, typist, transcriber, event planner, the movement can use your help! If you are a nurse, doctor, law enforcement agent, caretaker, service provider, social worker, organize workshops to inform people about how to spot victims of human trafficking. If you work for a shelter, food pantry, mental health clinic, housing office, women's health clinic, help start or join a task force of service providers who can respond to a person who has been trafficked in your area. If you cook, sew, farm, make art, teach English, do data entry or word processing, lend your skills to a survivor's job-training program at a local antislavery or other labor organization.

3. If you own a business or work for a major corporation, research the production chain through which your products are made and ensure that slavery is not a part of it. Require your suppliers to conform to fair-labor standards. Learn strategies to implement socially responsible

Antislavery Organizations

IF YOU WOULD LIKE TO CONTACT or make contributions to any of the organizations that were discussed in or contributed to this book, you can find their information here.

FREE THE SLAVES
Phone: 202-775-7480
Email: info@freetheslaves.net
Website: www.freetheslaves.net
Mission: "Free the Slaves liberates slaves around the world, helps them rebuild their lives, and researches real world solutions to eradicate slavery forever."

ALLIANCE AGAINST MODERN SLAVERY (CANADA)
Harriet Tubman Institute, York University
Phone: 416-736-2100, ext. 44544
E-mail: info@allianceagainstmodernslavery.org
Website: allianceagainstmodernslavery.org
Mission: "To research, educate, and aid in partnership with public, private, nonprofit, and governmental organizations to end slavery in our local and global communities."

ANTI-SLAVERY INTERNATIONAL (ENGLAND)
Phone: +44-0-20-7501-8920
Email: info@antislavery.org
Website: www.antislavery.org/english/
Mission: "Anti-Slavery International works at local, national, and international levels to eliminate all forms of slavery around the world."

ASSOCIATION OF ALBANIAN GIRLS AND WOMEN (AAGW, ALBANIA)

Email: info@aagw.org

Website: www.aagw.org/TheProblem.html

Mission: "A primary aim of AAGW is to help former victims of trafficking re-integrate into Albanian society. AAGW promotes this goal by supplementing and supporting job training, job placement, and handicraft production programs."

BOAT PEOPLE SOS

Phone: 714-897-2214

Email: info@bpsos.org

Website: www.bpsos.org

Mission: "We are a national Vietnamese American community organization with the mission to empower, organize, and equip Vietnamese individuals and communities in their pursuit of liberty and dignity."

CHALLENGING HEIGHTS (GHANA)

Phone: +233-302-256460, +233-302-256459

Email: info@challengingheights.org

Website: www.challengingheights.org

Mission: "To ensure a secure, protected, and dignified future and life for children and youth by promoting their rights, education, and health."

COALITION OF IMMOKALEE WORKERS

Phone: 239-657-8311

Email: workers@ciw-online.org

Website: www.ciw-online.org

Mission: "We strive to build our strength as a community on a basis of reflection and analysis, constant attention to coalition-building across ethnic divisions, and an ongoing investment in leadership development to help our members continually develop their skills in community education and organization."

COALITION TO ABOLISH SLAVERY AND TRAFFICKING (CAST)

Phone: 213-365-1906

Email: info@castla.org

Website: www.castla.org

Mission: "The mission of the Coalition to Abolish Slavery and Trafficking (CAST) is to assist persons trafficked for the purpose of forced labor and slavery-like practices and to work toward ending all instances of such human rights violations."

EMANCIPATION NETWORK / MADE BY SURVIVORS

Phone: 800-831-6089

Website: www.madebysurvivors.com

Mission: "We help survivors of slavery rebuild their lives after rescue from slavery, with sustainable income, education, and help reintegrating into society."

FAIRTRADE LABELING ORGANIZATIONS INTERNATIONAL (GERMANY)

Phone: +49-228-949230

Website: www.fairtrade.net/home.html?&L

Mission: "Fairtrade's vision is a world in which all producers can enjoy secure and sustainable livelihoods, fulfill their potential, and decide on their future."

GOODWEAVE USA

Phone: 202-234-9050

Email: info@goodweave.org

Website: www.goodweave.org/home.php

Mission: "GoodWeave works to end child labor in the carpet industry and to offer educational opportunities to children in Nepal, India, and Afghanistan."

GLOBAL CENTURION

Phone: 703-919-6828

Email: info@globalcenturion.org

Website: www.globalcenturion.org/

Mission: "Fighting modern slavery by focusing on demand."

HUMAN TRAFFICKING CLINIC

University of Michigan Law School

Phone: 734-764-4147

Email: carrb@umich.edu

Website: www.law.umich.edu/humantrafficking

NATIONAL HUMAN TRAFFICKING RESOURCE CENTER

Phone: 888-373-7888

Email: NHTRC@polarisproject.org

Website: nhtrc.polarisproject.org

Mission: "The National Human Trafficking Resource Center (NHTRC) is a national, toll-free hotline, available to answer calls from anywhere in the country, 24 hours a day, 7 days a week, every day of the year."

See also "Polaris Project."

NIVASA FOUNDATION

Phone: 617-996-9050

Email: info@nivasafoundation.org

Website: www.nivasafoundation.org

Mission: "Our mission is to educate people at home and abroad about the dangers of human trafficking and modern-day slavery and help victims live in dignity and freedom with the ability to provide for their children and their future. The Nivasa Sponsor a Child program provides financial support for victims of human trafficking to help them raise and educate their children in Sri Lanka."

POLARIS PROJECT

Phone: 202-745-1001

Email: info@polarisproject.org

Website: www.polarisproject.org

Mission: "Polaris Project's vision is for a world without slavery. Named after the North Star that guided slaves towards freedom along the Underground Railroad, Polaris Project has been providing a comprehensive approach to combating human trafficking and modern-day slavery since 2002."

PROTECTION PROJECT

Paul H. Nitze School of Advanced International Studies, Johns Hopkins University

Phone: 202-663-5896

Email: protection_project@jhu.edu

Website: www.protectionproject.org

Mission: "The goal of the Protection Project is to research and document the global scope of the problem of trafficking in persons and, through the dissemination of relevant and timely information, to influence policy and practice in the war against trafficking."

RESTAVEK FREEDOM FOUNDATION

Phone: 513-475-3710
Email: info@restavekfreedom.org
Website: www.restavekfreedom.org
Mission: "The Restavek Foundation exists to bring an end to child slavery in Haiti."

SHARED HOPE INTERNATIONAL

Phone: 866-HER-LIFE
Email: savelives@sharedhope.org
Website: www.sharedhope.org/
Mission: "Shared Hope International exists to rescue and restore women and children in crisis. We are leaders in a worldwide effort to prevent and eradicate sex trafficking and slavery through education and public awareness."

SOMALY MAM FOUNDATION

Phone: 347-766-2595
Website: www.somaly.org
Mission: "To give victims and survivors a voice in their lives, liberate victims, end slavery, and empower survivors as they create and sustain lives of dignity."

SURVIVORS OF SLAVERY

Email: survivorsofslavery@gmail.com
Website: www.survivorsofslavery.org
Mission: "To support survivors of modern slavery who want to lend their voices to the 21st century abolitionist movement."

WILBERFORCE INSTITUTE FOR THE STUDY OF SLAVERY AND EMANCIPATION (WISE, ENGLAND)

University of Hull
Phone: +44-0-1482-305176
Email: r.bloomfield@hull.ac.uk
Website: http://www2.hull.ac.uk/fass/wise.aspx

Mission: "As an interdisciplinary institute WISE will generate world class research; will provide a forum for academic discourse and interaction; and will actively partner others in advancing public understanding of both historic and contemporary slavery, thereby informing political and social change."

WORLD VISION INTERNATIONAL (EAST ASIA)

Phone: +66-2-3916155; +66-2-3818861

Email: asiapacific@wvi.org

Website: www.wvi.org

Mission: "As a non-denominational Christian agency, World Vision aims to share and demonstrate the love and compassion that Jesus Christ extended to all people, but especially to children, and particularly to those living in poverty or suffering from oppression and injustice."

Signs of Enslavement

MANY OF THE PEOPLE WHO HAVE told their stories in this book were rescued from slavery because a neighbor, friend, coworker, or client noticed that their situation seemed unusual or exploitative. With the aid of a stranger or a friend's courage and intuition, many survivors are able to escape the most gruesome conditions. The list of potential warning signs given here might alert you to the possibility that someone is enslaved.[1] Though any one of these conditions might not indicate slavery, each one of them is a sign that should be an alert to abuse, exploitation, and even possible human trafficking.

Be alert if a person

1. Appears to be working without pay.
2. Is not free to change employers.
3. Is being held against his or her will.
4. Shows signs of employer abuse, either mental or physical.
5. Appears to be malnourished among people who are not.
6. Wears the same clothes every day or does not appear to own many personal possessions.
7. Is not allowed to leave his or her home.
8. Is being watched or followed when he or she leaves home.
9. Works an excessive number of hours.
10. Is afraid to discuss himself or his work situation.
11. Has been abused or threatened for refusing to work.
12. Has an unquantifiable debt related to his or her work situation.
13. Has been transported across national borders.

14. Has had his or her passport or legal documents confiscated by an employer.
15. Lives in fear of his or her employer.
16. Has had his or her family members threatened.
17. Seems to have an unusual sense of obligation to his or her employer despite exploitation.
18. Seems to be treated differently than other members of a household.
19. Appears to be confined to a relatively meager living space, such as the basement or garage.
20. Is a child and performs most or all of the domestic work in a household.

If you meet a person who exhibits these signs, it is typically better to inquire about his or her well-being rather than to ignore the signs. If you think you have encountered a case of modern-day slavery, you should contact the **National Human Trafficking Resource Center Hotline** at 888-373-7888.

Suggestions for Further Reading and Viewing

MODERN-DAY SLAVE NARRATIVES

Bales, Kevin and Zoe Trodd, eds. *To Plead Our Own Cause: Personal Stories by Today's Slaves.* Ithaca, N.Y.: Cornell University Press, 2008.

Beah, Ishmael. *A Long Way Gone: Memoirs of a Boy Soldier.* New York: Farrar, Straus and Giroux, 2008.

Bok, Francis. *Escape from Slavery: The True Story of My Ten Years in Captivity and My Journey to Freedom in America.* New York: St. Martin's Press, 2004.

Cadet, Jean-Robert. *Restavec: From Haitian Slave Child to Middle-Class American.* Austin: University of Texas Press, 1998.

Fernando, Beatrice. *In Contempt of Fate: The Tale of a Sri Lankan Sold Into Servitude, Who Survived.* Merrimac, Mass.: Bearo, 2004.

Lloyd, Rachel. *Girls Like Us: Fighting for a World Where Girls Are Not for Sale, an Activist Finds Her Calling and Heals Herself.* New York: HarperCollins, 2011.

Mam, Somaly. *The Road of Lost Innocence: The True Story of a Cambodian Heroine.* New York: Spiegel & Grau, 2008.

Nazer, Mende. *Slave: My True Story.* New York: Public Affairs, 2005.

Muhsen, Zana. *Sold: One Woman's True Account of Modern Slavery.* London: Little, Brown, 1994.

ON MODERN SLAVERY

Bales, Kevin. *Disposable People: New Slavery in the Global Economy.* Berkeley: University of California Press, 1999.

——. *Documenting Disposable People: Contemporary Global Slavery*. New York: Hayward, 2008.

——. *Ending Slavery: How We Free Today's Slaves*. Berkeley: University of California Press, 2008.

——. *The Slave Next Door: Human Trafficking and Slavery in America Today*. Berkeley: University of California Press, 2009.

Bowe, John. *Nobodies: Modern American Slave Labor and the Dark Side of the New Global Economy*. New York: Random House, 2008.

DeStefano, Anthony. *The War on Human Trafficking: U.S. Policy Assessed*. New Brunswick, N.J.: Rutgers University Press, 2007.

Doezema, Jo. *Sex Slaves and Discourse Masters: The Construction of Trafficking*. London: Zed Books, 2010.

Kara, Siddhartha. *Sex Trafficking: Inside the Business of Modern Slavery*. New York: Columbia University Press, 2008.

Lee, Maggy. *Trafficking and Global Crime Control*. London: Sage, 2011.

Quirk, Joel. *The Anti-slavery Project: From the Slave Trade to Human Trafficking*. Philadelphia: University of Pennsylvania Press, 2011.

——. *Unfinished Business: A Comparative Study of Historical and Contemporary Slavery*. Paris: UNESCO, 2009.

Skinner, Benjamin. *A Crime So Monstrous: Face-to-Face with Modern-Day Slavery*. New York: Free Press, 2008.

Van den Anker, Christien, ed. *The Political Economy of New Slavery*. New York: Palgrave Macmillan Press, 2004.

Waugh, Louisa. *Selling Olga: Stories of Human Trafficking and Resistance*. London: Phoenix, 2007.

Zheng, Tiantian, ed. *Sex Trafficking, Human Rights, and Social Justice*. New York: Routledge, 2010.

FOR YOUNGER READERS

Bales, Kevin. *New Slavery (Contemporary World Issues)*. Santa Barbara, Calif.: ABC-CLIO, 2005.

Bales, Kevin and Rebecca Cornell. *Slavery Today*. Toronto: Groundwood Books, 2008.

Hunter, Zach. *Be the Change: Your Guide to Freeing Slaves and Changing the World*. Grand Rapids, Mich.: Zondervan/Youth Specialties, 2007.

FILMS

Angyal, Joel, dir. *Sex and Money: The Search for National Worth*. photogenX, 2011.

Bilheimer, Robert, dir. *Not My Life*. Worldwide Documentaries, 2011.

Callahan, Peggy, dir. *Dreams Die Hard*. Free the Slaves, 2005.

——, dir. *Freedom and Beyond: Bal Vikas Ashram*. Free the Slaves, 2008.

——, dir. *The Silent Revolution: Sankalp and the Quarry Slaves*. Free the Slaves, 2008.

——. *Slavery in Your Pocket: The Congo Connection*. Free the Slaves, 2011.

Dillon, Justin, dir. *Call and Response*. Fair Trade Pictures, 2008.

Kondracki, Larysa, dir. *Whistleblower*. Samuel Goldwyn Films, 2010.

Mistrati, Miki and Robert Romano, dir. *The Dark Side of Chocolate*. Bastard Film, 2010.

Schisgall, David and Nina Alvarez, dir. *Very Young Girls*. Swinging T Productions, 2008.

Spears, Libby, dir. *Playground*. Blu-print Films, 2009.

THE SLAVE NARRATIVE TRADITION

Andrews, William L. *To Tell a Free Story: The First Century of Afro-American Autobiography, 1760–1865*. Urbana: University of Illinois Press, 1988.

Carretta, Vincent. *Unchained Voices: An Anthology of Black Authors in the English-Speaking World of the 18th Century*. Lexington: University of Kentucky Press, 1996.

Davis, Charles T. and Henry Louis Gates Jr. "Introduction: The Language of Slavery." In *The Slave's Narrative*, ed. Charles T. Davis and Henry Louis Gates Jr., xi–xxxiv. Oxford: Oxford University Press, 1985.

Foster, Frances Smith. *Witnessing Slavery: The Development of Ante-bellum Slave Narratives*. 2d. ed. Westport, Conn.: Greenwood Press, 1994.

Gates, Henry Louis, Jr. "Introduction." In *The Classic Slave Narratives*, 1–14. New York: Penguin, 1987.

Hartman, Saidiya. *Scenes of Subjection: Terror, Slavery, and Self-Making in Nineteenth Century America*. New York: Oxford University Press, 1997.

Lovejoy, Paul E. "Freedom Narratives of Transatlantic Slavery." *Slavery and Abolition* 32, no. 1 (2011): 91–107.

Olney, James. "'I Was Born': Slave Narratives, Their Status as Autobiography and as Literature." *Callaloo* 20 (Winter 1984): 46–73.

FOREWORD

1. "Speak truth to power" is sometimes thought to be a biblical quotation, but it originated with Milton Mayer and other Quakers, including Bayard Rustin, as they prepared a pamphlet challenging the behavior of the two antagonists of the Cold War. The pamphlet was published as *Speak Truth to Power: A Quaker Search for an Alternative to Violence* (Philadelphia: American Friends Service Committee, 1955).

2. I emphasize the clarity of the narratives in this book. It is a sad truth that some authors and organizations have altered, edited, or reconstructed the stories told by freed slaves in an effort to make them more palatable, sensational, or sympathetic. In this book, the integrity of the stories of freed slaves has been preserved with great care. To do otherwise is to violate again the dignity of those who have been enslaved.

3. Toni Morrison, *Beloved* (New York: Knopf, 1987), 95.

INTRODUCTION

1. These figures and definitions are drawn from Kevin Bales, *Disposable People: New Slavery in the Global Economy* (Berkeley: University of California, 1999), 8–9. Because slavery is illegal everywhere, accurate numbers are not possible. Though Bales (a quantitative sociologist) admits that coming to a precise calculation of the number of enslaved people is impossible, his estimate stands as the most thoroughly researched, well-documented, and statistically

sound estimate we have. It has been academically vetted. In 2012, the International Labor Organization (ILO) released another thorough study that gives a conservative estimate of 20.9 million people in forced labor, a significant revision of the 2005 estimate of 12.3 million (ILO, *ILO Global Estimate of Forced Labour: Results and Methodology* [Geneva: ILO, 2012). Both studies use conservative definitions of slavery or forced labor to ensure that their numbers are not inflated. These two studies provide a firm scholarly foundation for future research to determine the statistical prevalence of global slavery.

2. U.S. Department of State, Office to Monitor and Combat Trafficking in Persons, "Introduction," in *2008 Trafficking in Persons Report* (Washington, D.C.: U.S. Department of State, 2008), http://www.state.gov/g/tip/rls/tiprpt/2008/105376.htm. It is important to note, however, that this number is also imprecise. The U.S. Government Accountability Office (GAO) questioned its accuracy in 2006, but it is still the best estimate the government has provided. See U.S. GAO, *Human Trafficking: Better Data, Strategy, and Reporting Needed to Enhance U.S. Antitrafficking Efforts Abroad* (Washington, D.C.: U.S. GAO, 2006), http://www.gao.gov/new.items/d06825.pdf.

3. U.S. Department of State, Office to Monitor and Combat Trafficking in Persons, "Country Narratives: United States," in *2011 Trafficking in Persons Report* (Washington, D.C.: U.S. Department of State, 2011), 372.

4. U.S. Department of Justice, *Attorney General's Annual Report to Congress on U.S. Government Activities to Combat Trafficking in Persons: Fiscal Year 2005* (Washington, D.C.: U.S. Department of Justice, June 2006).

5. U.S. Department of State, Office to Monitor and Combat Trafficking in Persons, "Country Narratives: United States," in *2011 Trafficking in Persons Report*, 373, http://www.state.gov/documents/organization/164458.pdf.

6. U.S. Department of State, Office to Monitor and Combat Trafficking in Persons, "Country Narratives: Mauritania," in *2011 Trafficking in Persons Report*, http://www.state.gov/documents/organization/164455.pdf.

7. Louisa Waugh, *Selling Olga: Stories of Human Trafficking and Resistance* (London: Phoenix, 2007). See also chapter 3 for the first-person experiences of enslaved women and their traffickers in these regions.

8. For extended discussions of the harm done by conflating chosen sex work with forced sexual slavery, see Kamala Kempadoo and Jo Doezema, eds., *Global Sex Workers: Rights, Resistance, and Redefinition* (New York: Routledge, 1998); Laura Agustin, *Sex at the Margins: Migration, Labour Markets, and the Rescue*

Industry (London: Zed Books, 2007); Jo Doezema, *Sex Slaves and Discourse Masters: The Construction of Trafficking* (London: Zed Books, 2010).

9. ILO, *ILO Global Estimate of Forced Labour*, 14.

10. Ibid., 13–14.

11. Sidonie Smith and Kay Schaffer, *Human Rights and Narrated Lives: The Ethics of Recognition* (New York: Palgrave Macmillan, 2004), 27.

12. Ibid., 5–6.

13. William L. Andrews, introduction to *African American Autobiography: A Collection of Critical Essays*, ed. William L. Andrews (Englewood Cliffs, N.J.: Prentice Hall, 1993), 1.

14. Charles T. Davis and Henry Louis Gates Jr., "Introduction: The Language of Slavery," in *The Slave's Narrative*, ed. Charles T. Davis and Henry Louis Gates Jr. (Oxford: Oxford University Press, 1985), xiii.

15. See James Olney, "'I Was Born': Slave Narratives, Their Status as Autobiography and as Literature," *Callaloo* 20 (Winter 1984), 48–49; and Frances Smith Foster, *Witnessing Slavery: The Development of Ante-bellum Slave Narratives*, 2nd ed. (Westport, Conn.: Greenwood Press, 1994), 85.

16. Paul E. Lovejoy, "Freedom Narratives of Transatlantic Slavery," *Slavery and Abolition* 32, no. 1 (2011): 91–107.

17. Bales, *Disposable People*, 5.

18. Ibid., 14.

19. In this text, the word *trafficking* is often used interchangeably with *slavery* for the sake of language variation. Recent U.S. laws do not require the transportation or movement (international or otherwise) of a person to qualify as trafficking, though in the past movement was a legal characteristic of trafficking. The U.S. Trafficking Victims Protection Act of 2000 defines trafficking as a "contemporary manifestation of slavery" and as the "recruitment, harboring, transportation, provision, or obtaining of a person for labor or services, through the use of force, fraud, or coercion." Transport is one means of trafficking, but simply obtaining a person for labor through force is sufficient. Thus, the word *trafficking* is synonymous with *slavery* as defined here. However, as this section describes, the word *slavery* has a particular political power and descriptive precision, whereas trafficking is often confused with illegal smuggling or as requiring the international transportation of victims, so the use of the term *slavery* is more effective and more precise. See Trafficking Victims Protection Act of 2000, Public Law 106-386, October 28, 2000, http://www.state.gov/documents/organization/10492.pdf.

20. Joel Quirk, *The Anti-slavery Project: From the Slave Trade to Human Trafficking* (Philadelphia: University of Pennsylvania Press, 2011), 243–247.
21. Segments of these news documentaries can be seen at docs.msnbc.com, search term: *sex slaves*.

1. THE ALLURE OF WORK

1. U.S. Department of Labor, Bureau of Labor Statistics, "Labor Force Statistics from the Current Population Survey," October 2009, http://data.bls.gov/timeseries/LNS14000000.
2. *Historical Statistics of the United States, Millennial Edition On Line*, ed. Susan B. Carter, Scott Sigmund Gartner, Michael R. Haines, Alan L. Olmstead, Richard Sutch, and Gavin Wright (Cambridge: Cambridge University Press, 2006), table Ba470–477; Robert A. Margo, "Employment and Unemployment in the 1930s," *Journal of Economic Perspectives* 7, no. 2 (1993): 41–59.
3. *CIA World Factbook: Unemployment Rate* (Washington, D.C.: Central Intelligence Agency), https://www.cia.gov/library/publications/the-world-factbook/rankorder/2129rank.html, accessed May 15, 2013.

2. SLAVES IN THE FAMILY

1. Ira Berlin, *Generations of Captivity: A History of African-American Slaves* (Cambridge, Mass.: Harvard University Press, 2003), 205 n. 74.
2. Ibid., 205.
3. The amount of money a pimp requires a woman in his "stable" to earn each day.
4. Fondasyon Limyè Lavi, an organization dedicated to ending *restavec* slavery in Haiti.

3. CASE STUDY: INTERVIEWS FROM A BROTHEL

1. Kevin Bales, *Disposable People: New Slavery in the Global Economy* (Berkeley: University of California, 1999).
2. Kevin Bales, *Ending Slavery: How We Free Today's Slaves* (Berkeley: University of California Press, 2008), 160.
3. Nick Schwellenbach and Carol Leonnig, "U.S. Policy a Paper Tiger Against Sex Trade in War Zones," *Washington Post*, July 18, 2010.

4. Podem is an underfunded shelter and detention center in Bulgaria for former sex workers who are minors. Ironically, the word *podem* means "economic boom" in Bulgarian.
5. Oral sex.

4. PAINFUL DEFIANCE AND CONTESTED FREEDOM

1. Harriet Jacobs, *Incidents in the Life of a Slave Girl* (Boston: Published for the Author, 1861).
2. Ibid., 31.
3. Ibid., 294.
4. This quotation is from separate testimony given to the Protection Project; used with permission.
5. Laura Lederer, director of the Protection Project at the time.

5. COMMUNITY RESPONSE AND RESISTANCE

1. U.S. Department of Justice, *Attorney General's Annual Report to Congress on U.S. Government Activities to Combat Trafficking in Persons: Fiscal Year 2005* (Washington, D.C.: U.S. Department of Justice, June 2006), 1. The Department of Justice admits that this number needs further investigation.
2. Oxfam America, *Like Machines in the Field: Workers Without Rights in American Agriculture* (Boston: Oxfam America, March 2004), 38–39, http://www.oxfamamerica.org/files/like-machines-in-the-fields.pdf.
3. U.S. Department of State, Office to Monitor and Combat Trafficking in Persons, "Country Profiles: United States," in *2011 Trafficking in Persons Report*, 372–378 (Washington, D.C.: U.S. Department of State, 2011), http://www.state.gov/documents/organization/164458.pdf.

6. CASE STUDY: MINING UNITY

1. Kevin Bales, *Ending Slavery: How We Free Today's Slaves* (Berkeley: University of California Press, 2008); Peggy Callahan, dir., *The Silent Revolution: Sankalp and the Quarry Slaves* (Free the Slaves, 2008).
2. Kevin Bales and Zoe Trodd, eds., *To Plead Our Own Cause: Personal Stories by Today's Slaves* (Ithaca, N.Y.: Cornell University Press, 2008).

3. Callahan was collecting Ramphal's interview for a film documentary, so in this question she is attempting to get Ramphal to put together several of his responses in a succinct manner so that she can include it in the film. Her interview style is typically open-ended.
4. Sankalp estimates that there were 3,500 people at the demonstration.

7. THE VOICE AND THE SILENCE OF SLAVERY

1. William Wells Brown, *Narrative of William W. Brown, a Fugitive Slave, Written by Himself* (Boston: Anti-Slavery Office, 1847).
2. William Wells Brown, "A Lecture Delivered Before the Female Anti-Slavery Society of Salem," in *William Wells Brown: A Reader*, ed. Ezra Greenspan (Athens: University of Georgia Press, 2008), 108.
3. Ibid.

8. BECOMING AN ACTIVIST

1. This quote comes from the same filming trip when Peggy Callahan interviewed Vann again, but this second interview is not included in this book.
2. Kevin Bales, *Ending Slavery: How We Free Today's Slaves* (Berkeley: University of California Press, 2008), 65.

9. CASE STUDY: COALITION AGAINST SLAVERY AND TRAFFICKING, SURVIVOR ADVISORY CAUCUS

1. See http://www.castla.org/caucus-of-survivors, accessed June 1, 2013.
2. Email from Vanessa Lanza, director of Partnerships, to the author, June 26, 2012.

APPENDIX B

1. Adapted in part from Free the Slaves' *Community Members Guide* (2008).

Anti-Slavery International (England), 281
antislavery organizations, contact
information for, 281–86
Asia, unemployment in, 24
Association of Albanian Girls and Women
(AAGW), 36, 56, 100, 190, 282
awareness: as antislavery strategy, 147,
149–50, 166–67, 171, 206, 249, 251,
266, 272, 276–77; oversimplification
of problem and, 5; raising of, danger of
becoming an end in itself, x; reluctance
to admit existence of, 13; slave narratives
as method of raising, 9–10, 12, 36, 185
Azad Nagar, India: children, education of,
140, 162, 169, 175; dreams for future
in, 144, 154–56, 157, 162, 164, 165;
freedom in, as product of knowledge,
155; freedom in, through collective
ownership of mining lease, 140,
144, 147, 154, 156, 162, 164, 169, 176;
meaning of village name, 140; sources
on, 145. *See also* Sonbarsa, India

Bales, Kevin, 13, 18, 52–53, 70, 209,
293–94n3
Bal Vikas Ashram, 38, 40, 41
Baumann, Ginny, 180–83
begging, forced, 19, 44, 54–55
Belgium, forced sex work in, 190–91
Bell, Inge: career of, 69; contacts in
trafficking industry, 72; former sex
workers, efforts to aid, 75; interview of
brothel owner in Macedonia, 72–73,
86–89, 185–86; interview of madam
in Macedonian, 83–86; interviews of
sex workers in Greece and Macedonia,
75–83, 92, 98–100, 107–11, 185, 188–90;
interview technique of, 71
Benitez, Lucas, 116, 122, 125
Berlin, Ira, 42
Boat People SOS, 27–30, 282
Border Governors Conference (U.S.), 249
Bosnia, forced sex work in, 73
"breaking in" of enslaved persons, 73, 87
Brown, William Wells, 184–85
Brownback, Sam, 96, 102, 105–6

Bulgaria: forced sex work in, 76; mafia, sex
trafficking by, 69, 75, 78
businesses, antitrafficking measures for,
277–78

Callahan, Peggy: films by, 58, 117, 145, 158,
163; interview of child soldier, 212–28;
interviews of antislavery activists,
165–79, 212–28, 231–46; interviews of
forced laborers, 38–41, 117–27, 145–65;
interviews of forced sex workers, 58–61
Cambodia: activism against forced sex
work in, 21, 208–9, 231–32, 238–39,
242–46; anti-sex trafficking law, 229;
culture of, and recovery from trauma,
208; forced begging in, 19, 44, 54–55
Cambodia, forced sex work in, 73,
231–46; customers of, 240–41; debt
bondage of sex workers in, 245;
driven underground, by new laws,
229; drugging of sex workers, 232, 235,
245; *vs.* free sex workers, 230, 239–40;
living conditions in, 234–36, 236–37,
241; minors in, 230, 236; police and
government aid in anti-trafficking
efforts, 229–30; psychological damage
to women in, 230, 237–38, 241, 242,
244, 245; recruitment into, 232–33,
239; restrictions on movement in, 232,
233; survivors, support for life after
enslavement, 242–43; violence and
intimidation in, 234–35, 236–37, 238,
240, 241
caring about enslaved persons, reasons for,
157, 172, 179
CAST LA. *See* Coalition to Abolish
Slavery and Trafficking Los Angeles
Chain Store Reaction, 278
Challenging Heights (Ghana), 186, 191, 195,
196, 211, 282
chattel slavery, as type of slavery, 3
child forced labor: definition of, 4;
difficulty of tracing enslaved persons,
194; elimination of in Indian villages,
140, 143, 144; in Ghana, 191–96; in
India, 25, 38–41; organizations devoted